MANAGING INTERACTIVELY

Executing Business Strategy, Improving Communication, and Creating a Knowledge-Sharing Culture

MARY E. BOONE

McGraw-Hill

New York   San Francisco   Washington, D.C.   Auckland   Bogotá
Caracas   Lisbon   London   Madrid   Mexico City   Milan
Montreal   New Delhi   San Juan   Singapore
Sidney   Tokyo   Toronto

Also by Mary Boone

- Leadership and the Computer
- The Information Edge (with N. Dean Meyer)

McGraw-Hill

A Division of The **McGraw·Hill** Companies

Copyright © 2001 by Mary E. Boone. All rights reserved. Printed in the United States of America. Except as permitted under the United States Copyright Act of 1976, no part of this publication may be reproduced or distributed in any form or by any means, or stored in a data base or retrieval system, without the prior written permission of the publisher.

1 2 3 4 5 6 7 8 9 0   DOC / DOC   0 9 8 7 6 5 4 3 2 1 0

ISBN 0-07-135866-8

This research was supported in part by grants from IBM Corporation and Teligent. The author appreciates the generous support of these corporations in making this research possible.

This book was set in Janson MT by North Market Street Graphics.

Printed and bound by R.R. Donnelley & Sons Company.

This publication is designed to provide accurate and authoritative information in regard to the subject matter covered. It is sold with the understanding that the publisher is not engaged in rendering legal, accounting, or other professional service. If legal advice or other expert assistance is required, the services of a competent professional person should be sought.
> —*From a declaration of principles jointly adopted by a committee of the American Bar Association and a committee of publishers.*

 This book is printed on recycled, acid-free paper containing a minimum of 50% recycled de-inked fiber.

McGraw-Hill books are available at special quantity discounts to use as premiums and sales promotions, or for use in corporate training programs. For more information, please write to the Director of Special Sales, Professional Publishing, McGraw-Hill, Two Penn Plaza, New York, NY 10121. Or contact your local bookstore.

This book is dedicated to my mother,
Mary Elizabeth Hobby Boone,
and my friend L. Jane Calverley

Contents

Introduction

Moving from "Tell and Sell" to "Ask and Engage"

If you've picked up a business magazine in the last 20 years or so, it's not news to you that technology can transform an organization. What you're less likely to read about is how technology creates the need for a whole new style of management.

In *Leadership and the Computer,* I explained how technology could help CEOs communicate, change corporate cultures, invert hierarchies, and help lead an organization. That was in 1990. Then the Internet took off.

Now we have Internet-enabled business models that challenge our definitions of what an organization really is. Boundaries between companies are more blurred than ever before. It's as easy to hold a virtual meeting with a colleague in Japan as it is to saunter over to the next cubicle. Teenagers can consult to CEOs on e-business strategies. The Internet has enabled record numbers of people to become free agents and entrepreneurs. This new environment has amazing consequences for how we manage people and execute strategy.

In a world of interactive technologies, new networked business models, and changed attitudes toward work and authority, *effective management requires a radically different approach to communication.* Getting buy-in isn't enough anymore. You need *ownership* of ideas, strategies, and initiatives and that requires going beyond participation to interaction. Creating and executing strategy in this transformed business environment requires managers to connect, inform, and engage people in new ways. That is the central message of this book. The skills of organizational communication are moving to the fore of business for the first time.

Certainly communication has always been central to management. We've all heard the adage "Communicate, communicate, communicate." However, the practice of management rarely includes a comprehensive, sophisticated approach to business communication. Business schools generally don't teach communication courses and communication schools generally don't teach business courses. Corporate training in communication is often limited to a few lame attempts at teaching people to make eye contact or to use phrases like "I think what I hear you saying is..." Many managers leave communication plans up to public relations or corporate communication departments rather than seeing it as an area where they need to develop competencies themselves. This is a big mistake. It's similar to assuming that you don't need to know anything about technology because you have a technology department. Certainly corporate communication departments have a lot to offer, but you'll need to partner with them instead of assuming they can do everything for you.

Communication in business is often considered soft or intangible—something that's incidental after the real issues of numbers, strategies, or business processes. This can be a very costly assumption. If you plan to innovate, leverage intellectual capital, and get things done in your organization, effective communication is key to your success. When the Royal Bank of Canada changed its communication approach with employees in order to implement a new business model, this resulted in an *$800 million increase in revenue in the course of one year.* That's tangible—and it's documented in this book.

Communication in business is also usually treated as a pronouncement. Typically, managers communicate primarily through memos, speeches, and directives. Corporate visions are delivered to employees in the form of "change management" programs—campaigns designed to gain compliance instead of participation. Things are different in a digital economy. Often the people you're "managing" work for another department or even another company. The people who do work directly for you may have different ideas about work than you do. If you're a change agent or what Gary Hamel calls a "corporate rebel," you need to articulate ideas clearly and build coalitions in your organization.[1]

All these activities require more than a good memo. In this business climate, the purpose of communication must shift from "tell and sell" to "ask and engage." Good communication is no longer just about broadcasting a message creatively. Good communication is also about listening and engaging people. In short, management (and communication) must become more interactive. Instead of managing by *telling* people things, to succeed in this new era we have to *interact* with people, taking advantage of their wisdom as we make things happen together. You'll discover how to do this—how to "manage interactively"—in this book.

It's ironic that most managers and executives spend a huge portion of their budget on communications bandwidth and hardware without stopping to think about their own communication skills or the quality of communication in their organizations. The *act* of communication is as important as the technologies we use to connect to each other.

Don Tapscott, a well-known author and Chairman of Digital 4Sight, an e-business strategy consulting and research firm, summarizes the situation with this analogy

> **With the Internet, we went from a three-foot-wide garden path to a highway a mile wide in terms of our communication capacity. We're opening up the channels for people to communicate, but we haven't thought of how to manage what's happening on those channels. We've myopically stumbled into this massive new communications environment without thinking it through.**

Leading management thinkers like Tapscott and Gary Hamel, author of *Leading the Revolution*, call on managers to participate in completely reinventing their businesses. In his book, *Digital Capital*, Tapscott and his coauthors explain how you can use new Internet-enabled business models called "b-webs" (defined in Chapter 11) to transform a traditional organization or create a new one.[2] Gary Hamel suggests that business concept innovation—the ability to reconceive existing business models—will be the defining competitive advantage in what he calls the age of revolution.[3] Both of their theories require that you step up to the plate to make these new ideas happen. If you take on this type of challenge, you'll need a plan for connecting, informing, and engaging people to make your revolution a reality. And if you create a new business model such as a b-web, you'll need new approaches to working across organizational boundaries.

Whatever your title, your industry, or the size of your company, your ability to communicate is essential to executing strategy and achieving the results you want as a manager. Whether you are a "corporate rebel" or in a more traditional managerial role, the ideas in this book are critical to your success. And you can put these ideas to work right away.

Managing Interactively shows you how to communicate in an era when human capital matters more than ever—when ideas and innovation fuel success. Departing from the traditional communication methods of persuasion and buy-in, it explains how to engage people in a truly interactive way, whether they're in your department or in your b-web. It provides both new and time-tested approaches—including the use of technology—to help you improve your communication with all types of business partners, including employees, customers, contractors, consultants, and alliance partners. It helps you create an environment where people are eager to share knowledge and learn about new ideas.

Chapters 2 through 11 present the ten communication competencies you'll need for managing interactively. In Chapter 12 you'll hear advice on interactive leadership from top executives including Bill Esrey, CEO and Chairman of Sprint. Throughout the book you'll find concrete, practical ideas generously shared by the 85 people I interviewed. These professionals come from a variety of disciplines, including communication, marketing, human resources, knowledge management, and information technology. Some of them are line managers, some are CEOs; they are all listed by name and title in the acknowledgments. What they all have in common is that they've thought about the issue of communication in management, and they know what it takes to get people engaged and involved. They gave me lots of great ideas and specific examples, and they pointed out potholes. When they didn't know answers, they told me that too.

If you use these ideas to adjust your management style to be more interactive, you'll find it easier to bring fresh ideas to your organization, take advantage of your intellectual capital, build better alliances, and improve bottom-line results.

Are You Truly Interactive?

As you read this book, consider your management style and your current approach to communication. Are you truly interactive? Do you ask more than tell? Are you really interested in getting input from others? Have you considered how technologies like expertise location software can help you build a coalition or community? Do you know good methods for efficiently and effectively tapping into the minds of your colleagues to improve knowledge sharing? If you want to be an interactive manager and improve your communication in a change-saturated, warp-speed business environment, then you've come to the right place.

Connect

Breaking Down the Barriers Between People in Organizations

CONNECTING PEOPLE SOUNDS simple, doesn't it? Just provide access to a corporate phone directory, right? Not quite. The people you work with now may be outside your department, or even outside your company if you're in a web-enabled business. These days it's a challenge to even know whom to talk to in an organization. And even if you have a list of names, connecting requires a lot more than a phone call.

Connecting is critical in an e-business era. Change agents and corporate rebels with good ideas need to connect with others to build coalitions of support for the changes they initiate. Everyone needs to have access to the expertise, experience, and knowledge of their peers. Managers need to connect with a variety of stakeholders including employees, customers, and alliance partners. Better connections between people result in greater understanding, increased knowledge sharing, and an improved ability to create and execute strategy.

You can connect people with technology, but that's only the beginning. Active use of good interpersonal skills—what I call "getting over yourself"—is an essential skill in an era where personal connections really matter. And you can create more significant connections between people if you know how to share power, create rituals and experiences, and design physical environments that encourage connection and collaboration.

Part I starts with an introduction to interactive management. The discussion of competencies for connecting people begins in Chapter 2.

Interactive Management: Why We Need to Connect, Inform, and Engage People

CLERKS CAN SEND e-mail to CEOs. Customers are setting prices and even creating products for companies on-line. Telecommuters and contractors work from their houses instead of under the eyes of a boss. Key employees often can change jobs at the drop of a hat, and when they do, they're carrying around your company's intellectual capital in their heads.

Power is shifting.

Monumental changes in the way we coordinate work have taken place over the past 10 years. In this new environment, every organization is hungry for intellectual and human capital. Ideas take precedence over production lines. Innovation rules. Therefore, we need to go further than simply asking for *participation* in management. We need a model for cooperatively creating products, strategies, and even organizational structures. This cooperative approach requires a significant change in the way we communicate and manage.

The term *participatory management* implies that someone is granting people the right to participate—it still has overtones of the "parental" model of management. *Interactive management* implies that we're all in this together and that we're taking action. Interactive managers know how to lead, follow, AND get out of the way.

Now, make no mistake, I'm not talking here about putting every decision up for a vote. And I'm not talking about "touchy-feely" or "soft" stuff. This isn't about being a nice manager or discussing things ad nauseum. Interactive management is about effective communication—taking full advantage of all of the intellectual capital in your organization and in your business web. This requires not only the right tools, but also the right attitude. All of the technology and clever ad campaigns you can muster won't make a whit of difference if you can't engage the right people and earn their trust.

Interactive managers recognize that the people who work with them have a huge storehouse of creativity and innovation waiting to be tapped. They know that the 20- and 30-year-olds in their organization often know more than they do about a lot of things, particularly technology. They also recognize that the people they work with in strategic alliances can't be "managed," and that it's not easy to even get the *attention* of someone who is getting 200 e-mails a day—whether they work "for" you or not.

Peter Drucker told us in 1993 that the terms "boss" and "subordinate" were outmoded and suggested that organizations be viewed as teams of "associates." Many authors since then have repeated this sentiment, including Peter Senge and Tom Peters.[1]

Managers at all levels, whether they're CEOs or virtual team leaders, are involved in a *collective process of discovery* when it comes to making things happen in organizations. They simply can't control all the complexities of their environments alone. To execute strategy, innovate, and stay competitive, they need the help of the team, whether that team is an organization of 40,000 people or three people located in England, China, and Akron, Ohio, who work for different companies.

And leaders aren't the only ones who "manage." So does everyone else in the organization.

Management literature in the last decade or so has been highly focused on leaders. The fact is, innovation and change are only partly driven by leaders. The real engine driving change in organizations comes from all the people doing the work.

Now that technology makes it possible to share information throughout an enterprise and across organizational boundaries, traditional notions of power and hierarchy are altered. As power shifts, so does responsibility. Everyone becomes capable of initiating change in organizations. In order to be effective and responsible in using that power, managers and executives need to develop the types of communication competencies described in this book.

Management in an e-business era must be interactive.

How the Need for Interactive Management Evolved

In the beginning, there was command and control.

Managers wanted conformity and compliance. In short, for many years managers basically told people what to do, how to do it, and when to do it. They didn't ask people to think and contribute. People were considered interchangeable parts of an assembly line. Command and control sustained itself in a simpler era, but now Taylorist models of efficiency seem like ancient history. Why did all of us laugh our heads off when Lucille Ball as Lucy Ricardo tried to work in a chocolate factory? The chaotic, human image of her trying to fit into that structured, autocratic, mechanistic environment made for some pretty good humor.

Of course there were some early voices advocating a different management approach. Mary Parker Follett, whom Peter Drucker calls "The Prophet of Management," was a management scholar who was about 80 years ahead of her time. In the 1920s and 1930s she was one of the first to talk about the concept of participatory management, advancing such radical notions as "power with" as opposed to "power over" employees, "joint responsibility," and "multiple leadership."[2] While other leading thinkers such as Mayo and Maslow shared her idea that workers were more than a cog in the machine, Follett took things further than simply trying to find ways to incent employees; she was truly advocating the benefits of sharing power. This idea of letting workers actively participate in coordinating work was echoed by the socio-technical systems scholars in the 1960s.

In the 1980s, we started to hear more about empowerment and teamwork. Employees were encouraged to participate in helping to improve quality in organizations. This trend took a big detour when the economy slowed and Michael Hammer's ideas about business process reengineering took hold. When the focus shifted to cost reduction, streamlining, and efficient processes, senior managers and executives viewed people as being less important than process. This caused a lot of confusion for people who were "empowered" out of a job.

In 1988 Shoshanna Zuboff's landmark work, *In the Age of the Smart Machine*, foretold with great clarity the impacts of "informating" the organization. She explained that putting machines and information into the hands of workers would cause a significant change in organizational relationships. She said a learning environment would be "posthierarchical" and that while differentials in knowledge, responsibility, and power would still exist, they could no longer be assumed. Zuboff anticipated the need for interactive management when she said that the dictates of a learning environment would call for more intricacy in organizational relationships and this would place a high premium on "interpersonal know-how."[3]

Peter Senge's ideas about learning organizations, Warren Bennis' approach to leadership, and Peter Drucker and Tom Stewart's ideas about the importance of intellectual capital reminded us that people were as important as process.

Throughout the development of management thought and theory, there has been more of an emphasis on purpose (mission), process, strategy, and systems than there has been on the social side of how people operate at work—how they communicate not only with their bosses but also with each other—and what that means for achieving organizational success. This social aspect of management, this attention to how people communicate, is central to my concept of managing interactively. *An emphasis on communication is the distinguishing characteristic of an interactive management approach,* including the use of technology as a tool to expand the depth and breadth of interaction.[4]

Don't get me wrong: There are volumes and volumes of books on communication. But they tend not to be associated directly with "management literature." They're treated as something separate. Certainly, books have been written about communication in organizations, but they haven't attained the level of recognition of the Peters, Hammer, or Senge books. Communication as a critical element of management success is not a notion that's yet been popularized. Studied and written about? Yes. Popularized? No.

Why haven't social roles and communication been examined in more depth in the management literature? Probably because it's messy stuff. It's hard to talk about communication in ways that people can grasp without sounding like you're spouting psychobabble or being overly simplistic.

But in an Internet-enabled age, we need to better understand communication. Not just from a theoretical standpoint, but also from a practical one. Working in new forms of organizations such as b-webs and including new stakeholders in the formation and creation of everything from products to strategy requires a new approach to management itself. It requires an interactive approach.

As organizations and as individuals, most of us just don't see the need for actively attending to our level of communication competence. We'll examine our business processes; sure, you bet. But take a hard look at our ability to connect with others? That's a different story. Most managers think they already know how to communicate. I say there's room for improvement. Even in an "information" age we're still hard pressed to find spaces for collaboration (shortage of conference rooms), strategic planning often takes place at the top of an organization, and technologies—even the ones that have interactive capabilities—are used more to *inform* than *interact.* In the collaborative world that the Internet has enabled, with unprecedented levels of business-to-business activity, we have to move to a whole new level of communication competence.

So what is good communication anyway?

The Purpose of Communication: Connect, Inform, Engage

Communication is a rather nebulous term. In fact, my dictionary defines it as everything from transmitting information to administering Holy Communion.

In this book, I define communication around three key concepts: connect, inform, and engage. To improve communication in organizations, first we need to connect—whether that's face-to-face or through some other medium. When we have interactions, we need to inform each other. And finally, good communication means that we are engaged. And by that I mean we are willing to share in the creation and implementation of ideas.

Some of my colleagues tried to discourage me from using the word "communication" in the title of this book because they felt that people wouldn't know what it meant or that it was too broad in scope.

I decided to stick with "communication" precisely because it is a word that needs to be clarified. Some people confuse the communications infrastructure—the *technology* of communication—with the *act* of communication. We know a lot about hardware, but not very much about what we're *doing* with that hardware.

Other people have been too narrow in their definition of communication, thinking of corporate communication as synonymous with gaining "buy-in" from people across the organization. Pamphlets, banners, posters, memos, glossy internal magazines, speeches—all the traditional means of doing corporate "campaigns" are what people envision when they think of corporate communication. We've operated with a sender/receiver, journalistic type of model and left out the concepts of *interaction* and *engagement.*

This is not to say that memos, brochures, and magazines aren't useful, or that journalistic skills are unnecessary. It simply means that the world has changed and we need to be more conscious and discriminating about the way we apply them as tools. And we need to recognize that most of our communication is one-way.

As we will see in the next section, there are a number of business trends that necessitate a departure from that one-way approach. The need for strategic interactive communication is more compelling than ever before.

Six Trends Affecting Communication in Organizations Today

In understanding why communication is so vital to businesses in a new era, it's helpful to take a look at six key business trends and the communication challenges they create. (See Figure 1-1)

Trend I—A Dramatic Increase in Organizational Alliances and Cross-Departmental Teamwork

Since the early 1990s organizations have started to take on a whole new look. Almost all of us have experience working on cross-functional or "virtual" teams that span traditional departmental boundaries. Not only have we ventured outside our organizational "silos"—many of us also work in organizations that require us to collaborate with customers, contractors, alliance partners, joint venture partners, etc. And many of us do this work in teams. New Internet-enabled business mod-

Figure 1-1   Business Trends and Communication Challenges in an E-Business Era
Source: Boone Associates © 2001

els such as b-webs (see Chapter 11) have all but erased our notions of who's in or outside our organization.

This cross-boundary phenomenon is forcing us (if we want to be successful) to have more open minds and to think about management and communication in new ways. You can't "control" people who report up through an entirely different organization. And even if your whole company consists of only 10 people, you very likely will have to collaborate closely with "outsiders" in order to get work accomplished.

We have to think completely differently about how we communicate in an age of alliances. For example, who is going to own the intellectual capital we create in a partnership or alliance? How do we make decisions about the information we share outside our department or organization?

Trend 2—More Autonomy on the Part of Employees

After the layoffs of the 1980s, people recognize that they have to be marketable, and their loyalty to organizations has changed. This realization has resulted in more free agents and more autonomy on the part of workers. According to *Fast Company* magazine, software engineers in Silicon Valley literally have agents—like actors or sports figures. People in their 20s and 30s have new attitudes toward work, which have more to do with interaction than instruction.

People of all ages in all types of jobs are crafting lives instead of blindly climbing corporate ladders. They're expecting more democratic work environments. They want balance in their lives between work and family, and they want meaningful projects with a chance to make a real contribution to the outcomes.

Autocratic, or one-way, approaches to communication in this type of environment are doomed. Interactive is in. This trend is putting a great deal of pressure on people at the top of the organization—CEOs and other executives—to improve the form and quality of their communication.

Trend 3—Increased Scarcity of Attention

Communication overload (Volume × Complexity) is here to stay. People are receiving more messages and handling more complexity than ever before. You know this. It's not easy to get someone's attention.

Michael H. Goldhaber, an independent thinker and writer on social change, is in the process of completing a book on what he calls the "attention economy." Goldhaber posits that economics will change because of the scarcity of attention: "The industrial economy based on production, consumption, goods and money is in the process of being replaced by an attention economy in which the exchange of real and illusory attention come to the fore...As attention becomes increasingly important, an organization and the people in it will both benefit from being more deliberate in their efforts to get attention."

In order to get and hold people's attention, we need to consciously attend to the quality of our communication—now more than ever.

Trend 4—Continuous Adoption of Technology for Communication

Stop for a minute and think about how many new types of software or equipment you've learned to operate in the past five years.

There's a cartload of technologies that we're already using for communication, including voice mail, e-mail, teleconferencing, and collaborative meeting environments. Each technology presents its own challenges in terms of effective use. And new technology development and adoption isn't slowing down, it's speeding up.

New technologies create requirements for new communication skills. Effective communicators must know when to apply the right technology and how to make those electronic experiences successful.

Trend 5—The People We Want to Reach Are Diverse and Dispersed

The spectrum of people we communicate with in the average organization is broadening in terms of age, race, culture, etc. At the same time, these diverse stakeholders are accustomed to receiving tailored information. An effective communicator has to develop ways of managing this paradox. Joseph Pine, author of *Mass Customization,* points out that the principles of mass customization are applicable within a company as well as with customers. We need to "mass customize" the messages we send to diverse stakeholders.

People are also dispersed. In a global economy and with the rise in virtual organizations, the person you're communicating with could be around the corner or in a different hemisphere. Technology can create new channels of communication, but managers have to craft their communication to accommodate differences in culture and style.

Trend 6—Intellectual Capital Has Become of Significant Importance

The Knowledge Management/Intellectual Capital movement has shown us the importance of managing the intellectual assets of an organization.

In order to create or share knowledge, people must have access to each other and be able to exchange their ideas. Seems pretty straightforward, doesn't it? Well then, think about this: There are 300,000 people in your newly merged organization, and you want to know who knows the most about well-drilling operations in Russia. As they say in the movies, "Who ya gonna call?"

Knowledge management is about a whole lot more than just getting tacit knowledge (the knowledge people keep in their heads) transformed into explicit knowledge (knowledge in storable, accessible form). And it's also about more than just building huge repositories of knowledge or "best practices." Connecting people is every bit as important to knowledge management as capturing, storing, and distributing information. As Don Cohen, editor of *Knowledge Directions,* the journal of the Institute for Knowledge Management, puts it: "Knowledge management means many things, but it means communication most of all. Sharing knowledge, learning from customers, improving working practices, turning innovative ideas into innovative products—the stuff of knowledge management—are all communication efforts."[5]

Even if you're in a small organization, knowledge management matters. For example, turnover is critical to small and medium-size businesses. Knowledge sharing between the person leaving and the person coming in can make a world of difference to your business.

The next big challenge in the area of intellectual capital will be related to sharing and creating knowledge across organizational boundaries. As web-enabled, internetworked business models such as b-webs emerge, partners in alliances will find they are creating intellectual capital together and sharing intellectual resources. This raises some interesting challenges in terms of trust and communication, which we'll discuss in more detail in Chapter 11.

Figure 1-2 Interactive Communication Competencies
Source: Boone Associates © 2001

Given these trends and challenges, there are a number of competencies interactive managers need to develop in order to connect, inform, and engage people for success in an e-business era. I want to interject one caveat. Even though I'm providing an overview of competencies, I don't purport to have a definitive list of the answers here. This book is full of ideas but not prescriptions. Everyone's business situation will differ. These ten competencies (see Figure 1-2) simply represent a good start on what all of us need to be thinking about as communicators in a new environment.[6] With that said, let's take a look in Chapter 2 at some ideas for how to make people accessible to each other.

Make People (and Their Knowledge) Accessible

To MANY PEOPLE, communication is about giving people access to *information,* but interactive communication is also about giving people access to *each other.* As organizations grow in size and scope, and as even small organizations build alliances and work in global teams, it's becoming a considerable challenge to connect people inside organizations and across what Cisco CEO John Chambers calls business ecosystems. To be truly effective in an e-business era, we need to find each other and share ideas in order to leverage intellectual capital.

Connections commonly happen by choice, chance, or through other people. You may know exactly whom you want to talk to, so you look them up in the company directory. Or you might bump into someone in the cafeteria who knows something about a topic of interest to you. Or one of your friends may introduce you to someone they know you have something in common with. Deliberate and chance connections happen all the time, but they don't happen frequently enough. And sometimes it's not so easy to establish these connections. What if you don't have the name of the person you want to speak with, but you know the person exists? What if you sit by the wrong person in the cafeteria? And what happens when your friends don't know anyone who's interested in your particular topic?

There are lots of new ways to help overcome the limitations we've faced in the past in terms of locating and connecting to each other. But we need to focus our efforts.

This chapter covers three of the most important things you can do:

1. Identify and establish dialogue with *all* of your stakeholders.
2. Make certain that people who have knowledge and information are available to others.
3. Build communities of practice, purpose, interest, learning, and support.

Identify and Establish Dialogue with *All* of Your Stakeholders

If you're designing a message, holding a meeting, or building a product, it's important to consider all of your stakeholders. This is a simple concept, but one that is often overlooked.

The term "stakeholder" comes from the communication field. I think it's an excellent term for interactive managers to use because *stakeholder* implies something different from *audience*. Stakeholders literally have a "stake" in a project, initiative, or organization. Interactive managers need to think about the people who are affected by the projects they initiate, and stakeholders play an active role in understanding and contributing to a project, as opposed to an audience that passively receives a message.

As business models change and organizations form new types of alliances, relevant stakeholders may be in your department, elsewhere in your organization, or outside the company. In an e-business era there are a lot more people to consider. For example, contractors now do a large share of the work in organizations. Don't they need to contribute the ideas and knowledge they've gained in working with your full-time employees? How about your alliance partners? And what about your customers? Oddly enough, many organizations don't recognize that customers can tell them a lot about how to build and design a product.

Whenever you approach a business challenge, stop and think about all of the people who have a stake in the outcome and who will have the opportunity to affect the outcome. As you do so, consult the list of stakeholders in Figure 2-1, and think about who might add value through an interactive exchange with the remainder of your team.

These are just a few examples. If you sit down with key members of a project team and brainstorm the potential stakeholders in your project or initiative, you might be surprised at the list you'll generate.

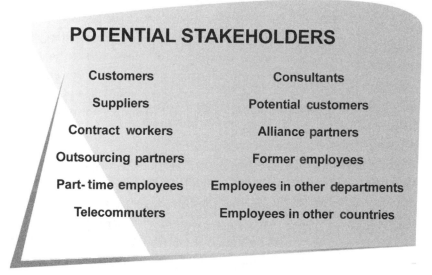

POTENTIAL STAKEHOLDERS

Customers	Consultants
Suppliers	Potential customers
Contract workers	Alliance partners
Outsourcing partners	Former employees
Part-time employees	Employees in other departments
Telecommuters	Employees in other countries

Figure 2-1   A Partial List of Potential Stakeholders for Business Initiatives

Source: Boone Associates © 2001

Let's take a look at how to successfully involve stakeholders.

Customers as Stakeholders

Billie Alban, an internationally known management consultant in the field of organizational development, and author of *Large Group Interventions,* tells a story of how Boeing actually put customers on the design teams for the design of the Boeing 777. Alban describes some interesting outcomes:

> **A customer from United Airlines said to the Boeing team, "No, this is an impossible design. If you put the engine here, I'm going to have to either hire eight-foot mechanics or get 1200 new trucks to fuel the plane, because it's too high for our equipment to reach." Now, that observation would never have come out in the usual way. And a Boeing customer from British Airways said funny things happened as they helped with the design process. For example, the covers to the toilet seats make a noise when they go down, and in a first-class cabin it makes a sudden crash-**

ing noise if there's a little jiggle in the plane. So not only was the crash disturbing the first-class passengers, often the pilots would hear it and wonder what the noise was. There's no way design engineers would know about those kinds of things without hearing from the people who use planes on a daily basis. The engineers want the latest gadgets, they worry about speed, and elevation, etc. The cover of the toilet seat making a noise would not necessarily occur to them.

Don Parker, a consultant who specializes in executive coaching and cultural change, provides another excellent example of the power of involving customers as stakeholders. One of Parker's former clients, who is now CEO of Cancer Treatment Centers of America, opens every board meeting with patients who talk about who they are, why they're a patient, what their illness has been like, what the company did well, and what they could do differently. Then that person has a dialogue with the board, and after the patient leaves, they start the business discussion.

Parker says that this has had a profound impact on their board meeting: "It changes the nature of the discussion because it reminds them visibly of what they're about and who their customer is, and why they're in business. And this is very dramatic. It's both real in that it gives them data, and it's symbolic at the same time."

Customer involvement is made even more feasible and convenient through the use of technology. Tom Sudman, President of Digital AV (a company specializing in Knowledge Management and virtual collaboration), works frequently with virtual design teams that include customers. One of his clients considers the inclusion of customers in the design process to be their number one competitive advantage. Sudman says on-line teamwork has advantages over focus groups in gaining customer input. Instead of taking lots of time coming up with product specs by running a focus group to get statistical data to take back to product design, Sudman points out that collaborative technologies can change the whole process and directly include the customer in new product design as it happens.

Contractors as Stakeholders

Customers are obvious stakeholders who are too often overlooked. But they're not the only ones left out of the communication process. Stakeholders may be right under your nose and you might not recognize them. Lindsay Eynon, Director, Change & Internal Communications, Hill & Knowlton (United Kingdom) tells the story of helping a client design a handbook for managers to support a change management effort. Her client was in Human Resources at a construction company, and the handbook focused on a layoff program. Sometime into the project, as Eynon was helping them write the handbook, she posed the question, "Do you actually call your people *staff,* or do you call them *employees?*"

It turned out that the word "staff" had a very specific meaning in their company, and it was dependent upon the type of contract the person had with the organization. In this organization of approximately 5000 people, 1400 of them were considered "operatives" as opposed to "staff." And the whole handbook had been written for "staff." Many "operatives" were employed on fixed terms on projects, but many of them also had been working there for as long as 26 years.

"It was an absolute eye opener," Eynon says. "The reality was, the 'operatives' wanted to know where the business was going and what was happening just as much as anyone else. And the managers who used the handbook we were writing were going to have to talk to both of those types of people. If this issue hadn't come to light almost by accident, the operatives wouldn't even have been given the same information that everybody else in the room had. None of us can make that kind of mistake in business today. If you're not careful, you can exclude or alienate an entire audience in seconds. You can't just make it up to people by going back to them and trying to involve them at a later point."

Shifting Stakeholder Groups

Stakeholder groups, particularly external ones, are constantly changing, and it's important for interactive managers to attend to such shifts. Few people understand this better than the public relations staff of the Poudre Valley Hospital System, in Fort Collins, Colorado. They were faced with the crisis situation of a lifetime when the hospital admitted Matthew Shepard, a young man who was beaten and left to die, tied to a fence, in Wyoming in 1998. This very sad incident caused a worldwide reaction.

Rick Muller, Coordinator of Marketing and Interactive Media for PVHS, said his group put most of their resources toward dealing with the crush of media people that descended upon them. They also did a Herculean job of keeping all the stakeholders—community leaders, employees, members of the gay community, concerned citizens, and a host of others—informed and involved. One saving grace was that they had just developed a website for the hospital, and this was used initially to inform the media throughout the country, but ended up becoming a primary source of information for individuals throughout the world as well. Interestingly, they didn't have a sophisticated intranet, so many employees used the external website to keep informed about the situation.

The website provided a way for all types of stakeholders to partici-pate—at an impressive rate of 810,000 hits during Matthew's five days at the hospital. It contained updates on his condition, and a place where his parents and hospital officials were able to issue statements to the press and the general public. What was surprising was the way in which e-mail provided a means of involving stakeholders. Muller notes:

> **People visited the website mostly to share their feelings. It was almost like a chat room. People basically said, "I came to the site to see what was happening firsthand." They expressed how they were feeling about the situation and they thanked us for providing sim-ple, straightforward information. We didn't provide that much information, but it was more than they expected. Through the site, we were able to offer a way for individuals to personally express feelings of grief, anger, frustration, isolation, and hope.**

As a result of web user feedback, Muller and his group set up a spe-cial mechanism for people to contact the Shepard family directly. "There were so many people who wanted to send a note to the family. We worked with our information systems staff to set up an e-mail box for the Shep-ards," explains Muller. The response? The Shepards received over 17,000 e-mails from people who wanted to express their concern and sympathy.

The website provided PVHS with a direct channel to its stakehold-ers. Instead of strictly relying on traditional broadcast media such as television or radio to simply inform people of Shepard's status, the hos-pital established an interactive relationship with a variety of concerned parties. By creating this channel for interaction, the hospital went far beyond simply diffusing a potentially explosive public relations situation. Responsiveness and caring—two very important qualities for a health care institution—were conveyed in the way they communicated with everyone involved.

Drawing the Line

Sometimes tough decisions have to be made about where to draw the line on stakeholder involvement. IBM has recently opened up its quarterly conference calls to individual investors. Hervey Parke, Director of Investor Relations, says he thought long and hard about whether to allow questions from the individual investors. In the end, IBM decided that access to the conference call, the text of the earnings release, and commentary in the financial press would give individual investors a complete picture of IBM's results. It was also concerned that allowing individual questions could take the discussion off-track. E-mail was also a consideration, but then the issue was volume:

> We have 1.8 million individual investors. It would be impossible to manage. E-mail is an easy thing to employ. And I worry about an individual investor wanting an answer and not being able to get one. It becomes a rather insidious process that the structure just can't support, so I'm disinclined to try to create that expectation because we would not be able to satisfy people's expectations. That's the issue. So, we'll let them participate in terms of listening to the conference so they can make their own investment decisions, which is useful, but I think you have to figure out where you pragmatically draw the line.

Identifying and involving stakeholders is the first step in making connections in an organization. Interactive managers also need to make sure that people throughout their area have access to the people and expertise they need. In the next section we'll see how to make the right people available to each other.

Make People Who Have Knowledge and Information Available

Locating knowledgeable *people* is as critical as locating *data*. It's ironic how much money companies spend on building databases when people get so much information from each other. While databases and repositories are useful, the most current information in an organization resides in the minds of trusted colleagues. The problem is that it's often hard to leverage access to people who have the most to offer in an organization. First of all, you have to find them, and then when you do they're often very busy.

As Mike Zisman, EVP of Strategy for Lotus Development Corporation, observes:

> **Expertise location is a big issue in companies today. The goal is not only to provide access to information, but to provide access to people who *have* the information. As you move up the organization there is much more of an interest in finding the *people* as opposed to the *information,* because you want their judgments about the information . . . I don't want raw data, I don't even want information, I want the judgments of people I trust.**

This approach is simple when you know the right people to call and when you can gain access to their phone numbers or e-mail addresses. But what if that's not possible? As businesses become more dispersed, this is becoming a hot issue.

Finding the Right People—How Technology Can Help

David Gilmour, CEO of Tacit Knowledge Systems (a company that develops automated knowledge discovery systems), points out:

> **Companies are transforming now at Internet rates of speed, and people don't do the same things on one day that they do on another day. Organizations are fluid, peoples' focus is fluid. So, you don't have a one-shot discovery problem [for finding people]. You have a process that has to be ongoing.**

Tacit Knowledge Systems has designed a "knowledge discovery" system that tracks people's interests, knowledge, and skills in a very flexible and fluid way. The software builds a profile of a person's interests and projects based on outgoing e-mail. For privacy and security reasons, the information in this profile is controlled by the individual, but the system generates all of the information about the person automatically, based on the content of the individual's e-mails.

Then, when someone wants to find a person with expertise or knowledge in a particular subject, he or she can simply type in key words and the system will search up-to-the-minute profiles of people throughout the organization and return an answer with a visual indicator of how deeply involved the person is in that particular subject area. Gilmour points out that e-mail is a better way to track people's interests than looking at self-generated profiles or CVs. He says that e-mail is the most up-to-date, accurate record of what a person is truly working on. "What people say they do and what they actually do tends to differ," he explains. Gilmour says this approach produces very rich information that is easy to maintain:

> **If the process of capturing information about people's interest or expertise is expensive or invasive, if people have to take too much time to fill out or update a profile, you're only going to get sort of coarse-grained crude approximations of the reality you're trying to capture. In this scenario, the system does all the work of keeping up with things.**

Gilmour also points out that people often don't want to share information when they don't have control over it. Giving people control over their personal profiles makes them much more comfortable sharing information about their work.

At Texaco a system has recently been put in place to help locate people with specific expertise in the organization. John Old, Director of Information Management at Texaco, says a recent presentation about the software to the president of the International Lubricants business demonstrated its value. During this presentation, the president mentioned he was trying to find someone who had expertise in a lubricant technology and who also spoke Russian. He admitted that calling people he knew hadn't worked very well. During the presentation, one of Old's colleagues put the president's query into the system and came up with five names that matched the president's criteria.

Knowledge management methods and technologies can be helpful in terms of expertise location. At AMEDD, the Army Medical Department, subject matter experts are a cornerstone of their knowledge management system, notes Steve Innanen, former Chief Knowledge Officer for the organization. The Army has always had subject matter experts, but after building an automated KM system called the KMN (Knowledge Management Network), those experts are easier to locate, and it is also easier for them to share their knowledge.

People can access the KMN, click on a link and pull up all the subject matter experts in a particular area. The system also allows them to send an e-mail to a selected expert. Experts themselves find the KMN useful because they can share their knowledge in a variety of ways. They can post information to the website, put information into a Frequently Asked Questions (FAQ) area, return an e-mail, or simply phone a person with an inquiry. The FAQ area saves them a great deal of time and effort, according to Innanen.

Bob Pinto, Practice Leader for the Government Sector of IBM's Knowledge Management group, also worked on the AMEDD project. Pinto emphasizes how access to this type of expertise is critical to good communication at a time when the military is downsizing:

> **In good times, the military logistics community would have a lieutenant colonel and a staff of 12 in logistics for an average size hospital. In this day and age, with the cutbacks, they're forced to have a major with maybe a staff of three or four. In the past there was a 30 to 60 day *overlap* for a transition when moving people around, so people were around to train incoming replacements. Now it's very common to have a 30-day *gap* before they replace a person who's left. No overlap. So you'd have these younger officers sitting out there trying to figure out how to solve specific problems. And with the subject matter expert directory, they could locate people with answers. The SMEs were both people who [were] currently in the military as well as people who [had] retired. It's amazing how many retirees still feel an affiliation with the organization and are willing to have people call and talk to them about things.**

Finding the Right People—A Nontechnical Solution

Technology is not always the answer to leveraging expertise and connecting people inside an organization. In some cases organizational structure can be the right solution. Gloria Feldt, President of Planned Parenthood Federation of America, describes how they make scarce expertise available to their whole federation of organizations located throughout the United States. Each of the affiliates operates very independently, but is a member of the Planned Parenthood Federation. Suellen Craig, Head of Affiliate Services, created an internal consultancy made up of top-notch experts in clinic management, finance, marketing, etc., that now serves the needs of the entire federation.

This organizational structure has allowed Planned Parenthood to consolidate their regional offices and to have the people in those offices working nationally instead of regionally. Therefore, the best experts are available to everyone, instead of just to the affiliates in a particular region. And these internal consultants can now work from home, or wherever they want.

By putting people in contact with each other instead of simply building databases, interactive managers can help leverage their organization's intellectual assets. Linking people is the first step in achieving excellence in communication and interactive management.

In addition to connecting individuals, it's important to also build communities of people who have like interests and expertise, so they can share information and communicate on an ongoing basis. In the next section we'll look at types of communities, and ideas for how to encourage their development.

Communities of Practice, Purpose, Interest, Learning, and Support

The term *community* is almost as nebulous as the term *communication*. In my interviews and in the Knowledge Management literature, I found a number of definitions. I define *community* as a group of people who share a common interest or purpose. Communities, regardless of their size, composition, or geography, are built on a foundation of trust and cooperation. By building communities, interactive managers can improve communication and information sharing in powerful ways in their organizations.

Why is this notion of community so important? Successful communities create esprit de corps, provide fertile ground for innovation and creativity, and speed the sharing of knowledge. Etienne Wenger, one of the premier scholars in the field of knowledge management, says communities "represent the new frontier for organizations, the promise of great opportunities for pioneers of the knowledge age. They must be acknowledged, supported, and fully integrated into the operation of organizations."[1]

Communities also represent a significant opportunity for Internet-enabled alliances such as b-webs. Relationships between organizations could be strengthened through the development of communities that cross organizational boundaries. As you look at the types of communities described in this chapter, think about how they might add value not only within your organization, but also across your b-web and strategic partnerships.

It's also critical to note that b-webs and alliances can be built around communities. For example, Consumerreview.com is a b-web built around communities of interest. It provides all sorts of enthusiasts—from snowboarders to new parents—with a place on-line to both submit reviews of the products they use as well as interact in a community of like-minded enthusiasts. Consumerreview.com receives over 1.2 million visitors a month, with at least 60 percent of them arriving at the site multiple times per week. The people visiting the site have created communities of interest around the passions they share. Business models could be built around all types of communities.

Much of what's already been written about communities in the knowledge management literature focuses on *communities of practice*, which are defined as self-organized groups that share common work practices, interests, or aims.[2] While I have the deepest respect for the usefulness of this term, I think it can be helpful for interactive managers to make additional distinctions.

In my interviews, people talked about different types of communities, which I have placed into five categories: communities of practice, purpose, interest, learning, and support. Of course, as in any other type of classification scheme, the categories overlap. Some communities start out as one type and then morph into another type. Other communities can be classified in all of the categories. But regardless of this overlap, I think it's useful to point out the different purposes for which communities are being constructed.

- Communities of *practice* are organized around people's roles or professional interests; for example, there are communities of physical therapists, salespeople, managers, and software engineers.

- Communities of *purpose* consist of people who share measurable goals or objectives that are to be solved within a specified time frame. For example, a project team might create a community of purpose.

- Communities of *interest* are more topical in nature and less associated with the practice of a profession. They tend to cross more organizational and professional boundaries. For example, while I might belong to a community of practice for physicians, I might also belong to a community of interest on a topic such as alternative health. This community of interest could include health professionals as well as people outside the profession.

- Although people learn in all these types of communities, communities of *learning* distinguish themselves by having a component of formalized training or knowledge transfer embedded as a professed purpose for the community.

- A community of *support*, which is familiar to the public on-line world, will often spring up around a particular psychological or physical challenge that a person is facing, for example, cancer support communities or support for parents of children with Attention Deficit Disorder. Communities of support are not well-tested in the business community, but I believe they have relevance to work in organizations.

The following sections discuss each type of community in more detail.

Communities of Practice.   Jon Iwata, Vice President of Corporate Communications at IBM, points out that the intranet is a great place to host communities of practice. At IBM, intranet sites have been created for its sales force community, technical community, and managers. Iwata stresses that these communities cross internal departmental boundaries.

These communities may cross physical and organizational boundaries, but the individuals within them share common professional interests. For example, says Iwata, there are more than 100,000 technical professionals in IBM, and while they may be computer scientists, mathematicians, or chip engineers, they have shared interests. "At some level, there is great commonality in what technical professionals want and need—intellectual property, patents, career development, technical conferences, publishing, etc.," he explains. "They share problems and are looking for answers. They can talk to their technical colleagues inside of their local group or division, but the technical community site provides a place to share information, tools, resources, and conversations with *all* of their technical colleagues throughout the company."

It's worth noting that this type of innovative application on an intranet pays off. Iwata estimates that the IBM external home page gets between three and four million hits a day, while their intranet home page gets about *13 million hits a day.*

Communities of Purpose. "We tend to build communities of purpose, which we think are profoundly different than communities of practice," says Tom Sudman, President of Digital AV. "Communities of purpose have goals, time frames, and metrics against which they are measured."

Communities of purpose often disperse and reform in different configurations around other purposes. Often you'll find communities of purpose embedded in communities of practice.

Coalitions of not-for-profit organizations have been forming communities of purpose for many, many years. As Planned Parenthood Federation of America President Gloria Feldt points out: "Coalitions have a sense of purpose, and may not last forever or may be dormant for a while and then be activated when there's a specific need." Feldt says that it is easiest to form a community of purpose when there is a pressing issue at hand.

Communities of Interest. These are open to everyone—regardless of their role or profession in an organization. This openness is a quality that many communities of practice do not share with communities of interest.

For example, Steve Innanen of the Army Medical Department says they ran into problems with the concept of communities of *practice* at AMEDD. Communities of practice on their network often turned into horizontal silos with interested people excluded from discussions:

Let's say I wanted to just join a community long enough to ask a question about something health related, like blood types. If the question is about something that's being researched or is not pub-

licly available, I might want access to a community of experts. There might be a group of phlebotomists on a network, but if I'm not a member of their community, I can't get access to their knowledge unless they've put some stuff in the library and marked it public. So, if I'm coming on as a first-time user, I may be fenced off from gaining access to that information. This just creates more silos in an organization, and that really doesn't sit real well with me, because I think we miss out on a lot.

While you may or may not agree with Innanen, he brings up an interesting point. And it is a point related to the need for what Mike Zisman, EVP of Strategy at Lotus Development Corporation, calls "just-in-time" communities. For example, the person Innanen describes as wanting to know about blood really doesn't want to *join* the phlebotomists on an ongoing basis. But the person is *interested* at that particular *point in time.* And a quick-forming community could coalesce around that person to help with a particular problem or question.

Innanen echoes the need for these just-in-time communities:

We just never could get our information technology minds to understand that a community is actually a point in time. If you have Person A and Person C and they both belong to different communities—let's say one is a finance officer and the other one is a medical officer—it may be that just for this one moment of time, the finance guy wants to know how much it costs to run a hospital. Those two should be able to link up, share that information, and once they've done that, the community goes away . . . I really agree with that. There is a lot to be said for communities of practice, and it is nice to put functional folks together so they can determine who their subject matter experts are and face the issues that their specific community has to face. But I also think that a lot of other communities face some of those same challenges, and by placing them in this silo, we miss out on some opportunities to truly share some good experiences and successes across the board.

Communities of interest exist for differing periods of time. That is, they are based around a shared interest that may be quite ephemeral, or conversely, quite long lasting. This is different from communities of practice whose interests in their profession are ongoing.

Communities of interest don't necessarily have to be based around a business topic in order to be valuable to the business. As John Old of Texaco points out:

> **A passion of mine is removing the barrier to bringing your personal life into the workplace . . . It encourages connections between people who have similar interests . . . I know several people in Texaco who like woodworking, and I've discussed it with them, but it doesn't take very long before that conversation drifts off into a work-related topic. So it's a way of generating more connections . . . Metcalf's Law says that the value of a network goes up roughly as the square of the number of connections or nodes in the network. So when you generate more connections, you make the network more valuable . . . That's the idea, you encourage connections around all sorts of *interests* people have, rather than just trying to keep work and personal life separate.**

If we're trying to get people to share *business* information, they're much more likely to do that if they have established personal relationships that build trust and collegiality. And communities of interest can provide a place to establish those relationships.

Communities of Learning. Teachers usually transfer knowledge to students. Communities of learning offer people the opportunity to learn from *each other* as well as from an *instructor.*

In communities of learning, teachers become facilitators, and students become both learners and teachers of each other. Teachers and students share power and learn together.

Steve Innanen of AMEDD says that a learning community sprang up among the physical therapists of the U.S. Army Medical Command who used their Knowledge Management Network. He noted that while a formal virtual schoolhouse had been set up for them, they opted to create their own learning environment using collaborative tools such as on-line discussion groups. (See Appendix 2 for a detailed explanation of on-line discussion groups.) They then discussed case studies among themselves with only minimal prompting from an instructor.

At Marist College, a liberal arts school based in Poughkeepsie, New York, a community of learners developed around an on-line course offering. As part of a pilot learning project, Rebecca Thomas, Assistant Professor of Computer Science and Information Systems, teaches a C++ course to IBM employees. She says that students who work together at the same IBM location talk about the course and learn from each other. Thomas notes that there are differences between the students who are isolated and those who interact with each other. She says that the creation of a learning community is something she is going to focus more on in upcoming semesters.

The course Thomas is teaching is part of a larger pilot project called the Learner Support/Knowledge Management system, which is aimed at creating a community of learning among Marist students and instructors. The structure of this system is designed to stimulate on-line discussions and provide access to catalogued information.

What's intriguing about this project is its capacity for creating a learning community not only at the school, but one that also stretches beyond the boundaries of the learning institution. The resources generated by the community could be used by students, and people from outside the organization might eventually be allowed to access all the resources on the system, including content experts, instructors, and students. This would extend the boundaries of the learning community. In fact, the people accessing the system would likely become sources of information and learning for people inside the university or college.

Communities of Support. These communities exist primarily for the purpose of communication and building relationships. They don't have objectives or agendas other than to provide a place for people to talk about the things that are important to them personally. Now, this may sound like a waste of time in a business setting, but stop and think a minute.

The fact is, work gets done around both emotion and intellect. The connections between people on an emotional level has an impact on their ability to work together. If I develop a friendship with you, trust levels between us will be high, and that will have a positive impact on our working relationship. It will also have a strong impact on knowledge sharing and communication. Communities of support tend to build very high levels of trust because of the emotional and personal nature of their exchanges.

Let me be right up front here: I didn't find any examples of communities of support that were officially sanctioned within a business context. However, I didn't really search for them, either. But regardless of my lack of data on this topic, I think it's interesting to contemplate the development of communities of support within organizations.

One example of such a community is made up of new hires at IBM. According to John Iwata, IBM has a site on its intranet that supports new employees through the orientation process, giving them a first-year critical survival kit. He says that one of the big benefits of the site is that new employees have a place to swap stories and support each other. "They go through the company together as a class," he says. "They can help each other out as classmates and share their concerns and interests about being new to the company."

Setting Up Communities: Tips and Rules for Operation

If you are involved in starting a community (whether it's on-line or not), there are a few things you can learn from the people who have been there. There are a host of factors in making a community successful. You have to be very careful if you're trying to set up a community. Communities already exist in organizations, and you'll be most successful if you simply form communities around existing clusters of people. If you do have an idea that you think will draw people together, the best way to help a community form is to set forth the opportunity for people to participate, and then allow the community to quickly take over responsibility for sustaining itself. Communities need to be highly self-governing.

In this section we'll look at four aspects of community building: gaining commitment, developing rules, enforcing rules, and use of technology.

Commitment. Alex Lowy of the Alliance for Converging Technologies, and coauthor of *Digital Capital,* describes five conditions that help on-line communities achieve retention, commitment, and loyalty:

- Shared interests
- Time spent interacting

- Ability to make contributions
- Common identity as a group
- Development of interdependence

Of these five conditions, Lowy points out that contribution and inter-action are most important. People must feel a sense of self-direction; that is, that they can make changes that impact the way the community operates, whether starting a new discussion group or deciding on the rules of operation. And, of course, interaction is key to sustaining and growing the community.

Rules. Communities also need rules. They're needed to avoid what I call communities of kvetching. Many organizations have been con-cerned about the creation of on-line communities because they've read articles about how they disintegrate into whining sessions. This can be avoided by paying attention up front to the way the community is con-structed and moderated. Good facilitation skills can help redirect con-versations and move them in a more useful direction.

Fred Schoeps, Program Director for KM at IBM, points out that it is important to have people spearheading community building efforts who are adept communicators and who will be good at helping the group to agree on these governance issues: "People need to agree on how they will conduct themselves and interact with other people. That's not necessar-ily natural for people to do."

What is interesting is that these rules will need to differ based on the situation and circumstances of the community. Some communities will need stringent rules of operation; others won't. Lowy explains that the community also needs mechanisms of enforcement, and these will vary as well.

Enforcement of the Rules. Lisa Kimball, Founder and VP for Professional Services for Caucus Systems, has moderated thousands of discussions in on-line communities over the past 20 years. Kimball says that most problems occur when expectations haven't been set up front properly. When there are no established rules, people tend to violate norms acci-dentally, for example, forwarding copies of on-line discussions or admitting people to teleconferences without informing others. Kimball says that the best way to restore trust in these situations is to have a frank and open discussion in which the "offender" apologizes without getting defensive about the problem, and all the parties agree on how to avoid the problem in the future.

Other minor violations of the community norms include degrading or abusive comments. This is a more frequent problem in on-line community exchanges, and in these cases the skills of a moderator become significant. And Kimball suggests that the moderator call the "offender" on bad behavior in public, rather than drawing that person aside:

> **The whole group experienced the exchange, so it's important to bring it out to the whole group and say that's really not okay, remember the norms of our group are X and Y and Z. And the same thing is true in person. That's what a lot of people don't do in person, which is a problem as well. If a group has experienced something, it's important for the group to process it.**

Technology. Most of the examples of building community that I chronicle here use some form of technology for sustaining interaction.

The same technologies that can be used to locate people in organizations can also be used to initiate and grow communities. Tacit's e-mail profiling software, described by CEO David Gilmour, and the software used to locate people mentioned by John Old at Texaco, would be good technologies for locating people with common interests or common professional roles who might want to form a community. Any software that helps you find the right people can help you build a community.

Communities can use a host of mechanisms for interacting. Audio and video teleconferencing, on-line discussion groups, instant messaging, chat rooms, web meetings, shared electronic "rooms," all are types of technologies that can support the interaction in a community. It's important to understand the functionality of a variety of software and how it matches the group's objectives and their way of working. (For an overview of interactive technologies, see Appendix 2.)

In the end, of course, it's not the technology but the experience and the content in communities that counts. You don't have to have technology to build a community. And as an interactive manager, you may find that you need very little technology, or you may need a lot. Technology can provide an infrastructure or a foundation to support the community, but it isn't the entire answer.

Mike Burtha, Executive Director of Knowledge Networking at Johnson & Johnson, points out that it's as easy to get tripped up by technology as it is to benefit from it. He tries to approach community building in ways that create the fewest possible encumbrances on people's work. He gives the example of a small community of five people who might only need to do a teleconference every other Friday for two hours. And in between meetings, they may only need to fax or e-mail a few things to each other. They don't necessarily have to implement a more complex, technology-laden, on-line system. Burtha explains the importance of keeping things simple: "There are a lot of technologies out there that are really intrusive on people when they are trying to get their work done. Understanding the impact of technology on people's behavior is essential." The use of technology for building communities should make things easier for people, not harder.

As Alex Lowy, coauthor of *Digital Capital,* says, people will put up with the hassles of technology if they're receiving the rewards:

Communities are about the ability to connect with people that we care about, to say things that we feel are important, and have a sense that they're being heard and captured in a way that we trust. When we feel that there isn't violation of trust and confidentiality and that we have control over where our communications are going, then these places become trusted and attractive to us, so we want to go back again.

By putting people in touch with each other, giving them access to the knowledge they all possess, and by building communities, organizations can create environments rich in creative ideas and intellectual capital. Making people accessible to each other is the first of our 10 competencies for managing interactively.

Key Ideas from Chapter 2

- Know who your stakeholders are and communicate with them.
- Leverage intellectual capital through expertise location.
- Include customers in product design.
- Harness the power of communities to build relationships with partners, customers, and coworkers.

The next chapter explores a second competency: sharing power. Putting people in touch with one another is only one step in helping them to connect. Sharing power, as we'll see, sets the context for an effective interaction.

Share Power

When I say the word "power" to you, what comes to mind? If you're like most people, what it means to you is the idea of power *over* something or someone. For a lot of people it means the ability to control people or things.

For me, power has a different meaning. It's about the ability to make things happen, to initiate change. Back in the 1920s, management "prophet" Mary Parker Follett said that power doesn't have to be *coercive*. When power is shared, when it is what Follett calls *coactive*, it can be, in her words, "the enrichment and advancement of every human soul." It can also mean the advancement and enrichment of your organization.[1]

Coactive power is compelling in light of the realities of Peter Drucker's "postcapitalist society." In his book by that name, Drucker explains that knowledge workers now own the means of production and take it home every night in their heads. Collectively, they also own the means of production through pension funds and mutual funds. This has interesting consequences for power in organizations.

One of the consequences Drucker describes is the inability to supervise people anymore. To illustrate his point, he points out that a marketing manager may give a market researcher the assignment to do research for a new product design, but that the market researcher tells the head of the company what research is needed, how it will be conducted, and the importance of the results. Drucker further extends the analogy to the military:

The commanding general of an air base decides how many planes and of what kind are needed for a certain mission. But it is the crew chief, though vastly inferior in rank (and usually not even a commissioned officer), who tells the general how many planes are airworthy and what repairs they need before they can be sent off on their mission. Only a very foolish commanding general overrules his crew chief, despite the difference in rank—and such a commanding general, by the way, will not last very long.[2]

A colleague of mine says Drucker recently closed one of his speeches by saying that in a knowledge economy, we're all *volunteers,* and we've trained our managers to manage *conscripts.*

But despite warnings from Drucker, Johnny Harben, senior consultant for the change management consulting firm Smythe Dorward Lambert Ltd., points out that there are still people in management who expect deference after a career of working their way up the ladder. "Some people say, 'Hell, I've worked my way up this business, the least I can expect now is for somebody to get my coffee ... And I also want to tell the world my view of things now that I've reached the top.' " But Harben says this reaction to making it to the top produces knowing smiles on the part of coworkers who silently (or verbally!) respond, "Don't automatically assume that your opinion is better than mine just because you've reached the top." These days, respect is based far more on knowledge and experience than a position on an organization chart.

We've already talked about managing people who report to someone else, working with people half your age who know more than you do about technology, and software engineers who have agents.

A power-hungry approach is a problem in any organization, but it is particularly ill-suited to a business web or alliance. In an Internet-enabled business model, it's influence and knowledge that count. Getting people to deliver on a goal in this type of environment is a lot different from telling your employees what to do. If you don't share power with your alliance partners, little will get accomplished.

The age of deference is over.

The age of parenting is over, too.

Regardless of where you sit in an organization, guaranteed jobs are a thing of the past. Everyone has to accept more responsibility for making things happen, both in terms of decision making and actions. We can't sit back and blame the boss for everything anymore. Shared purpose and shared work dictate actions instead of *people* dictating actions.

In this chapter, I want to take a brief look at the concept of power, talk about examples of power-sharing from above and below, and close with a discussion of the use of technology and its impact on power.

Giving Power from Above

There are a number of ways that leaders can share power. One of the most obvious ways is to allow someone at a lower level to change or influence your decision making. But there are other, more subtle ways that leaders can share power. For example, they can choose to sponsor or conduct events that send a message about power-sharing and interaction.

One form of power-sharing event is Workout, a method developed at General Electric and championed by Jack Welch. Workout is both a way of sharing power and a way of mirroring a power-sharing culture. (A full description of how a Workout session is conducted can be found in Chapter 10 in the discussion of large group events.) One of the initial developers of Workout, Steve Kerr, Chief Learning Officer at GE, explains that Workout is different from many events in that there is a tremendous amount of follow-through and structural support for what happens at the meeting: "It's not like some of these events where everybody hugs each other at the end and trades phone numbers ... You don't say 'Maybe' and walk out ... You have real-time decision making." During Workout events, employees not only have the opportunity to express their ideas and opinions, but they can also initiate projects and get management commitment for the time and resources to see them through.

Kerr goes on to explain GE's philosophy on power-sharing, which is not only reflected in their Workout sessions, but also in their focus on boundaryless organizations (i.e., organizations that remove internal and external barriers between people):

> **In a bureaucracy, you worry a lot about who's got the highest rank. In Workout and in boundaryless companies it's just not a relevant question. The question is who's got the most information. So on Monday maybe the general is a manufacturing guy when you're talking about manufacturing, because he knows**

**what we're talking about. He's the general until the day we've
built it, because then we have to learn how to sell it. Then maybe
a junior guy, the marketing expert, he becomes king for a day. It's
not anarchy, we're still going with power, but the power comes
from having information that's relevant rather than being of a
higher rank.**

RootLearning® Inc. is a company that helps organizations share
power by creating the capability to think and act differently on critical
business issues. Jim Haudan, President, explains how significant the
impacts can be when people are given the opportunity to contribute in
events like the ones his company facilitates:

**At a focus group in Canada, a participant once said to me, "I
learned more in the last hour than I have in the last 15 years,
because this the first time I ever had to really *think*." She said,
"The most important thing is the dignity that comes from [man-
agement] believing that I could really think and add something,
rather than just be told what to do." She talked about how most
communication was not about learning, it was about persuasion—the attempt to persuade her to do what somebody else
concluded was needed to be done, versus the real dignity
involved in trying to ask her what she thought she could contribute to trying to find a solution. That was extraordinarily
meaningful to her.**

Giving and taking power don't always come naturally to people.
Events such as these provide a safe opportunity for people to practice
the skills of sharing power.

Power can also be shared by leaders simply through modeling a
behavior. Steve Kerr recalls a story about Jack Welch using this technique. Kerr was putting together an educate-the-educator program for
platform skills because some of the senior managers needed them.
Welch got Kerr to announce it during the corporate executive council,
which consists of the top people at GE. Kerr recalls the event:

**I said, "If anybody needs help, I'm available," and immediately
Welch says, "Yes, I could use some help, come and see me." And**

of course he's a very good speaker, needs no help at all, but it was his way of signaling to the people that he wanted them to do it and that it was okay to ask for help. So immediately everybody goes yeah, yeah, yeah, and it became fashionable to ask for help.

In this instance, Welch was sharing power with Kerr in a very subtle but effective way. By volunteering for the training, Welch used his power to help Kerr achieve the objective of improving the platform skills of the rest of the team.

Sharing Power from Below

The importance of using power responsibly cannot be overestimated, and using power responsibly means recognizing that all of us have power and that we need to share it in productive ways. This also includes taking responsibility for sharing power with the people "above" us in an organization.

Here's an extreme example of what happens when we don't share power with our bosses. At the top of Mount Everest in the spring of 1996, Jon Krakauer, the author of *Into Thin Air,* was poised at the edge of the Hillary Step. He was out of oxygen. Nearby at the South Summit he saw one of the guides, Andy Harris, rummaging through some oxygen bottles. He called to Harris to bring him a fresh bottle. Harris shouted back that there weren't any. Krakauer, desperate at this point, came over to examine for himself and found six full canisters, but Harris (probably mentally impeded by severe altitude hypoxia) refused to believe him.

Krakauer says that his own lack of oxygen contributed to his inability to see at that moment that Harris was in trouble. But there was something more that prevented him from questioning the situation:

My ability to discern the obvious was exacerbated to some degree by the guide-client protocol. Andy and I were very similar in terms of physical ability and technical expertise; had we been climbing together in a nonguided situation as equal partners, it's inconceivable to me that I would have neglected to recognize his plight. But on this expedition he had been cast in the role of *invincible guide,* there to look after me and the other clients; we had

been specifically indoctrinated not to question our guides' judgment. The thought never entered my crippled mind that Andy might in fact be in terrible straits—that a guide might urgently need help from me . . . Given what unfolded over the hours that followed [Harris died], the ease with which I abdicated responsibility—my utter failure to consider that Andy might have been in serious trouble—was a lapse that's likely to haunt me for the rest of my life.[3]

In management we've often cast our organizational leaders in the role of "invincible guides." Questioning the direction of a leader—especially a charismatic one—is not de rigueur. But that has to change in the fluid, paradox-ridden, complex environment we're entering in business. It's not unlike that blizzard at the top of Everest. All of us need to help each other find our way to the summit and back to base camp.

Our next example of power-sharing from "below" comes from business.

During an important off-site meeting, Scott Gassman got a disturbing phone call from his senior VP of Human Resources. Gassman, Director of Organizational Development for Empire Health Care (a large health insurance provider), says he was really disheartened by the news he received. For months he had invested a great deal of time and emotional energy working to introduce the use of large group methods into his organization. The VP who called was an important cosponsor for implementing those techniques, and he told Gassman he was leaving the company.

As a bit of background, large group methods (which will be discussed at length in Chapter 10, and which we mentioned in the GE Workout example above) are designed to help organizations work more effectively, efficiently, and democratically. Some people are threatened by the use of these methods because they require sharing control and authority.

Two large group events had already been held in the company, but Gassman and his colleagues needed senior management support for bringing the methods to the rest of the organization, and the loss of his cosponsor was significant. The senior-level sponsorship decision centered on one meeting with a consultant who was brought in to speak to the senior officers about the benefits of large group events. In keeping with the large group philosophy, this consultant was very nondirective, and it was making the senior officers uncomfortable.

During a short break in the meeting, the senior officers expressed their concerns to the Acting VP of Human Resources (who had replaced Gassman's cosponsor). She in turn relayed their concerns to Gassman, indicating that they wanted to stop the meeting. It was a moment of truth. Gassman could have ended the meeting. Instead he decided to share power with his boss when he replied: "Look, even if it means I lose my job, I've waited too long to get this far. I'm just going to go with it." The meeting continued.

As a result of the meeting, several key executives decided to sponsor large group events in their areas of the organization, and now they are widely used throughout the organization with great success.

Gassman's courage is admirable. He recognized his value to the organization and the importance of the issue. He responded to the use of power by his new boss in the right way. Instead of simply taking her directive to end the meeting, he recognized his own power to affect the situation and stood his ground. She, in turn, listened. We've all got to develop this ability to share power.

Recognizing that you have choices and that you control your own destiny is the first step toward responsible power-sharing from below. In fact, what we say and do to ourselves often does more to deprive us of power than any outside influence. I remember sitting in a business meeting for organizational development professionals a couple of years ago. One member of the group, a man from a large utility company, launched into a long diatribe about the horrors of his job, the hours, the incivility of the people he worked with, and his feelings of utter powerlessness to make any changes to how things were done there. I turned to him and asked him several questions about actions he might try in order to effect change. His reply: "No way, they simply aren't listening anymore."

Then I asked, "Why don't you get another job?" He looked at me with utter incredulity and said, "I can't, I have a wife and two kids in college and a big mortgage and ..." I listened as he poured out the list of reasons, and then I said, "If they've stopped listening to you, what makes you think you'll never get laid off or fired?" He suddenly went silent. "I never thought about it that way," he said quietly. Finally he was ready to listen instead of complain. The group of people we were sitting with reinforced the importance of his taking power, pointing out to him that he had all the right credentials to be highly marketable in the current business environment. They also convinced him that he had a responsibility to use his talents well, whether that meant staying or leaving his current job. Three weeks later he called to tell me that things had really improved at work and that changes he wanted to see were starting to be made. He acknowledged that a big part of the problem had been his lack of recognition of his own power to effect change.

One important point to note is that if we're going to take power, we need to do so within a context. Simply trying to wrest power from leaders for our own purposes is as futile an exercise as it is to withhold it for no good reason. In the cases mentioned above, there were good reasons to take power: A leader was in trouble on Everest, and in the other two cases the employees felt they couldn't do their jobs well without taking power. Clearly we need context, purpose, and limitation on how we share power in both directions.

There are no longer guarantees about job security or job satisfaction, or anything else for that matter. Each of us has the responsibility to try to change the things we can in organizations, to make the best use we can of our talents. Part of that responsibility means that we will have to accept the fact that leaders are no longer a substitute set of "parents." To be effective interactive managers, we will have to take power from above and teach the people who work for us to do the same. And this will mean both taking more personal responsibility for outcomes as well as giving up a measure of control as a manager.

Approaches to Communication in Power-Sharing Environments

Up until the restructuring of business in the 1980s and 1990s, organizations took a very paternalistic approach to communication. This type of approach is highly inappropriate in an environment where people share power.

John Easden, Group Marketing Director of First National Bank in the United Kingdom, says that he found the communication really needed reassessment when he came into his position. He explains that their business (like many other businesses) had been focused on developing information technology, doing business process reengineering, and keeping costs down. In that environment, Easden says the communication remained largely paternalistic in tone:

> In the old-style communications, they were talking *at* you. It was very old-fashioned, very paternalistic. What we're trying to do now . . . is to actually be a lot more adult, to engage with people openly and honestly about where we're going in this business, the tough decisions we're making, and why we're doing these things. And we're trying to put in place mechanisms that allow you to tell us what you think. For example, we now provide a reply device on every written communication, and we also hold regular two-way, face-to-face briefing sessions across the whole group. We are developing electronic chat rooms and notice boards for our intranet.

Easden says that the communication approach is now much more reflective of the way in which the organization has changed in terms of power-sharing.

Communication approaches in organizations can reflect a lack of power-sharing by withholding information from employees. Interactive management requires sharing information. Rick Fetherston, VP of Public Relations at American Family Insurance, agrees:

> You have to trust your employees and agents with information. Many corporations are paternalistic, and they try to hoard information. I counsel my CEO and president, "There are no secrets. Don't even try to have any, because there are no secrets. You have 11,000 people in this organization, you have 11,000 leaks. So, if you really want to control the information, control it by getting it out early, getting it out accurately, and trust people." People are independent, they're less trusting of authority, they want to be treated as adults. So give it to them. Don't try to hold anything back . . . Even if you don't know, tell them you don't know. Tell them you'll give them an update in three months.

As Charlene Wheeless, Vice President of Corporate Communications at DynCorp, a company that provides IT services and solutions, puts it: "We had to stop treating our employees like an audience for information dissemination. They're partners in the business."

Technology and the Sharing of Power

Interactive technologies provide excellent vehicles for power-sharing in both directions in organizations. But note that technologies are only power-sharing tools when their interactive capabilities are used. So often, technology is used as a one-way tool to disseminate information rather than to provide a channel for feedback.

Much has been written about the fact that e-mail flattens hierarchies in organizations. By making people at the top of an organization more accessible to people at other levels, shifts in power have undoubtedly occurred. And there's no question that by far and away, e-mail is the still the most popular interactive technology (perhaps with the exception of cell phones) in use in organizations today.

But there's so much more people could, and should, be doing.

For example, in Chapter 12, Bill Esrey, Chairman and CEO of Sprint, explains how he used an interactive meeting technology that allowed him and the president of Sprint to share power during a meeting by getting rapid, candid feedback from a large group of people.

Julie Beedon, an independent organizational development consultant in the United Kingdom recounts two interesting stories of the use of interactive technologies for power-sharing. In the first story, technology was used by a top executive to share power in a large group event and uncover an important underlying problem. The second story illustrates the perils of using an "interactive" technology in a noninteractive way.

Example I: Take a Vote

Beedon and her team were slightly puzzled, but satisfied. They had run a large face-to-face group meeting for several days, and while the meeting had gone very smoothly, there was something happening, some sort of undercurrent that the team just couldn't bring to light. On the fourth day, the chairman of the company turned up to interact with the group and ask some questions. He began by displaying a version of the group's vision and asked them to use an interactive voting technology to give him feedback on how well people felt aligned with the vision. The voting technology allows a large group of people to use a push-button key-set to vote on a range of issues, and the results are immediately calculated and displayed on a large screen for the group to see. This was certainly an example of using technology to share power. The chairman was making himself quite vulnerable. That fact became readily apparent when the group answered back that only 30 percent of them were on board with the suggested vision!

Beedon says that the results sent the team back to the drawing board to work on strategy for the afternoon, and eventually the numbers improved significantly. The technology had elucidated the group's lack of alignment with the vision, and Beedon says the problem would have been hard to uncover without it.

Example 2: Using What You Ask For

Interactive technologies aren't worth a hoot if you don't manage interactively. This story illustrates why. Beedon worked with the chairman of a very large global corporation for months, trying to convince him to be more interactive in his approach to an upcoming large group meeting with 120 of the top executives from divisions around the world. The meeting focused on developing a common purpose for the overall organization. They decided to hold an augmented meeting, which is conducted using a large screen display with text-editing software. The problem was, the chairman had essentially already decided the direction he wanted to go with the wording of the purpose, regardless of what the group itself came up with during their interactions. Beedon predicted disaster because, in essence, the chairman was asking for input with no intention of listening to it.

At the meeting, the 120 executives broke up into 13 small groups and worked on the wording of the purpose all morning. They presented these 13 versions of the purpose via the large screen technology, and then the chairman proceeded to *tell* them what the statement was going to be.

Beedon's prediction came true:

> **We had superb technology, we had all these statements coming up on the screen live. We were thinking, "This is fabulous, this is wonderful, we should get a consensus really quickly with this technology" . . . But then, of course, [after the chairman presented his vision] the reaction was pretty well exactly as I predicted, only at a slightly louder volume than I had predicted. I think the thing that troubled the chairman the most is that some of the CEOs who had been the biggest advocates of change were the most angry. I mean they were incredibly angry, at a level of anger that was phenomenal.**

After this strong reaction from the group, Beedon met with the chairman over lunch and managed to convince him that they could use the large screen display technology to come to consensus, but only if he was really willing to let the group do the work and only if he was willing to use their input. "So we used the large screen to display the work that people had done already, and within 45 minutes after lunch we had consensus on one of those statements," says Beedon. "It wasn't the same as the chairman's, but we worked with all the different versions and people were comfortable with it."

E-mail, voting technologies, and augmented meetings are only a few of the ways in which technology can be used to share power. For example, on-line discussion groups are starting to be recognized more broadly as a means of sharing power across hierarchical levels.

Unfortunately, however, many interactive technologies are not used to interact and share power. Lots of e-mails are of the one-way, broadcast variety, and lots of audioconferences are used to tell instead of to solicit input.

A great deal of time and energy is wasted in organizations where people aren't sharing power and working interactively. Interactive managers recognize that the people who report to them are usually closer to issues of concern than they are, and will often have the answers to solving problems and addressing opportunities. Likewise, people at lower levels of the organization have to be courageous in *taking power* when they need to. Everyone has responsibility for power-sharing—not just the people at the top of an organization. If the competency of power-sharing is developed at all levels of an organization, work can happen much more efficiently and effectively.

Key Ideas from Chapter 3

- Sharing power isn't an act of altruism, it's a business necessity.
- Power follows ability, not seniority.
- Everyone is responsible for sharing power, not just leaders.
- Technologies such as e-mail, voting software, augmented meetings, and on-line discussion groups can help you share power.
- Avoid paternalistic messages and show trust in employees by sharing information.

Physical environments often reflect how power is shared in an organization. For example, think of how most top executive quarters are designed. In many cases they are set up to reflect an aura of control instead of shared power. In our next chapter we'll focus on how interactive managers can design their physical environments to encourage better interaction and communication.

CHAPTER

Design Physical and On-line Working Environments to Encourage Collaboration

A COLLEAGUE OF mine has this amazing desk. It looks like it should belong to Henry VIII. It's huge and imposing and he used to have it placed perpendicular to the far wall as you walked into his office. Two chairs (that look like they belonged to Anne Boleyn) were placed across the desk from him. The impression it conveyed was that he was in charge and granting you an audience. Now he is actually a very interactive, thoughtful guy, but you'd never have known it from his office set-up. When I pointed this out to him, he was surprised. He said, "When we moved in here, the furniture was already here and I kind of liked it so I just kept it." Actually, he didn't need new furniture, all he needed to do was move it around a little. Which he did. And it made an enormous difference. With the desk against the wall and placement of the chairs near a couch, his office is much more conducive to collaboration and conversation.

All of us intuitively know that our physical environment has an enormous impact on the way we communicate, and many of us give a great deal of thought to this when we design environments in our homes. We spend time thinking about what kind of furniture we want and where we want to put it, we choose lighting fixtures, and we think about what will make us and our guests comfortable. Unfortunately we don't spend a lot of time thinking about environments at work—especially on-line environments.

Why should you worry about physical environments in an e-business era? There are several reasons. First, people will never stop meeting face-to-face. (If you don't believe this, ask yourself how many empty seats there were on your last airplane ride.) Second, if you are only going to meet face-to-face infrequently, you need to make the most of those interactions. Face-to-face collaboration isn't cheap, and it's important to support it with the proper resources. Third, e-business is all about creativity and innovation. Creativity is greatly influenced by environment.

If you want to encourage communication and collaboration in your workplace, it's essential for you to think about the impact of environment on work. Skeptical?

Imagine two meeting rooms.

One is filled with auditorium-style seating facing a lectern. The floor is a cement slab covered with a thin layer of standard-issue gray carpeting. Construction noise from an overhead room is playing counterpoint to the buzz of conversation from the adjacent room. Standard black and white photocopied materials are placed on each seat.

The second meeting room is in the same building, but as you walk in, there is music playing at a low level in the background. The floor underneath you feels softer somehow. Plants, movable walls and furniture, books, and computer kiosks on wheels dot the room. As you walk into the space, you see that relevant articles have been highlighted and posted on the walls. The lighting is not fluorescent, and you actually catch a whiff of fresh air coming from outside the building.

As Matt Taylor, student of Frank Lloyd Wright, puts it, "Environment speaks." How do each of those meeting environments speak to you? Which of the two do you think will most enhance communication for your upcoming 10-hour meeting?

As we learn more about the way people collaborate and accomplish work, one thing is becoming quite clear: Environment has a powerful impact on how well people communicate and create. If we want an interactive environment, we have to plan for it.

The same holds true for on-line environments. Many people spend the majority of their day on-line or on the phone. As the Internet increases the amount of business we conduct on-line, many of our meetings will be held in web conferences, video conferences, on-line discussion groups, etc. To be effective, we'll need to design these environments in the same way we need to design our physical environments. Otherwise, we won't get the level of communication and collaboration we desire.

As Tom Sudman, President of Digital AV, puts it, virtual environments are dimensionless space. So often we invest in highly praised groupware packages and then become dissatisfied with the results in terms of productivity and effectiveness. Often the problem is that we haven't thought about how to design for an on-line environment. An off-the-shelf groupware package is like an empty building. You have to think about the virtual equivalent of walls, furniture, lighting, and tools in order to make these "places" good for work. On-line environments require thoughtful design just like physical environments.

In this chapter we'll explore ideas about how to make physical and virtual space purposeful, flexible, comfortable, and stimulating in order to encourage interaction and innovation.

Purposeful Environments

Before you design or choose a work environment, think about your purpose and objectives. For centuries architects have designed purposefully: Cathedral steps evoke a sense of reverence as they force you to walk slowly toward the cathedral itself. Frank Lloyd Wright designed residences to match the lifestyles of their owners. And in business we design buildings for maximum efficiency on an assembly line (unfortunately, many of us still do knowledge work in these same environments).[1]

What is your company's culture like? What do you want it to be like? How does the physical environment reflect that culture? What are the purposes of the meeting you're holding? How does the place you've chosen to hold that meeting reflect those purposes? How do you and your coworkers prefer working together? Do you need to do more collaborative or solitary work? How is the space designed to accommodate those needs?

Once you're clear on what you want to achieve, you can match the environment to your purpose. In this section we'll talk about three types of ments: office space, meeting space (especially for large group events), and virtual space.

Purposeful Office Space

At Federal Express Canada there has always been a strong emphasis on working in cross-functional teams, and a high value is placed on collaboration. The previous building the company occupied didn't reflect this culture or way of working. In 1997 the company was housed in a building where it occupied six floors. It only had two austere meeting rooms, and all of the best locations were reserved for the offices of the top brass.[2]

In a recent issue of *Knowledge Report,* an on-line report published by Steelcase, Joe Tibensky, Manager of International Properties and Real Estate for FedEx, points out that the company is process-driven as opposed to product-driven and that this necessitates an emphasis on open communication. The old environment created significant impediments to this business objective of working in fluid, fast-moving teams.

The new building emphasizes openness and ease of communication, and deemphasizes hierarchy. Private offices on the perimeter have been moved to the center of the building into identical glass-fronted offices. The exterior walls next to the windows now house places for small groups of people to work. There is three times as much meeting space for formal meetings, and informal meeting spaces are located in each floor's central area. Because the staircases are open and aesthetically pleasing, people frequently cross paths there and stop for a few moments of conversation.

The people at Owens Corning, the glass and building materials company, carefully considered the importance of environment in effecting a culture change within their company. The leaders wanted to create a more collaborative, participative, decentralized organization with a flatter organizational structure. Their vision for the new work culture included self-directed networks of employees working collaboratively and utilizing technology effectively. They started by having architect Cesar Pelli design a new corporate headquarters that is horizontal and open, as opposed to the 28-story Fiberglas Tower that served as headquarters in Toledo, Ohio, until 1996. (See Figure 4-1.) Next they began work on the internal space. A planning process conducted by Steelcase Inc. and Harley Elling Design involved leaders and workers in redesigning the workplace to fit the organization's cultural objectives. They created 120 informal interaction areas, 80 fully equipped teaming rooms that include presentation and teleconferencing capabilities, and of course individual

Figure 4-1 Owens Corning Headquarters, Old and New
Source: Photos courtesy of Owens Corning

workspaces that are open and highly collaborative. Private enclaves allow people to work in a more secluded space.

A survey of 400 Owens Corning employees after they moved into the new building showed that 75 percent found their meetings were more efficient, 60 percent saw an increase in their productivity, 88 percent reported a high level of teaming within their departments, and 66 percent saw a high level of teaming across organizational boundaries.[3]

Purposeful Meeting Space

When choosing the place for a meeting and deciding on what the space will look like, purpose is of the utmost importance.

If your purpose is to signal a change, according to Don Parker of Parker Consultants, you may want to change the venue of the meeting:

> **I was working with a large advertising agency that was trying to decide where to hold an all-employee meeting to announce key decisions about significant changes that would occur in the way the business was going to be run, both structurally and process-wise. When we started talking about it, we realized that we couldn't hold it at the same hotels we'd always gone to. If I say to you, "We're going into a new world, we're going to do things dif-**

ferently," and yet I'm in the same building, same room, with the same faces, same people, same PowerPoint presentation, then you're sitting out in the audience thinking, "Why didn't we start now if things are going to be different?" We ended up holding the meeting in a bowling alley, and people still talk about it.

Once you've picked the place, you also will need to think about the meeting room space in terms of your purpose. If you need creativity and innovation from the group, what you'll need are spaces that say, "This is new, this is different, this is not going to be the same old stuff."

I once worked with an information technology group that wanted to shift its culture to become more customer-service oriented. In the new culture people would need to work in highly fluid teams and they would need to greatly improve their communication and collaboration across different parts of the organization. This meeting was being held to get people to brainstorm creatively about the things in the organization that needed changing. Interaction was key, and I didn't want people sitting with their friends, I wanted them to sit with the *whole department.* I had given meeting planners explicit instructions that there were to be no tables in the room. Instead, 150 chairs were to be placed in a circle at the center of the very large room. When I arrived, the room was full of huge tables, each set up for approximately 10 to 15 people.

When I explained to my client that the room setup would need to be changed, he said there was no way to get the tables broken down in time and make the changes to the room I requested. I said I'd break down the tables myself. When he saw me go over and start taking things off the tables, he consented to get help and we made the necessary changes. The meeting ended up being extraordinarily interactive, and my client later admitted that taking the tables out made a huge difference in the quality and quantity of their interaction—reflecting the type of interaction he was seeking in the new culture. Why was I willing to go to bat on such a seemingly small point? I've seen the power of these seemingly minor changes to internal space firsthand. Billie Alban, an organizational development consultant who facilitates and provides training for people on the use of large group methods, echoes my sentiments:

My partner and I just came back from doing a meeting for the King's Fund of the National Health Services in England, which is a

very prestigious think tank for the British health-care system. I had a funny interaction with the person who first asked us to do this, a very innovative guy, Martin Fisher. I said, "I want five-foot round tables." He said, "Well, we're accustomed to auditorium seating." I said no. He then said, "Well, we could bring in some tables, you know, square tables or something." I said, "No, I want five-foot round tables." Then he said to me, "Well, we're going to have to hire them." I said, "Hire them!" They did, and it was a wonderful meeting and he told me afterward that people said it was one of the best meetings they'd ever had because people got talking to each other instead of sitting there passively listening. *They ended up buying the tables.*

Whatever your purpose, site selection, interior design, and room design will be key to communicating your message. So far we've only talked about physical environments. What about virtual spaces?

Purposeful Virtual Environments

When working in an electronic environment, purpose plays a role at two points in time. First, purpose should drive the selection of the technology you're going to use for an interaction. Second, once you've selected the right technology, you'll need to design the interaction. An analogy might be made to the physical: Picking the technology is like picking a site for a meeting. But once you've picked the site, you have to decide about room setup. The same is true on-line.

For example, Brad Meyer, founder of Collaboration Ltd., a firm specializing in virtual meeting skills, points out that video teleconferencing systems have differing functionality and that these subtle distinctions can have communication impacts. When Meyer began working with British Petroleum, they started with one brand of video teleconferencing system that focused primarily on the video picture, and the senior executives became heavy users of the system for their meetings. When it was decided that the system needed to be spread around the globe for use by people at all levels of the organization, another video system was selected, because people at other levels in the company needed to share documents, and the previous system didn't handle document-sharing as well. The new video system had good resolution and quality for documents, but less quality in the pictures of *people* that were transmitted. The senior executives quickly lost interest in the system. Meyer says executives are more focused on sharing visual information than on sharing data, and so the new system really didn't do a good job of meeting their purposes.[4]

Mike Zisman, EVP of Strategy at Lotus Development Corporation, has significant experience working in virtual collaborative environments. Zisman points out that the more sophisticated your purpose, the more you have to consciously design an on-line environment. If all you want to do is create an on-line repository, a sort of shared file cabinet for a group, then simply purchasing and installing a groupware product will suffice. But if you want truly dynamic teamwork to take place in virtual space, you have to design for it.

Appendix 2 goes into more detail on how to design purposeful on-line environments more effectively and how to match technology to purpose. But for now simply recognize that purpose plays a role in the design of virtual environments as well as physical ones.

Flexible Environments

Interactive managers need flexible environments because knowledge work is unpredictable and unwieldy. This morning I may need to have a discussion with two people from engineering. This afternoon I need to work in my office alone. Tomorrow I need to do an all-staff meeting with 400 people. Flexibility is the sine qua non of interactive environments.

Whether you're in an office environment or a meeting environment, movable tables, chairs, and other tools are essential. John Kao is the author of *Jamming* and CEO of The Idea Factory, a company that provides consulting services in the area of innovation and creativity. The Idea Factory is housed in a massive loft space in San Francisco, where we conducted our interview. Movable meeting tools are essential to Kao's approach to using their space for meetings. "Nothing in this space is nailed down," says Kao. "Everything is movable...there are no assumptions built into the architecture of your interior design that would create a kind of legacy problem...hard architecture design really in some respects limits as much as it enables...so here we remove as many of the boundaries as possible...so that anything that needs to happen can happen."

The knOwhere Store in Palo Alto is an extremely flexible learning and communication environment. "We've been designing furniture with wheels on it for 20 years," says Gail Taylor, cofounder. (See Figure 4-2.) Everything in the entire knOwhere Store space moves—including the walls and even part of the ceiling. And not only are the walls movable, they're designed to be written on. Therefore there is flexibility in both movement and function. Tables and kiosks have "wings" that transform their functionality and add or subtract surface space. Their beautifully designed tables fold up neatly so they are very easy to set up or move out of the way. "Sometimes a table interferes with the creative process. Sometimes it's essential," says Taylor. "So we make it foldable, rollable."

Easels, individual desks, and file cabinets are all movable. Even the *ideas* you put on the movable walls are movable because they can be written on 11-by-17-inch tiles, called hypertiles, which can be shifted from one wall to another.

The movable walls make it very easy to reshape the space. "Okay, so you want to break out a team of 10; great, we'll shape it for 10. You want one for three, we'll shape it for three. The philosophy used to be that people had to configure to the environment," says Taylor. "But knowledge work demands that the environment configure to people, to their work. And so that's what we do."

Figure 4-2   Movable Walls and Furniture in The knOwhere Store
Source: Athenaeum International © 2000

Even the entire concept of The knOwhere Store is flexible and portable. The Rapid Deployment Solutions® (RDS) environment allows for the creation of special environments in public spaces. These environments are usually set up in spaces between 7,000 to 10,000 square feet. "A truck shows up with all the walls, all the toys, all the music, all the video equipment, everything in it," explains Taylor. (See Figure 4-3.)

At CLW Real Estate Services Group in Tampa, Florida, the office layout relects flexibility and mobility in its use of mobile tables, pedestals, and markerboard screens. The mobile tables can be used to either expand an individual's worksurface or it can be used for an impromptu team meeting. The mobile pedestal can serve as a moving file cabinet, and markerboard screens can double as writing surfaces or privacy screens.[5]

A survey conducted by Steelcase indicated that respondents need work settings that "morph" between private and public space to promote innovation, and they need company rules that support mobility instead of obstructing it. When Steelcase asked people what prevents them from tailoring their work environments to suit their immediate needs, 43 percent said the furniture was too heavy or hard to move. Another 27 percent said they were held back by company rules that prohibited it.[6]

Figure 4-3　A Portable Meeting Environment
Source: Athenaeum International © 2000

Flexibility in On-line Environments

On-line environments offer many opportunities for flexibility. For example, if you are holding discussions on-line, whether in audio conferences or on-line discussion groups, you can easily modify how you bring people together. And in a virtual environment you can manipulate time and space more easily than you can in a physical environment. For example, you can bring everyone together in the same "room" or you can break them into separate rooms. This can be accomplished in audio conferences by partitioning off people into separate discussions or having them all meet at the same time in the general discussion. In an on-line discussion group, you can have everyone in the equivalent of a "general session" or you can break out the discussion groups in other ways, perhaps according to topic or stakeholder group.

Virtual space is highly malleable, and so is virtual time. You can decide to hold a meeting at one particular time with everyone attending together, or you can have people check into an on-line meeting at their leisure. The concepts can also be mixed and matched, as can the media you select. Suppose you want to hold a meeting and invite a famous speaker whom you want everyone to hear simultaneously. You could do this by holding an audio conference, a video conference, a webcast, or an on-line discussion. Perhaps everyone was not able to attend. You could webcast the event after the fact, and allow people to ask questions of the speaker via e-mail for a week following the event. Or you could hold an on-line discussion with the speaker moderating the discussion for two days (at their leisure) after the event. The flexibility is tremendous when you are designing virtual interactions. (For more information and definitions on each of these technologies, see Appendix 2.)

Flexibility is a definite advantage, but it can also be a liability if you don't design your interactions consciously. Time and space are important considerations when you're making choices about selecting and using media. As Tom Sudman, whose company, Digital AV, specializes in the design of virtual environments, points out:

When you're trying to make something virtual, you're engineering time and space out of the process. . . . And you have to engineer the concepts of time and space right back in again. . . . [If you don't do this] there is no feeling of space, there is no negotiated social struc-

ture in which people are meeting. And in asynchronous format, like a Lotus Notes discussion database, or something like that, you basically lose the essence of time. And time, again, is a very important business parameter. So in the absence of time, thinking tends to become purely divergent and never convergent. And so you will intellectualize all the alternatives but never synthesize down to the best. And so it really takes a mixture of methods and tools and concepts in virtual space to create what I call the tempo . . . without that, people can't sense what they're into. They can't find the sense of urgency, they can't reach their goals.

On-line environments also offer the flexibility of adding or subtracting context. For example, in an on-line repository you can create links to other functions, such as an on-line discussion group. Sudman gives the following example as a link to a discussion: "Suppose I find a white paper that interests me by a particular author. On-line, I could be linked into the discussion that led to the creation of that paper. I can add context to the document by linking to another space or I can subtract context by zeroing in on what I need—for example, conducting a very specific on-line search."

Developments in virtual reality (VR) provide some fascinating glimpses into the future flexibility of working in a virtual world. Mike Rosen of Mike Rosen and Associates, an architectural firm that specializes in the application of VR, explains his vision of the flexibility that will come from being in an on-line virtual environment:

Right now the Internet is a two-dimensional world. As information comes onto the screen, it comes on relatively slowly, and it comes on like a slide show. You get one static image after another, and then within the static images you can have animations and streaming video and things like that, but essentially you're looking at a fairly still environment. Our concept is to create a three-dimensional environment on the Internet.

So, for example, when you log on to our site, you'll be able to go into the city and then do in the city whatever you would do in the real city. If you want to go to a museum, if you want to go to a restaurant, if you want to go to a store and shop, you'll be able to

do that on the Internet through our site. Unlike a game, where it's a new world to you, and you don't know what's going to be around the corner, this is going to be something that's going to be familiar to you—it's like walking down the street.

While much of the work in VR is experimental in nature, it's easy to see how this type of technology could play a role in the design of flexible virtual environments in the future. Imagine being able to enter a virtual meeting space that contains VR capabilities. Instead of being restricted to a text-based discussion, you would be able to move into a three-dimensional conversation space with a strong visual component. And with a developmental technology called Network VR, objects in the space could become mobile. So if we were designing a product together, we could literally look at it and hand it back and forth to each other in real time, rather than e-mailing files back and forth, or simply sending a photograph or video shot.

Virtual reality is pretty heady stuff for most of us at this point in time. In Chapter 7, Rosen describes some current applications of VR for businesses, and in Appendix 2 we'll discuss a definition of VR. But it is interesting to think about the possibilities it offers now and in the future for creating highly flexible environments for accomplishing work and collaboration.

Comfortable Environments

Comfort is a critical consideration when you are trying to encourage interactivity, collaboration, and communication in either a physical or a virtual environment.

The importance of physical comfort to collaborative work is obvious, and it's pretty easy to recognize that there are lots of things you can do to make people more physically comfortable and productive. You can adjust the lighting, add music (which people in business rarely think to do), give people more comfortable furniture, rearrange the furniture, move walls, bring in fresh air, alter the colors...the list goes on and on. And what seem like small changes can have huge impacts on communication and productivity.

All you need is a little observation to see that people in most workplaces experience discomfort with lighting—you see fluorescent bulbs being unscrewed, lamps being brought from home, and people vying mightily for offices near a source of natural light. What's the first thing we do in a room at home when we want to change the mood? We change the lighting.

Comfortable chairs are another key issue. When we're asking people to sit in meetings all day and contribute their best ideas, we're not making sure that they're comfortable. Gerry Laybourne CEO of Oxygen Media, a company that provides women's programming on the Internet and cable television, says that one of her top commitments to the people who work for her is to have comfortable chairs. A friend of mine likes to say that in meetings, the mind can only contribute as much as the rear end can withstand.

Psychological Comfort

In order for people to psychologically feel comfortable in a space, boundaries have to be set and respected. And nowhere is this more apparent in human behavior than around our issues of privacy. In order for us to feel comfortable in an environment, privacy is key. In the physical world, this has implications for how office space is partitioned. We talk a lot about open offices, but in the process we have to strike a balance between our need for collaboration and our need for privacy. Companies are beginning to attend to the need for all types of public and private space, including enclaves for small private meetings or personal work and the addition of scores of conference rooms to encourage more interaction in organizations. We need to have both personal and public space in order to feel both a sense of privacy and a sense of connection to our coworkers.

In virtual space, boundaries are even more important because it often feels like there aren't any. Virtual "walls" need to be built in order for people to feel comfortable about sharing information and opening up to others. Almost 20 years ago I wrote about the importance of creating a sense of "shared space" in electronic meetings and the value of using metaphors like the concept of a "room" to make people feel they are in a bounded space. All of the things I wrote about then are still completely relevant today. People need to know what the boundaries are in an on-line environment. Who is in the "room" when you're on an audio conference or in an on-line discussion group? How do we separate what stays in our space and what goes outside it? All of these factors are critical to establishing a sense of trust and psychological comfort when we're working on-line.

On-line, there may be "rooms" where we talk to everyone, and rooms we only share with a few people—the same public and private distinction I mentioned in physical space. It's important to be very explicit about the boundaries in these situations; otherwise you might inadvertently overstep one. For example, publicly posting information that's created in a small private group requires that you get permission from the group. But people will only observe that norm if they know it exists. It's almost like being in a building blindfolded. Unless someone explains that you're in a small space with walls, you may think you're standing in a foyer. And the opposite is also true, you could be standing in a foyer and thinking you're holding a private conversation. The implications are obvious: Big mistakes can be made if everyone isn't clear about where the "walls" are on-line.

As work increasingly crosses boundaries both inside and outside organizations, psychological comfort becomes a real issue. Sharing information in an on-line discussion group set up for your own department is a lot different from contributing to a discussion group that is set up with b-web partners or strategic alliance partners. This is when rules about what is public and private are particularly important. Developing trust virtually is a bigger challenge than developing it face to face. People will work better together in virtual organizations if someone takes the time to design those virtual environments properly.

When using interactive technologies, remember the need for psychological comfort. It needs to be made clear where the "rooms" are, what's public, what's private, and what the rules are for negotiating that space. Good facilitation and interpersonal skills go a long way in making people comfortable in virtual environments.

Stimulating Environments

Knowledge workers learn and work in a variety of ways: auditory, visual, kinesthetic, and tactile. Innovation and creativity will thrive in environments that have elements that appeal to all of these types of preferences. Interactive managers know that it takes a stimulating environment to produce stimulating ideas.

I've already mentioned the flexibility of the environment at The knOwhere Store in Palo Alto, California. It is also highly stimulating. The room is filled with books that you are encouraged to pick up and look at—not just business books, but brightly colored (and carefully selected) titles ranging from children's books to cutting edge science—and posters and all sorts of visual stimuli to get your synapses snapping. When knOwhere facilitation teams prepare for an event, they do background research so the entire environment is tailored to stimulate the people walking into it. For example, walls are covered with relevant articles, highlighted to make them more tantilizing.

I wanted to touch every surface I saw when I walked into The knOwhere Store. Instead of the steely coldness of most office products, this furniture is made out of gorgeous wood, silky to the touch. Even the movable walls are extraordinarily sturdy and have a smooth, solid wooden base and trim. As Gail Taylor puts it: "When we were building our walls, we gave a lot of thought to that wood. We want you to touch it and we want you to feel its solidness. We're not interested in things that feel flimsy or tentative. We're asking something very bold of the people who work in this environment, and that's to put their ideas and visions out there, to let go of control as we normally think about it. And in order to do that, that's a risk. And it's something that people normally aren't comfortable doing, but our environment invites it, and in fact almost demands it."

The environment is intentionally designed to please, invite, surprise, and evoke creative responses. (Here you even get to transgress your childhood taboo of writing on the walls!) It is relaxed, but you never question whether it's a space to accomplish things. Technology is threaded throughout, from workstations where group work is captured to video screens to computer kiosks. It's clear that this is a place where work and innovation will happen. "Toys" such as Legos, modeling clay, and science kits are used to help people model concepts and do breakthrough thinking. Someone might use a children's book to illustrate a complex concept that needs to be grasped by people across different disciplines. A Lego model can be used to simulate a business environment. Every conceivable tool to help people think, create, learn, and communicate seems to be housed in some nook or cranny of this space. (See Figure 4-4.)

The Taylors have created an environment where people can build prototypes of ideas. Michael Schrage, a research associate at the MIT Media Lab, explores this concept in his book, *Serious Play.*[7] The psychology of play and humor and their relationship to creativity is well known by theoretical psychologists, but ignored in our society—particularly societies with a strong work ethic. Businesses seldom recognize the value of play. But the Taylors' philosophy is based on the premise: "If you can't have fun with the problem, you'll never solve it."

Electronic environments also need to be stimulating. There are mountains of books written on web design so I won't visit that territory here. But it's intriguing to compare the amount of attention we give to designing websites for our external audiences with the lack of attention we give to internal virtual environments—whether they be in groupware or on web conferences.

Video conferencing and webcasting can also use a little spice, and Bill Machrone, VP of Technology at Ziff Davis Media, a technology publishing concern whose publications include *PC Magazine, eWeek,* and *PC Computing* (now *Smart Business*) points out that a range of new video products is making it easier to create more engaging video experiences

Figure 4-4   Example of a Stimulating Meeting Environment
Source: Athenaeum International © 2000

in companies. For example, he describes a very reasonably priced product for webcasting:

> **It's a . . . digital TV studio in a box smaller than a dorm room refrigerator. You hook it up to a PC and the PC is your control panel. And it will do titling, superimposition, fades, and cross-fades, and all of the professional TV studio effects such as flyaways and green screens. You can have waving palm trees in the background while you and I sit and pontificate in the studio.**

Instead of simply having talking heads yak during a webcast, this type of technology allows for more creativity in the design of a virtual meeting, through the creation of special effects. The Globecaster product comes from Play Inc., a company that melds high-end video and graphics capabilities for PCs.

Even if you can't afford the latest technology or an investment in the best interior design, you can make environments more stimulating by simply using your imagination. Use music in an audio conference, bring outside speakers in for a webcast, get creative people in your graphics department to brainstorm ideas for your next on-line discussion group.

Lisa Kimball, Founder and VP Professional Services for Caucus Systems, an on-line meeting provider, explains that it's often our own fault that things are so boring on-line. If we don't think about how we design environments, we will often overlook the fact that a small design element can make a big difference. For example, even a seemingly minor consideration of the use of language can have an impact, as Kimball illustrates:

> **I was just in a meeting earlier today with a company where we're doing some work around their knowledge management effort. Everyone's constantly wringing their hands and saying, "We just created this most unbelievably great knowledge repository with all these best practices and we can't get anyone to go in it!" And I said to them, "Well, does the *knowledge repository* sound like some place *you'd* want to go?"**

At the outset of this book, I pointed out that it's getting harder to get people's attention and time. In order to get the kind of collaboration we want from stakeholders, it's necessary to create environments that encourage it. Especially if you're inviting people who don't report to you to a meeting, it's all the more important that you create an environment that incents and excites.

In the end, being stimulating is about taking some risks, having fun, and making some mistakes in the process. As Gail Taylor puts it, "Being creative involves risks. You have to let yourself wander and you have to let yourself fail. If you're in the middle where you don't take risks, you can't succeed."

Key Ideas from Chapter 4

- The design of work environments powerfully affects collaboration, creativity, and innovation.
- Physical environments need to be as interactive as on-line environments.
- Groupware applications often fail when managers don't consciously design the on-line environment.
- Purpose, flexibility, comfort, and stimulation should guide the design of on-line and physical environments.

The concept of "design" in interactive management also extends to the next competency: creating rituals and experiences. Rituals and experiences can be designed (or altered) to improve collaboration and communication in organizations. When interactive managers want to say things in powerful ways, rituals and experiences offer superb vehicles for those messages.

Create Rituals and Shared Experiences

W HEN TWO PEOPLE meeting for the first time discover that they're both Vietnam vets, they'll often say "Welcome home" to each other. The ritual was developed among the vets in recent years. "We say it to each other because we know what it took to get home," says Jack Maloney, team leader at the Manhattan Veteran's Center. "It's a rite of passage for us." When my friend Bob Balogh, a Vietnam vet, told me about this practice, it struck me as an example of how powerful a shared experience can be, even if the experience is not shared in the same place, at the same time, or in the same way. People who serve in the same war have an experience that often provides an immediate bond, even if they never served within 500 miles of each other.

Rituals and shared experiences communicate powerfully. The more dispersed your organization is, the more important it is to create experiences that bring people together and give them a sense of belonging. This is particularly important in new types of organizations such as b-webs. If you are managing people who don't report to you—especially if they're in another organization—somehow you need to create a sense of commitment to the work you're doing together.

At the outset of this book I talked about the challenges of getting people's attention in an e-business era. Rituals and experiences, when properly crafted, can be enormously effective tools for interactive managers who want to break through the noise of today's e-business environment.

A word of caution: You can overdo it or completely screw up with experiences and rituals if you're not careful. I'll start this chapter by talking about nonevents and empty rituals. If events miss the mark or if you fail to reexamine your rituals from time to time, you can end up communicating in ways that you don't intend. It's also important to recognize that before you interrupt an existing ritual, you need to observe it over time. It's easy to be too hasty in making changes to rituals—particularly if you're operating on assumptions rather than data about why the ritual is or is not important.

After we explore the dangers, we'll look at some examples of well-constructed experiences and rituals and talk about the impacts of these examples, how to integrate the use of technology, and how to extend the effects of an experience or ritual. By learning to use rituals and experiences, interactive managers can dramatically improve communication in their organizations.

Avoid Nonevents and Empty Rituals

Every organization has rituals. Among the most common of organizational rituals is the meeting. Sales meetings, end-of-year meetings, celebratory meetings, and numerous other types of meetings are used to certain effect in companies. However, when rituals or experiences become stale, they become ineffectual. It's a real trick to create experiences and rituals that can last over time without becoming boring or hackneyed.

Nowhere does "Been there, done that" apply more strongly than when you're trying to create an experience. If people attending your "experience" have already had a similar one, you're cooked. Rick Melvill, cofounder of The Blue Moon Group, a company that pioneered industrial theater in South Africa, echoes this notion:

> People used to open their meetings with, "We'd like to begin with a screening of our dynamic new corporate video." The more common that got, the more audiences clouded over every time they heard the word "video" because they'd seen so many with chopper shots of the factory edited to [the music of] Vangelis's Chari-

ots of Fire. When you're presenting in an environment where people are overexposed to media like video or PowerPoint, you need to do something new.

While doing something new is important, overdoing things is an easy trap to fall into. Instead of coming up with truly creative and instructive approaches to designing experiences, managers often make the mistake of trying to turn up the volume on the entertainment factor—and the result is usually a nonevent. "Avoid the mass rally of the troops to honor the adored leader," says Anthony Goodman, CEO of Smythe Dorward Lambert Inc., a consulting firm specializing in change management and internal communication. "You don't want to have the dry ice and laser lights rotating with Tina Turner singing 'Simply the Best' for the eighth time this year." People might enjoy the show, but you won't really have a lasting impact unless you design experiences carefully.

More important than doing something new is the notion of doing something *relevant* and then making sure there is some sort of *follow-up* to the event to ensure that the experience you evoke can be translated back into the work environment. Don Parker, a consultant specializing in organizational change and management coaching, tells the story of a large advertising agency that held a mega-event under a massive tent on the plaza around Lincoln Center in New York City. Speakers and participants from across a number of disciplines—everything from work and creativity to food and fashion—were invited to come and help communicate the company's new vision. Interactive discussion groups were planned to encourage dialogue about the new vision and what it would mean for the people attending. The worldwide firm wanted this global leadership meeting of approximately 300 people to be an unforgettable event. Indeed it was, but for the wrong reasons. Parker explains:

In itself as an event, you would say it was very creative and it was very successful. But there was zero follow-up and zero communication following the event. It should have served as the foundation for a whole range of communications, across the whole organization. Instead, it just went dead, went silent. So it had the opposite effect from what was intended. It became a cheerleading event instead of an event to spearhead a change in the cul-

ture. Quite honestly, I think it would have been better not to do the event at all. Because, ironically, the fact that the event itself was so successful raised people's expectations, and then when nothing happened, those expectations were violated. And there's nothing in an organization, or between people, that will sour a relationship like violating expectations.

I asked Parker what could have been done differently, and he said that during the event there were small group meetings to discuss the relevance of what was happening at the event to what was going on back in their offices. Some of the output of those small group meetings was captured by the meeting leaders and written down, but nothing was done with it. Parker explains:

People left the event, went back into their own worlds, literally, from Asia to Moscow to Kuala Lumpur and everywhere else in between, and then the organization at the center, the headquarters, that had planned the event and pulled it together, simply went on to other things. They didn't even ask the basic questions: Have you done what you said you would do in Asia? Have you done what you said you would do in China? So when headquarters didn't ask questions, the rest of the organization felt there was no need for answers.

In an upcoming section we'll explore in more depth what people have done and can do to extend an experience beyond the boundaries of a single event, including preparation for the event and follow-up.

In addition to nonevents, interactive managers need to watch out for empty rituals. Peg Neuhauser, a consultant on organizational culture and author of the book *Corporate Legends and Lore,* points out that one of the most common forms of ritual, meetings, are often still held even when their purpose has vanished. And many are held the same way for years, just out of habit. Says Neuhauser: "I gripe at organizations all the time about their formatted meetings like staff meetings and other standard repetitive meetings. You ought to, every year or so at least, just scrap the format of those things and redesign them and come up with a new way to do it, so that they don't get stale and outlive their usefulness."

One suggestion she gives for dealing with repetitive meetings is to dramatically shorten their length and hold a series of very quick meetings instead. She says one company she works with holds a stand-up meeting on Monday morning to set the tone for the week, then holds another quick bring-a-sandwich meeting on Wednesday, and they wrap up the week with another meeting on Friday. And she means *fast:* "These are like 10 or 15 minute meetings. I don't even know if the term 'meeting' really fits. We need a different word for it!" Neuhauser says holding meetings in this fashion helps people to be more open to the idea of getting together because it keeps people focused, informed, and doesn't waste their time.

The point is, nonevents and empty rituals will set you back. Avoid them.

With that said, let's look at how to inject life and relevance into the experiences and rituals at your organization.

Incorporate Theater into Your Experience Design

Joe Pine and Jim Gilmore have written a marvelous book called *The Experience Economy,* in which they propose that "work is theatre."[1] In an attention-scarce world, their ideas are valuable tools for thinking about how to recapture people's imaginations through the design of experiences. Most of *The Experience Economy* focuses on creating *customer* experiences, and the approach to creating those experiences is based on the theater paradigm. However, in an interview for this book, Pine agreed with me that his concepts about the experience economy apply equally well *inside* a firm:

> **Today you have less of a social contract, a psychological contract, for keeping employees forever . . . [and you need to] develop a learning relationship with those you want to keep . . . so you need to stage experiences for those employees. And we see that increasingly happening in companies.**

Rick and Sue Melvill are the husband and wife team who built The Blue Moon Company, a drama-based communications consultancy based in South Africa. Blue Moon, now a part of the Johannesburg media group Salami, is a business built around the concept of theater and experience creation. The Melvills combine innovative theatrical techniques with communications methods to develop what they call industrial theater. Rick Melvill points out that with live theater, you can really capture people's attention and imagination: "Your mind doesn't wander like it does when it's presented with some prepackaged message."

Companies come to The Blue Moon Group with highly diverse business and communication objectives, and the Melvills design experiences around those objectives. Their production process involves extensive research, scripting, workshops, rehearsals, internal marketing campaigns, facilitator training, road show planning, staging, and pre- and postaudience research in order to create a unique experience tailored to that company's culture and purpose.

Let's take a look at some of the experiences people have created to improve communication in organizations.

Experience 1: Drumming Up a New Business. When AngloGold, a large gold mining company in South Africa, wanted to create an event around their new organizational structure, they faced an enormous challenge. The company had operated as 13 separate entities (listed separately on the South African stock exchange) and they wanted to create a symbolic event around the fact that they were merging all of those entities together. Each of the mines had operated as very separate, autonomous units, and people would have to give up a measure of their identity with those entities in order to see themselves as part of the whole company after the restructuring. Rick Melvill says that the logic of the merger lies in the fact that by working together they can have a much stronger influence on the gold market than they could as separate entities.

The challenge? The company needed to communicate this message to 60,000 employees. And 5000 of those people needed to meet at one location. How do you design an "experience" for 60,000 people? Melvill explains:

> In a lot of countries, I think they might call 5000 people together into a giant meeting and have huge screens and the CEO would stand up with a PowerPoint presentation, you know, and do some business graphics. In our event, 5000 people arrived at one massive venue, and when they walked in, they found dramatic lighting

and the incredible sight of 5000 drums. There were no chairs, only drums. So they all sat on the drums.

It wasn't long before the crowd was quieted by the rhythmic beat of African drums. Dry ice vapor flooded the room. Lasers and computer lighting systems created an unforgettable buildup. Suddenly there was a dramatic blackout. Standing center stage under a lone spotlight stood a drum leader.

Using only mime, the drum leader invited people to take up their drums. He then started all 5000 of them on a half-hour drumming session that nearly lifted the roof in an explosive example of the power of many hands and minds working in perfect sync.

So that's when the new chief executive walks out. Everybody is totally silent. He starts talking about the craziness of going out and beating out our own little rhythms and making a cacophony of noise and having no impact. And then he talks about the power of beating as one.

Not only did this dramatic event have an impact on the 5000 people in the room with the chief executive, but the event was linked by satellite to the other 60,000 stakeholders. While all 60,000 people did not have drums, each location had a drummer and a drumming performance. And each of the remote locations had sent a representative team to the central event. The event was tremendously successful in marking the transition from a fragmented organization to a unified one, and drumming is now a core part of the culture of AngloGold.

Experience 2: The Wall of Commitment. In 1996, British Airway's World Cargo business had experienced a significant decline. Competing with FedEx and UPS against a background of underinvestment had taken its toll on the cargo business, and the future of the business was in jeopardy. A turnaround would require a huge change in how employees viewed and ran the business.

Smythe Dorward Lambert Inc., a consulting firm specializing in change management and internal communication, helped address the issues the company was facing by first getting the leadership team to go out and run a series of half-day visioning sessions with employees. This act alone had tremendous impact, says Anthony Goodman, CEO: "For the first time ever, senior managers of this business were actually going out and talking face-to-face with a cross-section of their employees." And they made a point, Goodman says, of including the unions in these visioning sessions:

> **This was done as a partnership with the unions, whereas in the past, the two groups had been very confrontational. The unions would have blocked it, but instead they became involved in the team that was putting all the change together. In these visioning sessions they had a few charts around the walls; there were no slides. It was managers, shirtsleeves rolled up, actually getting down and talking to their people about what they were trying to do with the business, why it was important, and what help they needed. And those proved highly, highly influential in starting to turn that organization around.**

Once the vision had been clearly articulated, Goodman says it was important to cement the understanding of where the organization was going with an experience:

> **We needed to create something experiential. It was no good just telling people in a newsletter or in small group meetings how the new organization was going to work, because people couldn't understand. There was going to be a whole new cargo terminal, totally new technology, everything about that business was going to be turned upside down and done differently.**

The Smythe Dorward Lambert team built a "virtual environment" in a warehouse at Heathrow that was designed to take people on a journey through what it would be like to be a parcel in the current business versus what it was going to be like to be a parcel in the new world. As employees walked in the door they were bar-coded. Some of these human "parcels" were lost and some made it to their destination. But all of them got a sense of what was happening in the current organization. The virtual environment was manned by actual employees from all over the world—not consultants. Everyone from the board at British

Airways and all of the employees in World Cargo went through the experience. At the conclusion of their "tour" people were asked to sign the "Wall of Commitment," explaining what they were going to do as individuals to help bring about the change in the organization.

This innovative approach to communicating with employees worked. Says Goodman:

> **It's had very good results. Initially, obviously, the issue was, "Is the airline serious about investing? Does it want to be a major player in the cargo industry?" The decision was yes, the leadership and the people in the business had committed to turn it around. Over time now it's been very successful in terms of the results coming through from that business. BA's numbers came out for 1998, and World Cargo was one of the bits that was growing while other parts of the airline were shrinking.**

Designing Experiences for Large Groups

Large group interventions are a class of methods specifically designed to allow participants to create their own experience. These approaches (discussed in more detail in Chapter 10) bring large numbers of people together for a diverse range of purposes ranging from strategic planning to product development. Almost all large group interventions are aimed at bringing about change in organizations. These methods take a variety of forms, but what all of them have in common is a high level of participation and self-direction. Facilitators play a different type of role in large group meetings. Instead of acting as traffic cops, they help set the context for the meeting, and then the group does most of the work of seeing to it that the experience is productive and useful. The facilitators are much more nondirective in large group meetings than in regular meetings.

What this high level of self-direction does is engender a very different sort of experience for the group. In running large group meetings myself, I've found that they often encourage the kinds of behaviors that many leaders are trying to foster in their day-to-day work environments: People take responsibility for making things happen, there's not a lot of whining, and they become resourceful and creative in solving their own problems and creating new opportunities. The experience of being in a large group meeting is hard to describe if you haven't taken part in one. You can view a video of what a large group experience is like, but it's hard to understand what happens in terms of the transformation of the group unless you attend one.

I believe the most profound part of a large group experience is the change it brings about in people at the individual level. It's difficult to explain why, but for some reason after a large group meeting, people have more of a sense of their own power to effect change and a greater appreciation of what they can contribute to an organization. They also learn in the course of the meeting to appreciate the views of others and to enter into productive types of dialogue. What's interesting is that no one teaches them these things. The experience brings it about.

Julie Beedon, a consultant in the United Kingdom who hosts large group meetings on a regular basis, says that the result of a well-designed large group meeting is that you "shift the way people work." She says that large group experiences engender a sense of possibility:

> **I think what it creates is a belief in individuals that things don't have to be the way they always were, and it creates that *critical mass* of people who believe that things don't have to be the way they were. It's an unfreezing experience that people go through. They start to think, "Hey, we can do this!"**

Large group methods vary in their approaches—some include heavy use of graphics, some use technology, some don't—but all of them are focused on creating an experience that transforms people's attitudes toward change. And these methods generate results. In Chapter 10, you'll see examples of how these events are used for real-time decision-making. The experience creates an environment that motivates people to act on ideas.

Don't Overlook the Value of Smaller Scale Experiences

Not all experiences have to take place on the scale of a large group event. John Kao of The Idea Factory describes how his company created an experience for a group of executives from Royal Dutch Shell. Kao's group was asked to help these executives consider the question, "What is the future of the big mature company?" Kao explains: "They wanted to know what's going to be important about managing in this world of the medium-term future." His group felt that it was important to approach the topic in an unconventional, creative way, so they created what he calls the "dilemma dinner party."

The executives flew in from Europe and attended a dinner party set up inside The Idea Factory. In the middle of the dinner a homeless lady wandered into the room and started speaking in a very incoherent way. "They were very taken aback," says Kao. "They were frightened. This was a woman that had been sprawled on the sidewalk out front when they walked in. And it took them several minutes for them to figure out that she was an actor playing the role of the person who does not have a seat at the table to talk about the big issues."

Kao's group also brought in other actors posing as "outsiders," such as an environmental activist, a young entrepreneur, and a specialist in business ethics. "And we hooked them," says Kao. "Because they were unable to be dispassionate and kind of clinical about the homeless lady. She was in their face, in their space, in their personal zone. And it was an incredibly effective meeting."

Regardless of the size of an experience, the important notion to recognize is that experience shapes people in ways that words on a page or screen cannot. If you want people to go beyond an intellectual response to a message, design an experience.

Extend Experiences Beyond an Event

Preparation and follow-through for an experience is paramount. All too often (as Don Parker showed us in his example of the tent meeting for the advertising agency earlier), people create an event or experience and then neglect to tie it back to what happens at work.

As Billie Alban, a consultant specializing in large group events, points out:

> Some of these large group methods naturally have follow-through, because they're a series of conferences until the work is redesigned . . . it's a process. Others tend to be one-shot events, and so the question is how do you structure them, what do you do for follow-through? And I think any planning committee has to start by asking that question. Is this just an event? I think many of these events should not be seen as a onetime thing, but as part of a process.

In the upcoming sections, we'll present some approaches to extending an experience.

Extending Experiences Through Technology

Technology can be used very effectively to extend an experience. For example, Lisa Kimball, founder and VP Professional Services for Caucus Systems, a company that runs on-line meetings and virtual events, says that on-line discussion groups can be a powerful way of extending an event or experience, particularly large group events. Kimball says that the facilitators of such events recognize that while in the face-to-face moment you can have very profound results, it's often a challenge to get those commitments and changes transferred into everyday work. On-line conferencing, she adds, is a way of extending the impact of large group events:

> [On-line] conferencing and the strategies we use can extend some of those same dynamics that you had in the face-to-face experience into the workplace. So a lot of our work is about bringing a group of people together in a different kind of space with the same underlying principles that these large group interventions have.
>
> All of these methods are about gathering together people [who] have passion about discussing something, and that's what makes the process work. What we do in the e-world is let people self-select into the conversations that they have passion about being in. We design a framework where that can happen within a conferencing environment.

In fact, this same type of technology can be used to *create* an event that is extended over time by actually holding the event or experience on-line in the first place. Fred Schoeps, Program Director for Knowledge Management at IBM, explains how they created an on-line experience for their public sector group. For a kick-off event, they traditionally like to bring people together for a couple of days for a conference. However, they wanted to bring together 2500 people in over 90 countries. How can you bring together this type of group affordably?

IBM's Public Sector management decided to try something different and created a place on the web where this massive, dispersed group of people, made up of employees from the public sector group and their business partners, could meet asynchronously over a period of three weeks. Schoeps said they moved into an e-space that was designed like a conference, with a café, general sessions, and concurrent sessions. (See Figure 5-1.)

One of the most important ways in which this format for the conference allowed people to extend the experience was that all of the questions and answers were captured on-line. Schoeps points out that this allowed people to go back and reflect upon what was exchanged. He says, "And this helped them to internalize what happened in a way that you can't do if you're running from one room to the next to listen to somebody at a face-to-face conference." Schoeps also notes that a large part of the value of the on-line conference was derived from the

KM Center

You are Scott Burns, MDG.
You can manage this site.

KM Blue 98
A Web Conference for Knowledge Management within IBM
| Objectives and Goals | Event Format | Week 1 Calendar | Week 2 Calendar | FAQ |

Cafe
KM Cafe
Conference
NEW

OpenSpace
KM Open Space
Conference
NEW

Keynotes
KM Keynotes
Conference
NEW

HotTopics
KM Hot Topics
Conference
NEW

Stories
KM Stories
Conference
NEW

RefCenter
KM Reference
Center

Bookstore
KM Bookstore
KM Guest
Author NEW

KMBlue98 is produced and hosted for IBM by Metasystems Design Group (MDG)

Caucus version 4.05/110 is a product of Screen Porch LLC.   Your browser is MSIE 5.0.

Figure 5-1   Example of an Opening Screen for an On-line Conference
Source: Illustration reproduced courtesy of IBM and Caucus Systems

relationships that were built when people "talked" to each other on-line, not just to the presenters—thus extending the experience through the network of new relationships that were built during the course of the conference.

Listening Teams

At British Airways soaring fuel prices, tight competition, and deep discounting, among other challenges, recently caused the airline to develop a strategy that had a clear focus on premium travelers, cost savings, and superb customer service. After their privitization in the 1980s, BA had in place a very successful program called "Putting People First." In light of the new competitive challenges in the industry and the radical approach BA planned to take to meet these challenges, they designed another program to involve employees in helping to shape the direction the company needed to take. "Putting People First Again" was the name of the program that was aimed at recognizing the importance of people (both customers and employees) as being at the core of the BA brand message.[2]

However, a one-shot event for 58,000 people isn't usually enough to get the sort of sustained changes in attitudes and behaviors an organization looks for.

Instead, the team from BA, in conjunction with the U.K.-based Marketing & Communication Agency Ltd. (MCA), is holding five 250-person events per week in four-week cycles over the course of two years. Three months prior to each event, "listening teams" are selected from a cross-section of the employee base. Departments have representatives on "listening teams" who go out into the company on behalf of their department to learn more about its business. Many of the conversations the listening teams hold are captured so they can be shared more effectively. The information they gather is used as part of the conference, and after the event the listeners form a network of people to help apply what they've learned across the organization.[3]

The events themselves combine group discussions and candid presentations from senior BA managers (including CEO Bob Ayling) and other highly interactive activities designed to help participants take part in understanding where the company is going and participants' contribution to strategy.

By putting the listening teams in place and having them work prior to and after the event, the BA/MCA team extended the value of the experience far beyond the conference event. As Kevin Thomson, Chairman of MCA, explains: "Most companies will have events, but then they don't sit within the life of the body corporate. It will tend to be an event for the sake of an event... So the significant moment needs to be shared by everybody, but then you need to create a loop back into the business."

Lifesaving Theater

Perhaps one of the most powerful examples of extending an experience comes from Ransom Paine, another gold mine in South Africa. Rick and Sue Melvill of The Blue Moon Group tell a moving story about how they created an industrial theater experience for Randfontein Estates that had a profound impact extending far beyond the presentation of the performance.

Safety production is always a big concern in the mining industry. Several years ago Ransom Paine was having a problem with its safety record, despite the fact that it had sessions every morning that included a lecture on the importance of safety. Sue Melvill points out that the sessions were dull and that people began to cut corners in terms of safety. There was also a focus on bonuses that contributed to the problem because workers were cutting corners in their pursuit of production targets. The Blue Moon Group worked to get involvement of people in determining the root causes of the safety problems. Rick Melvill says, "We wanted to tap into the knowledge of the people who are actually at the rock face in terms of how they could solve problems within the company. This was a novel approach, because the mining industry tends to have a paramilitary flavor in terms of management style."

Once they obtained management approval, the Melvills designed and presented a piece of theater that depicted what was actually going on in the mines. Bonus-hungry employees were depicted throwing caution to the winds in their relentless pursuit of cash. Miners were shown rushing and cutting corners to meet their quotas. People clearly saw themselves in the actors, and the response to the event was an emotional one.

After the presentation, people broke into small, facilitated groups to talk about their response. "That led to a lot of input back from the workforce as to the problems in their area," Rick Melvill explains, "and then there was a very strong response from management in terms of delivering on their suggestions. It was just a matter of getting the people to talk about their problems and listening to them and then acting on it." Gathering and using this input effectively extended the experience.

The results were impressive. Extending the experience by going to the "rock face" prior to the event, using the event as a catalyst, and then following up with methods of feedback and response, resulted in the program making a huge difference. The miners began observing the safety standards. In the course of one year, fatalities dropped from 14 people to 2 people.

Interrupt and Change Rituals

Sometimes interrupting an *existing* ritual can be as powerful as creating a new experience or ritual.

Jack Welch at GE used this technique very effectively to signal his commitment to adhering to values as well as making your numbers. Steve Kerr, Chief Learning Officer at GE tells the story:

> **Welch used an occasion to do something shockingly different. . . . At the beginning of every year there's an operating manager's meeting, which is the top 500 people at GE. They go down to Boca Raton and hang around for a few days and it's usually a celebratory occasion because, at least in recent years, there's been much to celebrate. It's good times. And the year in question was 1992, which was a remarkable year for GE because 1991 had been the last big recession year, and so many companies—most companies—had ruinous financial reporting, and GE actually made money. So people came in expecting it to be really a great good news session. And Welch got up and he started by saying, "Look around you. Five people you're used to seeing are not here, and they're not here because they were fired." And it was just so shockingly different than what the occasion was built for, let alone what should have happened. And then he said, "Of**

the five, one was fired because he didn't make the numbers, four were fired because they didn't have the values."

That's significant, and was also shocking, because it didn't make any sense that you could make your numbers and still have trouble at GE, and particularly the idea that you could make your numbers in 1991 and have trouble. Everybody still talks about it. . . . Welch described the five people, said they didn't behave in a boundaryless way and so on and so forth. I happened to be in his line of sight as he left the big auditorium during the first break and he asked me, "Do you think that was really harsh?" I said, "Well, it depends what you had in mind. It sure did dispel some myths." And he said, "Good, that's what I wanted," and he kept walking. So it was a really great example of staging an event to change the culture of the place.

Kerr points out that Welch not only interrupted the ritual, but he also extended the experience by coming up with a matrix for measuring adherence to values as well as numbers. "It had the results on one axis and values on the other. And that began to put flesh on the bones. To this day, if you have the values but you're missing the numbers, we'll give you another swing. If you make the numbers but you have no values, you're out of here."

Welch also interrupted a ritual to inform people of the importance of their Six Sigma quality initiative. Golf forms an important part of the ritual at the annual officers' meeting. Welch himself is an avid golfer, and Kerr says that at every officers' meeting, golf is on the agenda for the afternoon. On the day they started the Six Sigma initiative, Welch got up at the officers' meeting, without any warning or notice, and said, "This is the most important initiative I've ever heard of, and because of the unusual importance of this initiative, golf is cancelled." Welch had brought in a speaker to lecture, demonstrate, and entertain questions about Six Sigma during what was originally planned as golf time. Kerr says people quickly got the message about the importance of Six Sigma. Interactive managers will often find that the alteration of existing rituals can be as powerful as creating new ones. If you're trying to institute change in your company, you'll find that rituals and experiences can be highly effective communication vehicles.

Key Ideas from Chapter 5

- Be careful with rituals and experiences; you can overdo it.
- Extending an experience is critical to achieving real results.
- Experiences can be extended through technologies such as on-line discussion groups or methods such as listening teams.
- Interrupting a ritual can be as powerful as creating one.
- Rituals and experiences build and reinforce cultures.

Certainly experiences and rituals are ways of connecting groups of people, but in order for these experiences to be successful, the individuals who participate in them have to be proficient in communicating with their coworkers. Interpersonal skills can help make experiences more successful. Chapter 6 examines the next critical interactive management competency for connecting people: getting over yourself.

CHAPTER

Get over Yourself

I T WAS FUN doing the interviews for this book. With two exceptions, everyone I spoke with was delightful. Let me tell you about one of the exceptions.

I arrived at George's office five minutes ahead of schedule. (The name has been changed to protect the rude.) I was promptly greeted by his impeccably polite assistant, who ushered me to a couch in the middle of the reception area. I could hear George's voice as I waited because there were no walls to the offices. He was casually discussing the writing of a business plan with someone he wanted to hire to do the job. Twenty-five minutes later he came out of his office to meet me. The first few words out of his mouth were, "I'm not sure if we'll be interrupted, and I don't think I can spend the amount of time we planned together." Given that I had traveled about 2000 miles to do the interview, and that he was late for it, this seemed quite amazing to me.

It got worse. About 35 minutes into what was supposed to be our hour-long interview, he got a phone call on his cell phone. Without so much as a backward glance, without a whispered, "Sorry, I need to take this call," he turned his back to me and told the person on the phone, "No, you're not interrupting me, I was just finishing up an interview." I waited for a couple of minutes, then I went to ask his assistant if I should stay or leave. She suggested staying, and I did—for 25 more minutes. George never turned around to give me so much as a nod or a wink. I finally had to leave because I had another interview scheduled about an hour away.

Most of us could easily dissect this scenario and point out George's mistakes. But we rarely do the same level of analysis of our own behavior. If George reads this book, I predict he won't recognize himself in the example. We are amazingly blind to our own communication inadequacies.

Unless you're willing to take a good hard look at yourself and what you're like, it's hard to manage interactively.

Poor communication skills are often labeled "personality issues" and dismissed as unimportant or not resolvable. This is naïve. Lack of candor, defensiveness, self-importance, and careless use of language can destroy projects and ideas. Nothing kills innovation and creativity faster than a person with all the answers. Business ecosystems and b-webs narrow our margins for error because they are totally built around connections between key players. Crucial relationships can be destroyed instantaneously through thoughtless communication. Egos and e-business don't mix well.

Getting over yourself is also critical to retaining and attracting the best employees. You need to be the kind of manager that *you* want to work for. Whether you're in a hot job market or a recession, top people will always have other options. And even if you can lure people to work for you with money or other attractions, you won't get the best out of them if your communication skills are lacking.

It's not enough to simply do a onetime assessment of your communication abilities. Getting over yourself requires vigilance and, in some cases, training.

Many executives hire coaches to help them assess their skills and to give them candid feedback on how to improve their communication. I think this is a terrific idea. In the same way that it is hard to edit your own work when you're a writer, it's hard to assess your own communication and leadership capabilities and design a course for improvement. Coaches can be a tremendous help in this regard. You probably got some external help the first time you did a business process reengineering project. Getting help with interactive management and communication shouldn't be any different.

But you don't need a coach to start the process yourself. As you go through each of the following sections, give yourself a grade. Do you avoid risks when you communicate? Do you place blame instead of focusing on outcomes? Do you try to "fix" things by having the answers instead of asking questions? Be honest. And, interestingly, you just might find that some of the skills you develop will help you *outside* of work.

This chapter will cover eight skills that are essential to improved personal communication:

Skill 1: Tell it like it is
Skill 2: Focus on outcomes
Skill 3: Don't avoid conflict
Skill 4: Ask questions instead of spouting answers
Skill 5: Use words carefully and consciously
Skill 6: Pay attention to what's not said
Skill 7: Make adjustments for differences in culture and personality types
Skill 8: Take time to reflect

So far in this book we've discussed four of ten communication *competencies* that interactive managers need in order to improve communication in their organizations. In this chapter we'll drill down to the *skills* level because it's hard to develop competencies such as connecting people, sharing power, and aligning messages, etc., unless you and the people in your organization have developed good communication skills as individuals.

You may already know most of the lessons in this chapter. But some of it will be new. For example, technology ushers in a whole new set of issues around the development and use of personal communication skills, and there are stories about that here.

Despite your level of communication proficiency, read through this chapter for two reasons: (1) A little refresher course never hurt anyone, and (2) the stories people tell here are amusing, motivational, and instructive.

Of course, this chapter isn't comprehensive. Interpersonal communication is a whole discipline in and of itself. There are many, many skills not touched upon here. This chapter centers around the skills that I believe are the most critical for interactive managers in an e-business era.

Skill I: Tell It Like It Is

An e-business era demands candor. Why? For three primary reasons. First, technology brings with it *transparency.* Organizations are rapidly erasing organizational boundaries by sharing information across an enterprise or even across a b-web. For example, Cisco's information systems are directly tied in to all of their external partners. This gives them a clear line of sight deep into their partners' financial and operating data. What kinds of secrets can you keep in that type of environment? As we've seen in previous chapters, employees, partners, and customers have access to an unprecedented amount of information. If you don't tell it like it is, they're likely to let you know it.

The second reason an e-business era requires straight talk is because the era of e-business is also the era of *autonomy*. People are becoming less and less dependent on their relationships with organizations. As we discussed in Chapter 3, they have become partners in running the business as opposed to complacent "workers." Lack of candor with a business partner spells big trouble.

The third reason why candor is important is the increased need for *speed* in an e-business era. Telling the truth, quite simply, makes things move easier and faster in the long run. If we're honest with each other, regardless of our level of management, it greases the wheels for working more quickly, smoothly, and effectively with other people. Fast companies are usually candid companies.

Candor Must Come from All Directions.   Of course, in the same way that sharing power in a company is a two-way street, candor has to come from all directions, not just from above. As John Easden, Group Marketing Director and head of communication for First National Bank in the United Kingdom explains:

> One of the saddest things for me was that when we first started asking employees for feedback on our management approaches, most people said, "Oh, this is a great opportunity," but we got one or two people saying, "This is the worst company I've ever worked for." The really sad thing for me was not that they wrote about their dissatisfaction, but that they didn't feel they could put their name[s] down, so I could go and say, "Look, I want to know why." This is not a blame culture. I want to know why, so I can do something about it . . . . We're not saying that we're going to always change what we've been doing as a result of people's input, but we may have gotten things wrong. If those concerns are kept down below the surface, we can't address them.

Without candor at all levels, it's hard to initiate change or work at top speed. And interactive managers need to be candid about two things: facts and feelings. (Stay with me, I can hear those psychobabble sirens going off.) Most of us understand the need for candor around facts, but the fact is, human beings work and make decisions on the basis of both facts and emotions, and emotional candor can pay off handsomely.

Doug Loewe, VP of Global Sales for UUNet, a subsidiary of MCI Worldcom, works at a pace and with a travel schedule that would put me in the hospital. The man is always on an airplane, always moving. He's been through three major mergers in as many years, and most of his team has gone through those changes with him. Loewe points out that candor is an essential element for working in a warp-speed-everchanging environment: "First, you have to make sure you recruit people who *like* going down the M25 at 125 miles an hour with their hair on fire. Otherwise, this is a very difficult environment to exist in…then you've got to let people know the real poop, not sit on information, let them know the truth. You have to say to people, 'Hey, this is bothering me, too. I'm not sure I understand this, but here's what I think we can do to manage through this change.' " Loewe gives the example of talking to his coworkers about a management shift following one of the mergers. He says one of the incoming executives had a reputation for being difficult to work with. When people asked him about this, he told them the truth: He expected a bumpy road. But he also pointed out that the person coming in was extremely competent. His honesty about the newcomer's personality went a long way toward preparing people to deal with the realities of working with this person.

In searching for root causes of problems in organizations, candor is essential at all levels of the organization, from top executives to line workers. John Moro, Division Manager for Integrated Customer View at AT&T, tells the story of how candor helped his organization move forward with an internal client on a critical issue:

With root cause analysis, when you have a problem or a breakdown, you keep asking why it happened . . . the hardest part is getting to the root cause because most people don't want to acknowledge mistakes . . . . Once, we had a situation where some things went fundamentally wrong between our organization and

another part of my boss's organization . . . . So we had to discuss the issues. My boss, my peer, and our customer held a conference call. And I decided to try something.

I said, "Listen folks, for right now my team and I are going to take responsibility for this breakdown." Everyone was kind of surprised when I said that. I could tell they were ready to jump down my throat. But as soon as I took responsibility, the attitudes shifted. They ended up having respect for that. Most of the time when someone makes an error, they get defensive about it. And when they get defensive, they lose credibility.

And I told my team, "Listen, we definitely made mistakes, let's not argue with them. Let's learn from this." And as it turned out, we did make most of the mistakes, but they made a few, too. I told my team, "Sometimes it's best to just admit things, so we can get past them and fix them. It's easy to spend too much time pointing fingers and not even discussing productive issues. So, let's just accept that the mistake was made and get to work." People make mistakes, they're not perfect.

What's interesting about candor is that it begets candor. When one person takes the risk to ask a tough question or call things as they see them, it elicits the same sort of response from the others. Ironically, the more vulnerable we make ourselves by being honest about both facts and feelings in communication situations, the more powerful those interactions become.

Candor and Difficult Decisions. Johnny Harben, Senior Consultant for Smythe Dorward Lambert Ltd., a change management and internal communication consulting firm, tells the story of eliciting a candid emotional response from a CEO when he was head of communications at Grand Metropolitan, a large food and beverage conglomerate, during its merger with Guinness. Harben captured the story when he was recording the CEO for an audiotape about the merger:

The whole company was watching what would happen with regard to the merger in the period between May and December.

One of the top level appointments was a man who was *loved* by the company. He had a combination of personal charisma, absolute integrity, and brilliance. He was president of the company in Europe. However, there was another equally qualified candidate for his position. The news came out in the media that this fabled president wasn't going to be in the new company, and it sent a shockwave around the business.

I said to Keenan [the CEO], live on the tape, "How do you feel about losing Ned?" He immediately said, "I don't want to talk about that, Johnny, can you turn the machine off? We didn't agree we'd talk about this. Anything else?"

He closed up his book and disappeared into his office. I was thunderstruck. I thought, "Damn, I've probably blown it completely with the guy now." I began to pack up my things . . . . Suddenly he came back into the room and said, "Turn the machine back on." There was audible emotion in his voice. He said, "I've got to tell you the decision that we made about Ned was the toughest business decision I've made in my whole life." On paper that doesn't look like a very emotional statement. But he could have said a whole lot of other things, like, "I personally feel very sorry that he's going, blah blah blah." But for the professional businessman, Jack the Knife, Keenan the Barbarian, to say "that was the toughest decision of my life" was a shocking statement. It was about emotion, friendship, and personal regard, and it really had quite an impact. It got people thinking, "Great, we have done that and now we can move on."

Harben's taking the risk to ask a tough, candid question set the tone for Keenan's honest response—another example of how candor begets candor. This example illustrates the importance of being honest about emotions as well as facts. Keenan could have simply avoided the whole issue or given a dry statement of the facts about the decision. Instead, his candor put the organization in a position to proceed instead of spinning its wheels about an emotionally charged issue.

Harben says that executives are not always eager to be emotionally candid: "When you ask a chairman to tell you how he's *feeling* about a merger, you're likely to get a response like, 'Well, John, I'm not sure anybody would be terribly interested in what I'm *feeling.*' You can almost see the English cartoon books with the word, 'Harrumph!' " But Harben says it is important to ask these questions because these are the type of questions employees want answered during a merger. People want to know the truth about both facts and feelings, because they recognize that key decisions will be made based on both.

Candor and Vulnerability. *Vulnerability* is not a word that's used very much in business. But it's an important word, and vulnerable is how people usually feel when they're being candid about their emotions. Phil Harkins, author of *Powerful Conversations,* explains:

> **Vulnerability is the essence of powerful conversation. You've got to be willing to risk the threat, the fear, the embarrassment part of it, you've got to be willing to stick your neck out there . . . . Trust breaks down because people are afraid to talk about things . . . . They're afraid that [being honest] is going to interfere with their ability to get what they need . . . . And the great leaders, the Jack Welches, they just step right up front. That's where Workout [sessions at General Electric] came from—get everybody in a room, and let's get everything out in the open . . . that is total vulnerability: Let's talk about everything.**

Bill Machrone, VP of Technology at Ziff Davis Media, writes for some of the top technical publications in the world, and he'll often write an article explaining a problem he has installing software or getting a network to work in his own home. Now this is a big exposure when you recognize that some of the world's smartest techies are among his readership. "Readers are very sensitive to your level of expertise," says Machrone. "Most of the time they expect you to be knowledgeable and authoritative. There's a fine line in the readers' reaction, between regarding you as empathetic or just pathetic. The confessional seems to work best when everyone is in the same boat—when they can identify with the experience you're having. It puts you on a common footing with the audience and increases rapport."

Leaders and interactive managers are perhaps most vulnerable when they admit they're wrong. But they're also most effective. Don

Tapscott, Chairman of Digital 4Sight, an e-business strategy consulting and research firm, tells the story of giving a speech to the top 200 people in the military for a NATO country. The strategic planning meeting centered on the theme of communications.

Tapscott was the second speaker on the agenda. The first speaker welcomed everyone to the conference on communications with a slide presentation. "I'm thinking, this is going to be a tough audience. Communication with this group is going to be about traditional command and control, and this has been going on for centuries," recalls Tapscott. "So then the admiral gets up to the mike and says, 'Well, communications is a very important theme, I agree, but communications is a two-way street.' And I'm thinking, 'Yes! Okay, maybe I was too hasty, maybe he'll say some good stuff here.' And then he says, 'We as senior management have a responsibility to communicate down to the rank-and-file, but they have a responsibility as well, to be open and *receive* our communications.' So I'm thinking, 'I'm really toast, because my message is about *nonhierarchical* communication.' "

Tapscott persevered with his own definition, telling the audience about how the Internet is enabling new forms of human communication: "I told them that for me, communication was about communicating from all directions, not just top down, but also bottom up and side-to-side. Okay, the body language was not so good, but a quarter of the way into the talk I see people starting to think 'Aha!' " At the close of his speech, Tapscott wondered what the admiral would say:

> **The admiral returns to the mike and says to the crowd, "Communications is a two-way street. I really got that wrong, didn't I? If one of my subordinates gave me a really strong suggestion, I'd view that as quite inappropriate. Maybe we're going to have to rethink fundamentally how we communicate. Command and control makes a lot of sense in the battlefield, but what proportion of our efforts are spent in the battlefield? Is that how we should develop software and do planning? I'm real interested in this new medium for human communication. Let's have a real open discussion here."**

> **So "Aha!" is *really* happening now. There's a wave of sentiment that moves across the room, and people are lined up at the**

microphones. It was like this one person, this admiral, had the ability to let that happen. And that's what really struck me. It took a lot of courage to do that, because it's in front of his superiors, his peers, and his subordinates. But he kind of let it go and the whole thing just blew wide open.

This is a terrific example of candid interactive management. This leader not only made himself vulnerable by saying "I was wrong," but he also used it as an opportunity to open up the discussion to the entire group, releasing the power of all of those pent-up ideas and contributions.

Candor is particularly important when you are working in widely dispersed organizations or in new forms of organizations such as b-webs. People are naturally predisposed to trust others from their own organization before they trust people in other departments or other companies. Trust across boundaries is essential to effective working relationships, and candor builds trust.

Using Technology to Encourage Candor.   Technology can be used as a medium to either encourage or discourage candor. Phil Harkins, CEO of Linkage Inc., says that even e-mail can be used to encourage open, honest dialogue:

> **To send out a powerful e-mail, you can start by being a little vulnerable yourself. You can say, in the very beginning, "I've been giving a lot of thought about the sales plan, and I'm feeling it's not completely out of whack, but I just don't know where to go with it." For a senior person in the organization to say "I don't know where to go with it" is very vulnerable. I'm looking for help. You talk about an accolade, an affirmation of their power, by saying to that person, "I need your help because I don't know where to go with this." That is so much more powerful than saying, "I've given this thought, I know exactly where I'm going."**

Lisa Kimball, founder and VP Professional Services for Caucus Systems, an on-line discussion software provider, says that the right on-line environment can promote candor and vulnerability: "For a lot of people, an on-line discussion feels safer. We've seen topics brought up on-line that were initially not easy to discuss in person. Then, after having them brought up on-line, the next time the group got together in person it became part of the conversation. An example would be something tough to discuss like, 'Who's really going to be in charge of X, me or the other guy?' "

Sometimes people have to be prodded to be candid. Rick Muller, Coordinator of Marketing and Interactive Media at Poudre Valley Hospital System, where Matthew Shepard was taken after being the victim of a hate crime incident in Wyoming, says that initially his administration did not want to release information about what was going on:

> **The initial challenge was that the CEO did not want to address the issue. His initial reaction was to avoid the situation, to not provide information to the media, and to lock all the doors. To his credit, he listened to our explanations. He had a choice. He could provide the information as we suggested, or allow the media to get the information any way they could, which usually means asking employees about what's going on, which puts the employee in an awkward situation. As he began to understand the larger context, the CEO became an enthusiastic supporter of providing more information, especially through our website. He became the spokesperson, offering a sense of credibility that no one else could have provided. By being up front, we avoided several conflicts and were better able to anticipate needs.**

Wherever you sit in the "hierarchy" of your organization, you have a responsibility to yourself, your coworkers, and your organization to tell the truth about the facts and about how you feel. Otherwise your organization will struggle to compete in an e business era. Technology such as e-mail, discussion groups, and websites can be used to encourage candor—but only if the people involved are willing to be candid themselves.

Skill 2: Focus on Outcomes

When communicating, especially around situations that are challenging or emotional, it's all too easy to lose sight of shared purpose. Instead of centering discussions on outcomes, we diverge.

Purpose gets clouded because we're focusing on the wrong things. As Julie Beedon, a communication and large group intervention consultant, explains:

> **People need to become more purposeful. When you stick to the purpose, you create a totally different quality of conversation. If you and I are arguing about how we should do something, if we shift the conversation into talking about *purpose*, we'll have a totally different kind of conversation. When we first set up our consulting company, we were all very different and we used to disagree about things. Typically, consultancy companies of three or four people don't survive the test of time. When we had disagreements, one of my colleagues always used to say, "Wait a minute, wait a minute, do we all want the same thing here?" He would just remind us that we had that shared purpose when things were really low.**

Without a focus on outcomes, it's easy to get caught in what Phil Harkins, CEO of Linkage Inc., a human resources consulting and research firm, calls "the Swamp." The Swamp is the place where people sometimes get stuck when they're trying to communicate. A number of factors contribute to getting stuck in the Swamp, which is characterized by complaining, frustration, and resignation.[1] One of the ways to get out of the Swamp is to focus on outcomes instead of placing blame. Harkins gives an example of how someone with an inventory problem in a large company used a purposeful, fact-based e-mail as a way to get of the Swamp:

> **People had been shooting back and forth e-mails about how we better solve this inventory problem, and there were a lot of threatening kind of statements that were being made, like you better, you will, or if you don't—that kind of thing. This was really getting into the Swamp. What happened is that over time we were able to get the key person to write an e-mail that was really perfectly scripted, that started with, "Let me tell you what I've been feeling about a lot of these e-mails. What I'd like to do is to start in the beginning and sort of retrace our steps. And let's talk about what's up. Let me see if I've got it straight in terms of**

where everybody's at . . . . And then let me give you three or four facts that emerge from this, and what I'd like very much to hear back from you is confirmation as to whether these facts are accurate. Because if we get the facts down, I think we can get to the underlying assumptions, and that will bring us the possibilities . . . ." And their inventory discussion went to a whole new level, and within four or five good solid e-mails back and forth, they were able to get to a place where they've never been able to get to before.

On-line work is already widespread and becoming increasingly prevalent. It offers both opportunities and risks. It is no longer unusual for work relationships to exist solely on-line. E-mail, telephone, and other technologies may serve as our only link to people we work with in complex, long-term projects. In this context, virtual conversations take on more weight and interactive managers must pay closer attention to their communication. A purposeful approach excludes blame and defensiveness and makes on-line work much more productive and profitable.

John Moro, Division Manager, Integrated Customer View, at AT&T, says that sticking to the facts and staying focused on outcomes is critical to succeeding in fast-paced organizations:

We still have a long way to go, but we're much more open and we do speak from the data. It's really driving up performance. My team has become a very high-performing team. I can see it. I can leave them in a room now and just let them go at it, because they're going to be open with each other and they're going to use data as a foundation for their discussions.

Projects go much more smoothly when people keep their purpose in mind, and stay grounded in the facts.

Skill 3: Don't Avoid Conflict

A couple of years ago I was doing some work in an IT department at a large midwestern insurance company. I've become very accustomed to easy, open relationships with all of my clients, and what distinguished this group is that there was one guy I just couldn't reach. Not only did he not like me, he was working actively to undermine the work I was doing with the group. I let this guy get to me. I didn't like him, either, and I used my position as a consultant to the organization to tell his boss just exactly what I thought of him. But I made a mistake: At first, I didn't say anything to the guy directly.

Later I faced down the conflict. On this type of engagement, part of my consulting involves a series of coaching days. I was scheduled to meet with each member of the internal IT consultancy for a coaching session. I was sure he would find a way to bow out of the meeting, but his boss *ordered* him to come. Needless to say, neither of us was looking forward to this. I thought I'd say, "Look, you don't want to be here. I don't want to be here. Let's just pack up our stuff and go on to our next meeting." Then I decided it was time I stopped avoiding a direct confrontation with this guy. I mean, hey, I'm supposed to be the communication expert, right? But the fact is, confrontation isn't any more fun for me than it is for anyone else.

So, I started the meeting like this: "Look, Bob, you and I aren't crazy about each other. That's pretty clear, right?" He nodded vigorously. I continued, "So I figure we can either use this next hour and a half to learn about ourselves and each other or we can totally waste it by being scrupulously polite and avoiding the real issues. The fact is, I feel like I haven't been able to reach you as an instructor or a coach, and I really hate the feeling that I've failed here. Because obviously there's some stuff I haven't been doing right. You're a smart guy, you've been to a million workshops and coaching sessions. Tell me what I can do better."

Whoosh! The floodgates opened up. And miracle of miracles, Bob had some really good points to make about my shortcomings. And as soon as he saw that I really wasn't going to get defensive about his comments, he started to soften and listen to some of my comments as well.

Now, don't get me wrong. Bob and I aren't best friends. But at the very least we both learned something from that interaction and we used the time really, really well.

The fact is, conflict exists whether you address it or not. And it costs organizations time, money, and energy.

Sarah Fasey, Internal Communications Manager for Microsoft Ltd., the United Kingdom and Ireland, tells the story of observing a constructive conflict at the executive level. Microsoft U.K. places serious emphasis on their "values" program, which had been in place for over a year and a half when some feedback came in that one of the executives had not "lived the values" in a public meeting. A number of employees had witnessed this and were upset about it. Fasey explains:

> I was privy to the exec meeting where they spent considerable time discussing the incident and their responsibility as role models for values-consistent behavior. You know, it was absolutely top of their mind that the behavior had been unacceptable. They have a very open and honest dialogue with each other, so it was actually handled in a very mature and honest way. I happened to be in the meeting, waiting for another piece of the agenda. I was both surprised and pleased that it was such a candid discussion.

Fasey says that the conversation was constructive because the values program gives people a language to help with difficult conversations:

> I mean he didn't like what he was hearing, but I think the values give us a useful way of questioning people's behavior. It gives us a common language, so if you fail to turn up for a meeting, fail to do what you agreed to do, fail to, I don't know, cooperate with me on an issue that I needed your help on, I've got a language I can use. I can say, "Look, Mary, I'm a bit concerned, you know. I thought we'd agreed that we were both going to do this. One of our values is integrity. Can I have a conversation with you as to why we didn't do this when we said we would?" So it opens the conversation. If we didn't have the values, I think it would be harder to find the starting point for that conversation.

Technology adds an interesting dimension to the whole notion of conflict—particularly e-mail. Because of the lack of verbal and nonverbal cues available on e-mail, conflicts can easily arise, and therefore they need to be confronted. Steve Kerr, Chief Learning Officer of GE, says that it's important to confront people who seem to be doing the e-mail end-run around the people they work with:

> I'll often write back and say, "What did George say? What did Jean say about that?" You should permit people to talk to you, but you can't let it be an end around. You've got to let them know: "We can always have a private exchange, and I'll respect

that, but I can't act on what you're going to tell me if you don't let me talk to anybody about it." So you can vent to me, but I may ask permission to go talk to somebody about it after we finish our e-mail exchange. That's my ground rule.

Lisa Kimball, founder and VP Professional Services for Caucus Systems, a company that runs thousands of on-line discussion groups a year, says that e-mail can really activate people's imagination when it comes to conflict, especially on virtual teams. She says it's much easier to confront people constructively when you see them every day than it is when you're in a virtual environment.

Kimball goes on to say that on-line discussion groups present some interesting dynamics when it comes to conflict. She notes that it's important to be very explicit about group norms and rules up front in order to avoid unnecessary conflict, but that when it does occur, it's important to address the conflict quickly and publicly:

The individuals who are observing a conflict between two people [in an on-line discussion group] are all thinking, "Oh God, what's going on, what's going to happen?" So the facilitator really needs to make it public and explicit that it's not okay for people to act out. So it's not good enough to just call the bad person aside and say, "Quit being such a jerk," and call the [victim] and say, "Gee I'm really sorry." The whole group experienced the conflict, so it's important to bring it out to the whole group by adding a comment into the on-line discussion that says, "That's really not okay, remember the norms of our group are X and Y and Z." You'd also want to do it in the same way in person, really. That's what a lot of people don't do in face-to-face meetings, and it's a problem there as well. If a group has experienced something, it's important for the _group_ to process it.

And the fact is, technologies such as voice mail and e-mail can be used as a shield to avoid conflict. As Betsy Pasley, Communications Planner at financial services company USAA, points out: "Leaving a voice mail at a time when you know that person's not going to be there is really a chicken way of getting out of what should be a face-to-face, or at the very least, a telephone, encounter."

But don't assume from all this that e-mail is an inappropriate medium for dealing with conflict. David Specht, CEO of Seeing Things Whole, an organization focusing on values-based decision-making and conflict management, says that e-mail can be very effective in mediation. He notes that while proposals from different parties in a mediation are usually delivered to people in the context of a face-to-face meeting, some of this type of work is starting to happen via e-mail. But Specht notes that the mediator still needs to be in the loop:

> **We've used e-mail as a way for participants in a negotiation to submit proposals. In low conflict situations, such proposals are frequently e-mailed out to all the participants—including the mediator—in the negotiation. In high conflict situations, the proposals should be e-mailed instead to the mediator, who will then rework any inflammatory or unclear language, without changing the content, in order to get the proposals into a form that can be heard by everyone. In instances where the conflict is extremely high, the mediators, again using computer technology, literally do their work in a shuttle diplomacy fashion, where the participants may never see each other.**

What it boils down to is this: If you're willing to take the chance to confront someone directly and you're willing to take responsibility for the way you handle that interaction, it's likely to be successful, regardless of the medium you choose. However, each medium presents a different set of constraints, so it's important to consciously think about how you will adapt your communication to deal with those constraints. Appendix 2 addresses the functionality and constraints of different media.

Given the pace and complexity of work in an Internet era, conflicts are more likely to arise. Whether it's a conflict between you and a local coworker, or a misunderstanding with a strategic alliance partner, address the issue early and directly. It will save you time and may well save the relationship.

Skill 4: Ask Questions Instead of Spouting Answers

In "Choruses From the Rock," T. S. Eliot says, "Be prepared for him who knows how to ask questions."

All of us like to have answers when we're faced with challenges, whether the challenges belong to us, coworkers, family or friends. But asking good questions can be as valuable as having a lot of answers.

"The language of powerful conversations is not to respond, but to say, 'Tell me more,' " says Phil Harkins, CEO of Linkage Inc. Harkins says that in order to gain people's trust, you have to inquire. Telling does not build trust in the same way that asking does.

Jim Haudan, President of Root Learning® Inc., has built a product line and a business around a philosophy grounded in the Socratic method. His company helps people at all levels in organizations to have a deep, profound understanding of company strategy and where they fit in delivering that strategy. This level of learning comes from asking, not telling. Says Haudan:

> **We're leading not by giving answers but by engaging people in the most critical questions. . . . A Socratic approach is important because it is really based on learning. It is based on discovery and curiosity and searching and connecting and linking . . . .**
>
> **I've worked with a number of senior executives who have struggled with this question. They'll say, "Okay we'll do all this stuff you suggest . . . but what if our people don't get the right answer?" And I say, "What do you mean? What is the right answer?" And once asked that, and pushed hard, they realize there really isn't a right answer. Dialogue becomes the engine that allows the exchange to have a greater richness than just the simple answers that might come from teaching or presenting or providing a conclusion.**

Haudan provides an example. While working with a retail distribution client, he and his staff asked people at all levels in the company, "What's more important, profitability or volume?" The RootMap™ tools the people had been working with to understand the business allowed them to wrestle with that question from a knowledgeable standpoint rather than by simply providing their opinions on the matter. The dialogue that took place between people from all levels of the organization was tremendously productive because they were well-informed. More important, senior management didn't give them the answer. By using the collective intelligence of that group of people, who were engaged in a dialogue, Haudan says that complexities of the business that had not been clear for four or five years became crystal clear in a matter of hours.

It's a challenge to get people inside a single organization to understand and execute strategy. That challenge becomes even tougher in alliances and new business models such as b-webs. Interactive managers know that dialogue, rather than broadcasts, can fire enthusiasm for cross-boundary projects.

Skill 5: Use Words Carefully and Consciously

If you've ever learned another language, you know how easy it is to make a mistake, and not just with vocabulary. Language is a maze of nuance. Even when two people share the same language, it's not always easy to understand what the other is trying to say.

Interactive managers understand the complexities and power of language. A simple change of words can mean the difference between a project's success or failure. You think I'm overstating the case? Here's an example: The head of communication at a very large financial services company wanted to introduce the use of on-line discussion groups into her company. Apparently, some of the top brass had been reading their airline magazines because they were strongly opposed to the idea based on some articles they had seen about these discussions suggesting they could disintegrate into whining sessions. "We floated the idea of discussion groups and it just got an absolutely horrible response," says one of the people who worked with the group. "So then we called them *professional forums.* Just by putting the word 'professional' in there, the executives got the sense that the discussions would be moderated. Then they were comfortable that these would be business-based discussions." After the name change, the project got the go-ahead!

Language becomes even more critical in an e-business era. As Glenn Gow, CEO of Crimson Consulting Group Inc., an Internet-based marketing consulting firm, explains:

> **With some of our consultants, our relationship today is limited to the web and e-mail. So we have to be very, very conscious of the words we use in our e-mails and the words we put on our website. Because we recognize that those words may be all that people know about us.**

Be Specific in Your Choice of Words. Technology gives us new pathways for confusing each other when it comes to language. John Moro, Division Manager for Integrated Customer View at AT&T, points out that this is particularly true if we don't take care to be specific in what we ask of others: "If you're not specific, it can cause problems. Take an e-mail, for example. Let's say you send someone this message: 'Here's the status, get back to me when you get a chance.' Well, when I come to you and say 'What's the status?' you're likely to reply, 'I left him an e-mail last week and he hasn't gotten back to me, boss.' "

In this instance, a lack of specificity is a way of passing the buck, and Moro doesn't see it as an acceptable way to communicate, pointing out that both in e-mail and face-to-face communication, people have a responsibility to each other to be specific with what they want and need. Moro says people often use a lack of specificity to put things off or pass off responsibility, and e-mail and voice mail aid and abet that type of behavior: "If you leave somebody an e-mail or a voice mail, the monkey's on their back now. Technology gives you more channels for passing on responsibility."

Moro also uses specific language to reflect his action-oriented approach to management: "At the beginning of this project, people were doing things like bringing me a problem without a solution, or putting something on the table without thinking it through. That's when I taught them to communicate for action."

Moro asks his team to turn *concerns* into *requests*—in other words, make them specific. Then the other person's choice is to accept, deny, or renegotiate. Moro says this approach has had very powerful effects on communication in their organization.

Everyone always has concerns, but what I want is for people to communicate in a way that allows someone to take action. So I'll say, "Hey, Brian, sounds like you have a concern." He says, "Yes, I do." So I say, "Well, what is it?" He elaborates for three minutes. I say, "Okay, Brian, try it again. Be very concise and specific. What is your concern?" They don't get it. It's like you have to really work on this. Then finally they get it. I'll say, "Brian, I think what I heard was that your concern is you don't have the right resources to do this project. Did I get it right?" Yes. So then I'll say to him, "Turn it into a request and be specific about who you're making the request to." And he struggles, until finally he

says, "Okay, I'm really placing this request to my teammates, is there anyone on the team that has Oracle 8I database knowl- edge, because I have a project for the next two weeks." And somebody says, "I can help you out." Bang. So, what could have started as a whining session, and usually does, is transformed into a positive action. I tell my group: "Listen, we really don't have time to go off and boil the ocean on all these issues. Think what your concern is, turn it into a request, and when you make your request, be very specific."

While specific, action-oriented language is critical in an e-business era, it's also true that interactive managers need to be *less* specific in some situations, as we'll see in our next section.

Create a Common Language for Diverse Groups. Sometimes we need to use highly tailored, highly specific language, and other times we need to use what Johnny Harben of Smythe Dorward Lambert Ltd. calls "high variety language"—language everyone can understand, regardless of their background or orientation. Harben explains: "Low variety lan- guages are very precise and very accurate; one thinks about analytical mathematics or computer language. Then you move into jargon, as you move up toward high variety language, which constitutes the far end of the scale with something like music or great art, something completely languageless, it's so powerful and compelling of the emotion. In busi- ness, when IT people or HR people talk to a general audience, they often rely too much on the jargon of their trade, rather than going to what I call high variety language, which is an interpretative and sum- marizing type of language."

High variety language is particularly important when you are work- ing in large cross-disciplinary groups of people. Gail Taylor, cofounder of The knOwhere Store, which hosts collaborative design meetings, talks about the importance of a group developing a common language during the "scanning" phase of its workshops—a time when the group is creatively scanning their environments for ideas related to the issue it's exploring:

The accountants have their language, the marketing people have their language, the business people have their language, the IT people have their language, and those are all terms of art, and

they're all important. That's what they've gotten their degrees in. So there's all this specialized language. When we bring people together, we create a metalanguage [high-level, jargon-free language] and a way for them to play with metaphors. They're creating, they're chunking up to a higher, more neutral language. It's so important. Because if you don't do that, you've constantly got people warring with each other about not understanding the language.

Strategic alliances and b-webs are causing people from different companies and industries to work together, and this presents interesting new challenges to developing a common language. Jeff Weiss, a founding partner of Vantage Partners LLC, an organization that consults to organizations regarding alliances, explains the need for a common language:

When you have organizations that think and operate differently, there's a real tension in making the boundary between them porous. One of the biggest challenges is creating the ability for them to communicate effectively with each other. Each organization is likely to have its own vocabulary—its own "speak"—and often even internally people have trouble communicating effectively. I'm not talking about managing 400 e-mails—that's a problem in and of itself—but translating the codes people use for how they refer to things. I recently spoke with a client about creating mechanisms in [his] organization for telling stories to share information and create a common understanding among people in different parts of the company. He talked about the particular challenge of bringing new people into an organization, because when they arrive they don't know the language. He said it's analogous to entering a foreign country or joining a new tribe.

Clearly in strategic partnerships, b-webs, mergers, acquisitions, and other forms of organizational alliances, the use of high variety language can help improve understanding and enhance effectiveness.

Use Metaphors for Clarification.   Gail Taylor of The knOwhere Store explains that metaphor can be a powerful tool in helping diverse groups of people to develop a "high variety language" for creating and working together:

We use metaphors. We'll have people go read different books about ants or rain forests and then we'll say, "How do rain forests organize?" Suddenly, they're building new models, speaking differently, and having fun with it. I remember one group we had that created a powerful metaphor about tide pools. Tide pools contain the richest nutrients in the world, but they're very short-lived, and if you don't make use of those nutrients, what happens is they die out. So they developed a whole research plan around a tide pool. They discussed how the approach to research is wasteful because it does things in a linear way rather than put ting all those nutrients together in a pool .... Groups create metaphors and say, "How does this apply to our business?"

David Sibbet, President of The Grove Consultants International, uses metaphor in group facilitation work as a means of providing a common language. He describes his work with Sematech, an industrial technology consortium:

During the late 1980s, after the United States got hammered in the chip industry by the Japanese, some people said "Why don't we get together and start sharing knowledge and create a learning community among semiconductor companies?" So a dozen or so of the biggest ones all sent executives to Sematech. So here's this organization composed of people from Intel, National Semi-Conductor, Texas Instruments, etc., and they all have a different idea about how things should be organized. And so they were really having problems managing this consortium, and so they wanted to have a seminar to help clarify things.

Sibbet ran the workshop for them, and he started by asking them to describe experiences that had had the greatest impact on forming their ideas about teams. Some people mentioned the military, others performing arts, and several had gotten their ideas about teams from working on a ranch. Sibbet separated the group into affinity groups, so the ranchers got together at one table and the military people got together, etc. Each table was asked to answer the question, "Sematech is like a ..." ranch, or platoon, or whatever their metaphor might be. And they created pictures on flip charts to illustrate these metaphors.

Metaphorical thinking is one of the ways you can do whole system thinking. You take something you know intimately in its elaborate wonder, and you compare it to something you don't know. And you explore the resonance, you explore what fits and what doesn't. That's the way we tend to move into new territory as humans. We take what we know, compare it to the new data, and map it.

Sibbet and the group used the ranch metaphor to produce a fascinating discussion. Sibbet became the graphic "scribe" for the group, and as they spoke he drew pictures illustrating their conversation. When Sibbet asked the group what kind of animals were on the farm, one person called out "predators." Sibbet said, "What are the predators?" Someone else replied, "This partner's projects. They run around eating up all the other projects." Consultants were rodents. The group spent 40 very productive minutes using the metaphor to explore what was happening with the consortium. It gave them a common language for understanding their management issues and opportunities.

In summary, when there's a need to create a common language across diverse groups of people, interactive managers should think both about the need for "high variety" language, as well as the need to be specific when the time comes to take action. Most important, in an e-business era, choose your words carefully. Your language may be your only means of representing yourself to a virtual colleague or a distant customer.

Skill 6: Pay Attention to What's Not Said

Social scientists know a great deal about how people communicate without words through their use of space, their tone of voice, and their facial expressions, among many other cues. What fascinates me is that, according to communication research, we get much more of our information through what's *not* said than we get through what *is* said.

Phil Harkins, CEO of Linkage, Inc., a human resources consulting, seminar, and research firm, notes that breakdowns in trust in organizations is most often around what people *don't* say:

People are stressed from overcommitments. Trust is breaking down because of system overload, hidden dialogue, and not getting things clear on the front end. For example, if we were sitting in a meeting together, I could go through something in detail and

you might sit and watch me. I might think you agreed with me because you didn't voice any objection. But you might be disagreeing silently. You and I have a totally different story about what really happened. It's what's *not* said.

What's not said is also important to on-line interactions. In the 1980s I analyzed the skills of audio-conferencing facilitators. The 66 skills I identified were largely based around how those facilitators overcame the lack of verbal cues from the participants in the meeting. They used metaphor, they used pictures, they listened for shifts in tone of voice, and they watched for who wasn't talking as well as who was talking.

All of us need to attend to the fact that virtual environments call for attention to the ways in which we say things without words. Tom Sudman, President of Digital AV, which consults to organizations regarding virtual work, says he has developed a means of reading people's "body language" on-line:

You start to interpret not only what people are saying, but what people are *not* saying. In an on-line group discussion, if Susan is contributing a lot and suddenly Susan doesn't contribute, I know she is uneasy about something. So as a coach it becomes my task to try to ask the right question to draw her out and find out whether she's just having a bad day, or if somebody offended her with their word choice. That's probably the most simplistic situation—where you've got to read the lack of what's being said as much as what's being said. And so it starts it there, with the presence of words as well as the absence of words. . . . [Face-to-face] you would go to body language and look for a frown versus Susan not saying something. So you're mapping to that level.

Sudman also points out the importance of attending to word choice in order to determine how someone is reacting in a virtual environment:

I may sit there and think, "Susan recently said she was really *enjoying* something. And now she just said something is *okay.*" So, maybe she isn't too happy right now because she's gone from really *enjoying* down to *okay.* What Susan is doing is giving me subliminal clues, as body language does, to what some of her real feelings are . . . .

Paying attention to what's not said goes beyond choice of words. And as a student and observer of nonverbal communication for the last two decades, I'm noticing some interesting developments. I believe that some of our accepted norms about nonverbal behavior are being challenged and changed by people in their teens, twenties, and thirties. Especially when it comes to the concept of listening.

Most of us have traditionally indicated that we're listening to each other by maintaining eye contact, orienting our bodies toward another person, and periodically through nods of our head indicating agreement or disagreement with what's being said. But these days people are "listening" in new ways. I've watched the teenagers of my friends do their homework, listen to the radio, have the TV on, be on a chat line and get instant messages—all at the same time! So they listen in a wholly different way than I listen.

And Bill Machrone, VP of Technology at Ziff Davis Media, says that it is sometimes hard to know who's listening in meetings these days because of the heavy use of instant messaging and e-mail during the meeting:

> **When we have our weekly manager's meeting, some of the people have wireless LAN connections on their laptops. And they're IM-ing [instant messaging] other people around the table or those who are teleconferencing in. So you have several layers and channels of communication going on—while one person is talking, the other guy is typing, "This guy's a bozo," but it's only going to one other person. It's like passing notes in school—you just fold it up and slip it so the teacher doesn't see it . . . .**

I pointed out to Machrone that if I were the speaker in a small meeting, it would be disconcerting to me if people didn't look up from their screens throughout the meeting. He replied: "I guess in the technology business we're more used to it, because we take our damn laptops and PDAs everyplace and we're tip-tapping away. . . . And you as the presenter can't know whether someone is instant messaging a friend or writing down every one of your golden phrases."

Machrone is right that the presenter can't know for sure what you're doing when you're working on a laptop or PDA. And of course the same thing has been true of pen and paper for years, but for some reason, most of us are comfortable with someone writing while we're talking because we often (erroneously, I might add) assume that the person is "taking notes."

The point is that technology is introducing confusion around what is considered good or bad communication behavior, and I think all of us are going to have to think about how we address these issues. One way of approaching the challenge of attending to what's *not* said is to be explicit about our communication behavior. If we check in with each other about what's going on, particularly when we're using a technology such as teleconferencing, then we're less likely to offend people or misunderstand them.

If you're a skilled interactive manager, you'll attend to what's *not* said, whether you're on a video conference, on-line discussion group, or sitting across the table from your colleagues.

Skill 7: Make Adjustments for Differences in Culture and Personality Types

In an e-business era, we're doing business globally and making connections with people in places we might never visit. We're also working across organizational boundaries with people in companies that are very different from ours, and even our own organizations are made up of increasingly diverse audiences in terms of age, nationality, and numerous other factors.

To communicate effectively in this new environment, we have to learn ways of bridging the gaps that place, time, geography, social structures, and personalities put between us. Part of the secret of doing this lies in understanding that while we're all different, in many ways we're also all the same.

In this section I'll talk about how differences in cultures (both organizational culture and nationality) need to be attended to when you communicate. I'll also briefly address how differences in personality and communication style call for tailored approaches to communication.

I approach this part of the chapter with caution, because part of the process of adapting your communication for cultural and personality differences involves typing people to some extent. Whether you're determining their Myers-Briggs profile (a personality-typing process based on Jungian psychology) or determining what a German or Lithuanian audience will best understand, you will be making some assumptions about them. This is both valuable and treacherous at the same time. What we expect from others and our ideas of what they're like have a huge impact on our communication.

Whatever approaches you use to help you address people "where they're coming from," do so with great care. It's all too easy to think we've figured someone else out. The biggest mistake you can make in communication is to lose sight of the fact that people are complex, and that the best way of getting to know what they're really like is to listen to them.

With that said, there are some interesting ways in which observations on cultural and personality differences can be useful, and some fascinating tie-ins with the use of technology. Let's take a look.

Cultural Diversity. The first step in adjusting your communication for cultural differences is to think about using inclusive language when you're talking about numerous stakeholder groups as part of one larger group. Frequently, people from parent companies or headquarters' locations can be chauvinistic in their use of language. Bob Buckman, Chairman of Buckman Laboratories, a chemical company, has 1300 employees based in over 80 countries. Buckman explains that language choice is crucial to making people feel part of one organization:

> **First of all, you don't use the word "foreign." Second, you don't use the word "subsidiary." We're all *associates*. When half of your associates are outside the United States, we're foreigners to *them*. So we've tried to eliminate the word "foreign." We just don't use it. And if we catch somebody using it, we say that's almost a violation of the code of ethics. . . . We're all equals in this thing. Somebody in South Africa is just as important as somebody here in the United States to the organization as a whole. Because we're a global organization. We're not just a U.S. company. Our mission statement and our code of ethics are written in our literature in multiple languages.**

Where you locate your organization and hold your meetings is a powerful way of communicating to your employees. Doug Loewe, Head of Global Sales for UUNet, a networking subsidiary of MCI Worldcom, says that he intentionally has not chosen a "headquarters" site in Europe for his group because he wants to communicate to them that they are a virtual organization, inclusive of all the countries his group represents:

> **We do not have a corporate headquarters in Europe. We have a very diverse group of people who live in multiple cities. It's critical that we not stay in an ivory tower, always getting together in Cambridge or London. This is a big challenge with a lot of American companies in Europe—they set up where they're comfortable, which is often London, or at least the U.K., because of the language. So while it's a challenge—trying to get people together is not an easy thing to do—it keeps you fresh and out there and in front of people. Fortunately, I'm very lucky because when I do travel, my team really is based in every one of the major countries, which is great.**

In attention to sensitivity to language and location, interactive managers need to understand how cultural differences will affect their daily interactions. Liz Richards of Smythe Dorward Lambert Ltd., a communications consulting firm, found a book called *Riding the Waves of Culture* to be useful in looking at cross-cultural communication issues when she was working with a European management team at Microsoft:

> **These ideas helped with even simple things. For instance, the French don't see meetings as a place where you come to conclusions and decisions. So if other people don't know that, you get a huge amount of frustration because British people would see meetings as a place to come to a decision. So there was a whole piece of work about actually getting that group to understand their cultural differences . . . not just so they could operate in a meeting environment with some degree of effectiveness, but also as the start of understanding how you remote-manage people who are also of a different nationality.[2]**

In addition to symbolic communication such as headquarters and meeting locations, other ways of crossing cultural boundaries include metaphors, analogies, stories, and theater. But interactive managers must pay close attention when using these approaches. Having recently set up a training program in the Czech Republic, Lisa Brooks, Director of Performance Management at Verizon Wireless, explains the challenges of working with a translator and the importance of choice of analogies:

> **The translator was terrific and his command of the English language was excellent. But it was important for me to be mindful of the analogies I used. Analogies don't always translate well into other languages. For example, if I were to use a sports analogy, I'd have to refer to soccer, because football is clearly American. And in Czech, the word "football" translates to "soccer." On the other hand, there were certain icons that would translate. I could use a Michael Jordan analogy. I had to pay very close attention to the translator, reading his face and his body language, because I really needed to be clear about how he was going to translate things.**

Dave Sibbet, President of the Grove Consultants, an organization specializing in group graphics methods, tells an amusing story about trying to use pictures as a means of communicating cross-culturally:

> **We were doing some work with nurses in Kenya, and we did these beautiful illustrations, knowing they'd respond to the pictures. We had tourniquets around the hands, illustrating all the different things they had to do as nurses. The project team in Kenya was redoing the materials one day and saw our drawings and said, "What are these severed arms doing in our book?" There's no concept of body parts being drawn on a page in their culture, unless they're body parts. If you just see the forearm with a tourniquet, it means it's a severed forearm with a tourniquet. There's no implied body. Where our culture is much more used to abstraction, in Kenya, they're really grounded and literal.**

Sibbet and his group understandably thought they were using a good method for communicating cross-culturally by using graphics. We can all learn from his example that it's worthwhile to include someone from a stakeholder group or culture when you're in the *planning* phases of putting together materials for people in a culture that's different from your own.

Technology can have some surprising impacts in terms of cross-cultural communication. Lisa Kimball of Caucus Systems says that technology can sometimes help people overcome cultural differences:

There was a Chinese guy who was a member of a group in a Fortune 500–type company, a global organization. He was very difficult to understand in person, because of a combination of style of English, a very soft voice, and a heavy accent. He was involved in an on-line conference with the group and was just completely, stunningly brilliant when he made contributions to the on-line discussion. People gave us feedback later that as a result of working with him in that medium, they gained a whole new level of respect for him. And when they were with him face-to-face after that, they put much more effort into being able to hear him because they knew there'd be a big payoff, so it had a nice carry-over effect.

In the case of an alliance between IBM, Infineon (formerly Siemens Microelectronics), and Toshiba, Laura Rothman, Technical Controller for the alliance, says that different cultures responded well to the use of different media: "The Japanese like to see things in writing. If they read something, they like to think about it. And when you're dealing with them, usually at a meeting they'll say yes, but they don't mean yes. They mean, 'I see what you're saying but I really need time to think about it.' So they would then be able to read the information in the [on-line discussions] and actually reply to it after they had time to think about it and form their words a little bit better." Rothman says that while video conferencing was also heavily used, some people preferred to use on-line discussions because it was easier in terms of language differences. When they did use video and audio conferences, Rothman says the groups tried to be careful to speak slowly and give people time to respond.

Differences in organizational cultures become more significant as people in companies start to work across organizational and geographic boundaries. Interactive managers look for differences and similarities in cultures and take those into account when they communicate.

Diversity in Personality Styles. Tailoring your communication on the basis of culture is important, but it's also critical as an interactive manager that you take into account similarities and differences at the individual personality level. Numerous psychological profiling methods exist, but one of the most widely accepted methods used in business is the Myers-Briggs Type Indicator. Isabel Myers, the inventor of the Myers-Briggs Indicator, used Jungian psychology as the basis for her method of characterizing differences in personality types. The Myers-Briggs approach is widely used in organizations as a method for putting together teams and helping people to work more effectively together.

The Myers-Briggs Type Indicator includes a series of questions that individuals answer for themselves, which indicates their preferences on four dimensions:

- Extraversion versus introversion
- Intuition versus sensation
- Thinking versus feeling
- Judging versus perceiving

An understanding of the differences and similarities in people's personality types is useful in interpreting what they say to you and in formulating what you say to them.

The Myers-Briggs approach is being used to help improve communication on both regular and virtual teams, according to several of the people I interviewed.

John Old, Director of Information Management at Texaco, says that the Myers-Briggs approach helps them build virtual teams and he encourages people to share information about their Myers-Briggs types:

> When we roll out . . . technology tools to a team, we don't just concentrate on the technology; we concentrate on helping the team members understand how they'll interact. Because in many of our teams there may be one or two members who are stationed somewhere else in the world, or some of us may travel a lot and we'll only be able to teleconference in. So we think it's very important that we help teams come to a really good understanding of how the particular individuals in the team will interact with each other. . . . We get them all to do a Myers-Briggs profile; we have an instructor who's certified in giving the Myers-Briggs profile and analyzing it. And she works with the team members so they

**understand when Joe's talking to Bill, this is going to be the style
of interaction. To be really effective, these are the kind of things
that you need to think about when you're trying to communicate.**

Bill Machrone, VP of Technology for Ziff Davis Media, says that
while some people scoff at the idea of doing this type of psychological
profiling, he believes there is value in understanding the similarities
and differences between people on teams, particularly virtual teams:

**I think this is just the leading edge of the wave, but I've been
hearing about people using Myers-Briggs on virtual teams. And
I've heard some people making fun of it, like, 'I'm an ENTJ [a specific Myers-Briggs personality type], har har, isn't that funny.' But
other people are just quietly going about doing it. . . . They get
profiles on people, and that way when the linear guy and the intu-
itive guy have to work side by side, you can smooth the troubled
waters. I've heard that people are starting to use it on virtual
teams in corporations because there are entire projects—from
conception to production—where people might only meet face-
to-face for the first time at the celebration party when it's all
over, or only see each other at a really big status meeting or
something like that.**

Another method of characterizing similarities and differences in
people is called Neuro Linguistic Programming (NLP). NLP was developed by John Grinder and Richard Bandler. Grinder's background is in
linguistics, and Bandler's background is computer programming and
mathematics. They drew on the work of famous psychotherapists, lin-
guists, and anthropologists to develop their approach.

Neuro refers to the way in which people use their senses to translate
experiences into thought. *Linguistic* refers to how you use language to
describe your experiences to yourself and others. *Programming* involves
looking at your experiences, recognizing patterns, and then "coding"
those patterns so that you can better understand yourself and others.[3]

There are a number of elements to the NLP approach and I'm necessarily oversimplifying things, but essentially, NLP involves characterizing the ways in which people think and learn in three ways: Visual,
Auditory, and Feelings.[4] The way people process their experiences will

usually fall into one of these categories, and by knowing your own preferences and their preferences, you can adjust your communication to be more effective. Even if you don't know a particular person's preference, you can pick up on verbal or nonverbal cues that they give in order to guess it. And when you're facing a larger audience as a speaker or writer, you can incorporate all three approaches in presenting your material. For example, if you're trying to illustrate a point about the importance of communication in organization, you might show a slide with people talking to each other (visual), play an audiotape of an effective interaction (auditory), and tell the audience how you felt about a particular communication experience you had (feelings).

NLP can also help you use technology more effectively, as Brad Meyer of Collaboration Ltd., a communication consulting firm, explains:

> **I apply NLP within the video conferencing arena . . . [For example,] if I'm looking down and to the right . . . to more than 50 percent of the people in the Western world, it will appear as though I'm accessing my feelings. Even if I am not. So, I may appear vulnerable and not know it. If I want to convey a message that I might normally draw on a white board, I will use my hands as anchors, as markers for things . . . The NLP world simply focuses in on what human [beings do] to communicate effectively. When people communicate, we base our understanding seven percent on words and 38 percent on tonality, the way we say the words, and 55 percent on physiology. So a lot of this stuff can help when you're using technology.**

Meyer notes that NLP principles can be useful across a number of different media, including audio conferencing and e-mail. With audio conferencing, he says you can match the way a person speaks or listen carefully to the words they use. In e-mail, you can attend to the words they use and even match the way they type—for example, using bullets or paragraphs.

Skill 8: Take Time to Reflect

There's no question that in a warp speed, Internet-based business world things have to go quickly. But interactive managers must cope with a paradox: the need for speed and the need for *conscious* communication—

which requires reflection. Without reflection, the wheels may move at top speed, but the vehicle may not be going anywhere. Remember George Jetson and Astro on the treadmill?

We're all focused on getting smarter. We want smart companies, smart communication, and smart people. What reflection offers us is the ability to not only become *smarter,* but also to become *wiser.* And there's a difference. Wisdom implies that we are not only smart, but also that we learn from our experiences and the experiences of others.

In the era of the Internet we can communicate and connect more quickly with people, but as we develop relationships with people inside and outside our organizations, *reflection* will be as important as *speed* when it comes to accomplishing work, building relationships, and sharing knowledge.

Unfortunately, most people don't set aside time for reflection. Organizational change consultant Don Parker says he often encourages his clients to literally create space on their calendars: "I look at their overbooked calendars and ask 'Where's the white space?' This is really important because when people fail to actually schedule open time on their calendars, they end up postponing personal reflection. They also have no space to handle unexpected emergencies without setting off a whole chain of scheduling disasters for other people." All of us need to schedule white space for reflection, and we need to encourage our coworkers to do the same. We also need to find methods to help us reflect—both on our work and on ourselves.

Needs Assessment. We've already talked about the importance of asking questions instead of providing answers. Good questions can be part of useful reflection prior to a project. Once again, this sounds simple, but it doesn't happen nearly enough in organizations. One of the areas where this is most evident is in the lack of communication to assess needs before beginning a project or making purchases in organizations. Interactive needs assessment should be a built-in communication process before you install a technology, develop a new compensation system, design a new brochure, or before you do any number of things that will absorb organizational resources such as time and money. Not only will this lead to better decision-making, but the process of communicating about needs can often bring to light valuable business knowledge and a clear focus on what's important.

Interviewees for this book wholeheartedly agreed on the value of good needs assessment as a communication tool. "People often come to us and say, 'Can you just get a quick bulletin out to everyone for us,' " says John Easden, Group Marketing Director and head of communications at First National Bank in the United Kingdom. "We'd question what they're trying to achieve. We'd ask why they're sending it, and quite often they actually realize that they don't have that much to say. What we try and get into people's heads is that they need to reflect about what they're trying to achieve and whether they need to do things in the first place. By asking them questions, we'll often change their perceptions about what they should be doing. It's really only after you've gone through that sort of reflective process that you find out the best way of doing things." By using a formal, reflective technique up front, we can save a tremendous amount of time and money.

In our rush to get things done we also forget to take the time to learn from the successes and failures of others who have gone before us. Capturing and reviewing lessons learned in an organization is a critical component of many knowledge management efforts, and it has paid huge dividends in terms of time and money.

After Action Learning.   In the KM arena there is a technique called "After Action Learning" that is a valuable tool for collaboration and knowledge sharing. After Action Learning simply refers to the idea of having an individual or a group reflect on experiences and then capture lessons learned in a structured format that they, and others, can access. By taking the time to communicate and learn from the experiences of others, a great deal of time and money can be saved, by reusing creative ideas, for example, as well as avoiding the repeat of costly mistakes. This is a way of operationalizing what Peter Senge calls "the learning organization."[5]

In a strategic alliance among IBM, Siemens, and Toshiba, applying a lessons-learned process was quite valuable, according to Sheri Feinzig, a Senior Consultant with IBM specializing in knowledge management who did consulting work with the alliance. "One of our original findings was that since there were so many projects going on at once, and all of them with tight deadlines, not very much information was being shared across the projects," Feinzig explains. "This resulted in mistakes being repeated, which is very costly. So we recommended that they implement a lessons-learned process, where they formally stepped back at the end of the project to say what went right, what went wrong. Then those lessons were applied to other projects. That's been *very* beneficial to them."

Technology and Reflection.   Technology not only increases the speed at which we work, it also provides us a means of reflection. Lisa Kimball, founder and VP Professional Services for Caucus Systems (a company that conducts thousands of on-line meetings per year), explains that on-line discussions allow for reflection: "On-line discussions give you the opportunity to go back and read what everyone said prior to making your own comment. You can reread the whole thread of the conversation. In face-to-face conversation you rarely do something like listen to a tape of the conversation. A lot of times you may get a whole different perspective on an conversation when you go back and look at it again."

Unfortunately, we don't always take advantage of the reflection capabilities technology provides. Many people experience what I call "send button regret." It's very easy to rush things in an ASAP era. The need to hurry often results in ill-considered communication. With e-mail, you can at least save a message and reread it before you send it. With voice mail, you have to perpetually be ready to be recorded when you dial a number. And with most voice message systems, you can't take the message back once it's been recorded. This can have serious consequences in terms of business and personal relationships.

Steve Kerr, Chief Learning Officer at General Electric, underscores the importance of reflection when using e-mail and voice mail and offers a practical suggestion: "Anger can be a great motivator to get a message written, especially if you're working at 9:30 at night. The trick is not to hit the send button. I can think of at least once when I responded angrily to a voice message. It's just so easy to push *8* to reply. But you have to stop and think, 'Will this help or hurt?' I also find it useful to send the message to someone I've trusted for a long time and ask them how it sounds."

The point is, whether it's a personal relationship, a professional relationship, or both, before you add a comment to an on-line discussion group, reply to an e-mail, or pick up the phone to call, reflect on what it is you *really* want to say.

Personal Reflection. True reflection goes beyond taking a couple of minutes to think before you send an e-mail. It also goes beyond remembering to capture what you know after a client engagement or team project. As we've seen, this type of reflection is certainly important, but it just scratches the surface when it comes to effective communication.

At the core of truly deep reflection is self-knowledge. In order to get over yourself, you first have to know yourself well. Self-knowledge is more important than *any other aspect* of managing interactively. To be interactive you have to be open to the ideas of others, okay with being wrong, not attached to particular outcomes, and above all you have to be a superb listener. Reflection allows you not only to hear the voices of others, but to also develop an ear for that internal voice that will tell you whether you're communicating in ways that will enhance your work and your relationships both inside and outside your company.

When management was about telling instead of engaging, interactive communication skills and personal reflection weren't nearly so critical to success. Managers could get away with a lack of self-knowledge and poor listening skills, as long as they were clear when issuing orders. Not anymore. Imagine an old school manager trying to head up a knowledge management effort in a strategic alliance or manage a top software developer who has 10 other job offers. New times call for new skills.

Getting over yourself is critical to your effectiveness as an interactive manager. And the more you develop your own communication skills and the skills of the people who work with you, the better you will be at establishing powerful connections between people in your organization.

Key Ideas from Chapter 6

- Nothing kills innovation and creativity faster than a person with all the answers.
- Lack of candor, defensiveness, self-importance, and careless use of language can destroy projects and ideas.
- E-mail, teleconferencing, and on-line discussion groups are good media for encouraging candor and accommodating cultural and language differences.
- Needs Assessment and After Action Learning can help you reflect.
- Methods such as Myers-Briggs can help you accommodate personality differences on virtual teams.

This fifth competency ends Part I, which explained how to *connect* people by putting them in touch with each other, creating the right environment, and building your own capacity to communicate well. Part II examines the second cornerstone of interactive communication—*informing* people.

Inform

Enhance Knowledge Sharing by Getting the Right Information, in the Right Form, to the Right People, in the Right Context

INFORMING PEOPLE IS a major challenge in an era where we're flooded with information. It's also a challenge to inform people who don't work directly for us. For example, how do you capture the attention of b-web or strategic alliance partners? And how do you encourage people to inform each other?

Making information available, useful, and enticing is critical to execution of strategy. In this part you'll learn how you can use visual grammar, find new ways to structure information, and apply fascinating methods for tailoring information to make it more useful and appealing.

You'll also find out how to use storytelling as a tool to capture information for knowledge management efforts, communicate with customers, and build brands.

To properly inform people, messages must be consistent. Part II closes with one of the most important aspects of communication: achieving alignment in both words and actions.

7

Make Information Available, Useful, and Enticing

IN AN E-BUSINESS era, we're facing a paradox: too much information and not enough information. We want to "share knowledge" in organizations while we're suffering from information overload. People don't have the information they need to do their work, so we build "knowledge repositories," and no one uses them.

If we want to make our organizations fast, efficient, and effective, then we all have to use each other's time and attention wisely. We can only inform people if we have their attention. To get it, we have to structure and tailor our messages and make information both visible and visual. In short, we have to be smart senders of information.

Make Information Visible

It's a real trick in organizations to get the right information in front of the right people at precisely the right time. Some people see this as a technology issue, but that's naïve. Intranets and other technologies are not a panacea for the challenges of information sharing and information overload. Can they help? Yes. Will they solve all of our problems around making information visible in organizations? No.

"If you looked at the intranets of most companies today, there's a lot of information sharing and publishing," says Jon Iwata, Vice President of

Corporate Communications at IBM. "And our surveys show that employees are inundated with information. There's just too much of it. The Internet, intranet, and e-mail have just made it worse because now there are even more ways for people to send things, both externally and internally. At IBM, the intranet comprises more than two million web pages. There's an ocean of information that employees have to wade through to find what they need. They complain about information overload, but on the other hand they also say, 'I don't have the critical business information I need to get my work done.' It's a really interesting paradox."

Most intranet sites today resemble websites from the early years of the Internet; they serve primarily as "brochureware"—offering static content such as marketing and sales information or press releases. Today most commercial websites are transaction-based, offering visitors a much higher level of interaction. Iwata sees a similar transition going on inside organizations: "We are moving to a world where employees can go to the intranet not just to read things, but to actually get business done."

Iwata provides a compelling example of how IBM uses its intranet to make critical information visible to employees. When IBM Chairman and CEO Lou Gerstner first came to IBM in the early 1990s, he created a year-end bonus program for all employees. The size of the bonus depended on the annual performance of the company, the employee, and the employee's division. It's a program that pays some $1.6 billion a year in bonuses to employees.

There was only one problem. Employees didn't have information to help them understand how their actions affected the company's performance. Iwata explains: "We didn't tell employees what the metrics were, nor how they performed against those metrics throughout the year... We were saying, 'Beat the competition, delight customers, and work really hard. And if you do that well, your bonus will be good.'" This resulted in a situation where employees worked hard all year, only to discover the reasons for underperformance after the fact. For example, they'd learn at the end of the year that expenses were up when it was too late to do anything about it. "So we decided to use the intranet to tell employees what the metrics are, and then inform them, at least once a quarter, about our progress."

Executives were understandably concerned about disclosing proprietary, competitive information. Many companies face internal political issues when they begin to share financial performance information. It is a test of a company's culture to get executives and managers to make their numbers available on intranets, because then their numbers are available not only to the people that work for them, but also to the people *they* work for.

"In the end, we found the right metrics," says Iwata. "Now, every quarter on the intranet, the *minute* after we announce earnings to the Street, we send out an e-mail from the chairman to inform all employees about how we did. The intranet also offers very detailed performance information that employees can examine and explore on their own. It is one of the most heavily trafficked sites in the entire intranet. There is an incredible spike in traffic as employees go to specific sites to find out how their business units are performing against their targets." This specificity gives employees the knowledge to make mid-course adjustments in their focus and the way they work each quarter. And, says Iwata, "executives are learning that if you inform employees about the reality of the business performance, they will find a way to help. The employees are making these things happen."

Iwata's example of making performance information visible is impressive. But making information visible gets even more complex. Performance information is routinely gathered and stored. What about all the information that people carry around in their heads? Interactive managers have to find creative ways to make both tacit and explicit information available.

Share Both Tacit and Explicit Knowledge

In the area of knowledge management a distinction is made between two types of knowledge:

- *Tacit* knowledge is the knowledge you carry around in your head.
- *Explicit* knowledge is knowledge that is captured and codified.

In organizations, we need to make both tacit and explicit knowledge *visible,* but that involves encouraging people to *share* that information. Most of the knowledge used in organizations today is explicit knowledge, but as David Gilmour, CEO of Tacit Knowledge Systems (a knowledge management software provider), points out, that may be a problem:

The explicit stuff is on the servers and in the repositories. The private stuff is never going to be on the servers. There's a great underworld of knowledge that today never makes it out into the open on an intranet . . . Knowledge sharing based on the paradigm of gathering stuff and sharing it through searches is always going to miss a huge amount of the action. Huge amount. And worse, it's old. It's the stuff that's gone through the process, the percolation, it's yesterday's news, driving through your rearview mirror.

Mike Zisman, EVP of Strategy for Lotus Development Corporation, agrees with Gilmour about the importance of tacit knowledge, and adds that it is important not only to gather it, but also to validate and distribute it:

If I want highly reliable information on Microsoft, I can go to the SEC and read their 10-K. Highly reliable, highly accurate. But that's probably much less useful than overhearing someone on the elevator at a conference who I don't know, say to someone else, "Microsoft is about to do boom boom boom boom." Totally unreliable, but if it's true, it's incredibly important. How do I validate that? How do I bring that in and determine who at IBM can tell me if it's complete B.S., or say to me, "Gee, that does triangulate with three other things we've heard." It's about collaboration, it's about a process that says discover, validate, distribute. You collect lots of information, validate it through some form of expertise, and then distribute it very broadly.

In Part I we talked about the first step in getting people to share knowledge, which is to *connect* them to each other. But once we've connected people, how do we encourage them to share what they know? A huge part of knowledge management efforts today are aimed at finding ways to encourage people to communicate by sharing their tacit and explicit knowledge. Steve Kerr, Chief Learning Officer at GE, explains that they have a very straightforward approach to encouraging the sharing of both tacit and explicit knowledge. He says that knowledge sharing is much more about *psychology* than *technology:*

I was invited to the Fortune CIO [Chief Information Officer] conference, and I'm a CLO [Chief Learning Officer]. They were curious

about what a **CLO** does. So I'm sitting quiet until the third day, and when it got to be my turn, I said, "Look, I've really enjoyed hanging around with you guys for two days, I've learned about hardware-software compatibility and protecting data on the Internet. But you know, in **GE** we take the view that the most important reason people don't share information is because they mostly don't want to. And in three days I haven't heard you guys talk about that. If people don't want to share, it doesn't happen. I don't know any computer that waits till its master goes home and it turns itself on and sends information around the company. In every arena, including knowledge sharing, ability times motivation equals performance. You guys focus on *ability* by helping people to communicate. So you've got technology, and I.T., and software, but a **CLO**'s job is focused on *motivation,* to think about why people don't want to share. . . . Why do honorable, bright people not want to share information? What is it about organizational life that stymies that? That's what being a CLO is about."

Kerr says the approach to information sharing at GE is simple—remove the barriers that inhibit communication: "We take the view that if there are barriers to sharing, and you remove the barriers, people are more likely to share. Duh. So that's what I do. I worry about removing those barriers."

Here's how he does that. Kerr explains that in the average company, if you have a good idea, you don't tell anyone until it's to your advantage to do so. So if the CEO happens upon you, you might brag and get rewarded for it, or you might brag to your boss. But for the most part you're not going to share unless you benefit from doing so. And in many cases, even if you do want to share an idea, it's often difficult to figure out whom to tell—especially if you don't want to seem as though you're bragging. "If you're sitting in a branch office in Shreveport, Louisiana, or Spartanburg, South Carolina, how do you know your idea is the best in the company?" Kerr asks. "And how do you know that someone won't say to you, 'How arrogant of you to say so!' Even if you thought so, who are you going to call, the home office? Who would you tell? So people sit there, they don't share, they've got no way to share."

Kerr also points out the dangers of sharing a best practice and then being studied to death: "The only thing worse than not having a best practice is having one, because after five minutes of fame come the pilgrims. You talk to the Baldridge winners, it's terrible, because they make a commitment to share; that's a condition of winning. There was a sausage company that won the award, and they had to go out of the sausage business, because they were so busy giving tours they couldn't make the sausages anymore. So people say the hell with that, I don't need the aggravation."

Other impediments to making information visible come on the receiving end of things. Often, people don't want to accept what's being communicated to them because it doesn't seem relevant. They conclude it's NIH ("not invented here"), or they think that a best practice in one area isn't generalizable to another.

Kerr says GE addresses these problems by:

- Encouraging the sharing and "stealing" of ideas as opposed to hoarding them and taking credit
- Providing a simple, easy mechanism for people to share a best practice
- Providing a centralized place for sharing best practices with other parts of the organization or other companies, thus avoiding the "tour" syndrome

As Chief Learning Officer at GE, Kerr's office encourages knowledge sharing by serving as what he calls a "911 clerk." Crotonville, where Kerr's organization is located, is the central location for people to call when they want to share good ideas:

> I'm a 911 clerk, that's what a **CLO** does. So Monday my phone rings and there's somebody on the phone saying "I think I have the best sales training program in GE." My people know training, we go check it out. When we get there we may or may not be impressed. If we are impressed, we make it portable. We will take it off their hands, generalize it, create a business game or CD-ROM or put it on the net or write a little case study, and we teach you the program. Tuesday, my phone rings, some guy says we think we have the best new product introduction process in the company. How would I know? But the research lab would know, and Lonnie runs the lab. I'm a 911 clerk, I pick up the phone, say, "Lonnie, we may have a great product in Pittsfield, could you go

**check it out?" I'm a clerk. I send people out, we validate stuff,
they check things.**

"In GE you get rewarded for sharing or stealing ideas," says Kerr.
"You do not get rewarded for coming up with an idea. In fact, coming
up with an idea is really bad news, because you're at risk. In an average
company, you wait for the chairman and say, 'Look! I've got the best
idea in the company!' and you get rewarded. If you say that here to
Welch or the vice chairman of GE, there won't even be a pause for
breath: 'That's fantastic, who else is using it?' 'No one, Jack, I'm special.' Then you get killed. You know why they call me? Because that's
an integrity violation at GE.... You don't mess around with this. If
you're hoarding ideas, you can't work here. So now my phone rings.
And who's on the phone, it's a nervous business leader: 'I think I've got
the best process in the company, for God's sakes get down here and
take it off my hands because Welch is coming and I don't want to get
caught holding this thing.' So you have a simple 911 system and you
have norms that support it... if you dropped in on our meetings, you'd
laugh. Everything starts: 'We took this idea from Hewlett Packard. We
stole this idea from lighting.' They're terrified that somebody will
think they thought of it themselves. We shared, we stole, we took, we
borrowed...."

Kerr stresses the simplicity of this approach, pointing out that there
are no best practice databases involved. He says all you need is a CLO and
a telephone, calling it a "low cost, simpleminded way to get in the game."
He says he doesn't keep databases because he doesn't want to maintain
them: "The big databases that people keep, mostly are not accessed...
we do have a new system going in and I'd like to be able to store this knowledge so it's not all in my head, so we'll see about the database. But the database isn't going to make people share information."

Regardless of the approach you take to making tacit information
visible, the most fundamental step to getting people to communicate
their knowledge is to make it easy and reward them for it.

One form of reward is results. Mike Burtha, Executive Director of
Knowledge Networking at Johnson & Johnson, says that one of its
global organizations was planning to build a system from scratch to
track business and industry information. Using one of the Knowledge
Networking Workspaces at J&J, they identified another J&J company

that had already done something similar, but it was in a completely different arena, in an entirely different field of work. Burtha says it's highly unlikely that they would have thought to look in that area or know whom to ask about the project. The key to success, he says, was that they were able to access the tacit knowledge by first finding a similar initiative and then speaking with the people engaged in that effort. As a result of their collaboration, the team was able to save approximately six months of development time and over $1,000,000 in direct costs to build the system. Burtha notes that this is just one of many examples of knowledge sharing success stories that he's witnessed.

Don Tapscott, coauthor of *Digital Capital* and Chairman of Digital 4Sight, an e-business strategy consulting and research firm, says that the sharing of knowledge forms a fundamental aspect of on-line alliances: "It's all inter-enterprise. All of these systems are hooked up with each other. Cisco can look right into their partners' systems and see how much inventory they've got, what the costs are, everything. It's all transparent. Everyone's naked." Tapscott's observation is that many b-webs have powerful sharing of explicit knowledge such as inventory and financial results. Interactive managers should also consider how to encourage the sharing of tacit knowledge in b-webs.

In the world of e-business, the sharing of tacit and explicit knowledge isn't a desired outcome, it's a necessity. Interactive managers have to find ways of encouraging their coworkers to interact with *each other* and share knowledge in order to stay competitive—particularly when they're sharing information across organizational boundaries. (We'll talk more about cross-boundary information sharing in Chapter 11.)

Put Information Where People Can Find It

This section heading seems ridiculously simple, right? Of course you want to put information where people will find it. But anyone who has ever lost their keys knows that it's not always easy to put things where they're logically supposed to be. Now take that problem and multiply it exponentially—it's a real challenge to put information in the right places in organizations with complex projects and multiple locations. And if you're in a b-web or strategic alliance, it's an even greater challenge to find things.

There are a variety of ways to make information easier to find. Some involve technology, some don't. Let's look at a few.

Using Technology to Find Information. Buzzsaw.com is a company that provides an Internet-based collaboration and commerce environment for construction projects. The company keeps track of all the documents needed for the various phases of a construction project, allows all of the people working on the project access to those documents, and provides an environment for real-time collaboration and purchase of building materials on-line. This new type of business model is allowing people much more flexible access to extensive project information. Anne Bonaparte, cofounder, explains:

> **A typical building project will have hundreds or thousands of drawings, documents, and spreadsheets. We provide the ability to search for a detail or design element that an architect might have used on a commercial project a couple of months ago and wants to reuse. We provide tools for them to share information and search for specific elements. That's very powerful because about 60 to 70 percent of design is really reuse of existing design elements, and a big problem architects and engineers have is they can't find what they designed. There's also a lot of information about how well a project was managed . . . and we are seeing customers begin to seek this kind of best practice information to improve their performance.**

The next phase of Buzzsaw.com's development will be construction administration, when a building is actually being built. Jason Pratt, Director of Product Marketing, says that this phase of the project also presents challenges in making information easy to find, particularly when changes are made during the construction phase:

> **A subcontractor will say to the project foreman, "Hey, this drawing says I need to put the electrical outlet right here, but there's a window there, because you moved that other thing three weeks ago, so where do you want this outlet to go? I can't do any work until you tell me what to do. Does the architect want it on the left or on the right?" The foreman needs to be able to communicate that to the general contractor, the general contractor needs to look at it and say, "Yeah, this is a real issue," and send it over to the architect. The architect has to say, "Is this something I can**

answer myself or is this something I need one of my consulting engineers to answer?" Maybe there's a fire code issue, so a building inspector has to get involved. In any case, once the architect looks at it and says "here's the resolution," then it has to travel all the way back down the chain, sometimes being approved by the owner along the way. Now you can imagine, even if that was a perfectly efficient fax process, it could be eight hours before that guy could get the answer to his question about where to put the outlet, whereas if it's on-line, it could literally happen within seconds, minutes. People can look at the issues, they have all the information there, they have the documents available, they have the entire set of project information they need to make the decision and make it quickly to respond at the speed of the Internet as opposed to at the speed of mail or faxes or paper.

Another interesting use of technology to make information visible is pattern recognition software. Particularly with the use of survey data, pattern recognition software can improve communication by highlighting feedback from the organization that otherwise would go unnoticed. Fred Schoeps, Program Director for Knowledge Management at IBM, says that the use of this type of software with HR survey data was particularly valuable:

For years we've had an employee survey to assess how employees view our business, what's working, what's not working for them. In addition to just being able to provide a range response, there's also write-in response. And when you're doing that with a sample size of 40,000 people, it becomes really difficult to see what sort of patterns are there. And so we applied a business intelligence tool to it in order to look for patterns, and it was exciting because we basically saw very quickly some patterns that I don't think we would have seen, even if somebody had read all the stuff. If you read 100 things, what do you remember? This software basically allowed us to be able to make visible the patterns and then use judgment. For example, one of the patterns we found is that there are areas where we're not acting the way we talk. I mean, it's a fairly powerful statement, and it forces us to say, "Gee, we didn't see that that clearly." Now all of a sudden you can say, "Wow, how do we deal with that? Let's consciously work on that."

Sometimes technology can make it *harder* to communicate and find the information you need. Numerous interviewees told me of problems that arise from too many electronic team rooms, too many e-mails, and too many on-line discussion groups. Bob Pinto, Knowledge Management Practice Leader for the Government Sector at IBM, says that there are enormous challenges to finding information when you are doing KM projects, particularly with large organizations. He says, "How do you find a discussion group that you're interested in when you have 80 different discussion groups among 20 different communities of practice?" Pinto recounts a story where this inability to locate things quickly had a serious impact in an governmental organization:

> **The general gave an order to one of the colonels to start a discussion on a certain topic. The colonel carried out the order. The general then decided he would log on and join in the discussion, but he couldn't find it. And so he called the guy up and reamed him out because he hadn't done what he was told to do. The colonel explained that he *had* started the discussion. The problem was that the name of the discussion thread heading didn't mean anything to the general. And when he was trying to do his search by name of discussion, he couldn't find it anywhere.**

In fact, the KM group in this government organization had developed a tool to do "fuzzy" searches. "Fuzzy" searches do not require the level of precision other types of searches, such as keyword searches, require. With a fuzzy search you have more leeway in terms of knowing what you're looking for. Unfortunately, this "fuzzy" tool wasn't operational when the general was doing his search; otherwise it would have been more likely that he could have found the discussion group he was looking for.

Finding Information Without Technology.   Making information easier to find doesn't necessarily mean that technology is always involved.

In his work with a large advertising agency, Don Parker, a consultant who specializes in communication and systemic organizational change, discovered that use of physical space was the key to making information visible for large ad campaigns:

> **The creatives were seeing a piece of the project, the account people helped generate ideas, but each group got a very narrow view**

of what was going on. So we created rooms that show all of the work for, say, the Burger King account—the print, the TV commercials, promotional support, direct mail, etc., and they held their team meetings in the room. It's a very visible reinforcement to the business, rather than sitting in a sterile conference room around a table, only talking words.

Interactive managers need to use their imaginations, as well as technology, to make information visible.

Use a Variety of Interactive Media but Don't Overdo It

All too often we get accustomed to using certain media and don't feel comfortable outside our "zone." Instead of using the media our stakeholders prefer, we simply use the ones we like best. To make information visible, you need to use a variety of media.

As Paul Sanchez, former Communications Consulting Practice Director at Watson Wyatt, an HR consulting firm, points out:

Look to the allocation of your resources across the spectrum of media applications. Electronic media ought to be seen as one of a number of possible approaches or applications, along with print, face-to-face, etc. The idea of putting entire summary plan descriptions detailing a health and welfare plan on the web is a waste. The most efficient approach would be to post a summary and headline about where and how to get the entire printed document when you need it.

Sanchez's point is well taken. Interactive managers need to consider a full range of options when they communicate, and the existence of new electronic media doesn't mean that it's time to throw out all the paper.

What's tricky about using a variety of media is that you don't want to contribute to the problem of overload. To address this issue, Smythe Dorward Lambert Ltd., a communications consulting company, has developed an exercise it calls "media match," which helps companies determine the most effective media for reaching different organizational audiences. The tool is customized for each client, taking into account what media stakeholders prefer, what media they currently have, and what media they may want to create or acquire. This methodology is based around the use of focus groups to gather information about the supply and demand for information in the organization. Then a tool, which can be net-based or paper-based, is developed that allows people in the organization to generate the top options for how to send messages.

If you do a good job of assessing how your stakeholders like to receive information, you'll have a better chance of targeting them appropriately in ways that will make your information easy to find, easy to use, and enticing. As Christine Smith, Senior Director of Sales Support and Operations for RIA Group, a taxation software developer, explains: "We found that different people, different ages, of different backgrounds, find some methods of communication work for them and others that just don't. The best thing to do is to constantly use all forms of media and to keep it mixed. At the same time, you need to keep some things consistent. For example, people know that they can always go onto our external website or our intranet for certain things."

And don't forget, interactive media are comprised of more than technology. In the interviews for this book, people mentioned the use of regular mail, radio drama, theater, murals with comic strips, and even painted tablecloths, for helping make information more visible and useful.

Make Information Visual

When you think about it, it's really remarkable how often we leave out visual approaches to communication, even in an e-business era. What are the most popular ways of communicating? The telephone and e-mail. E-mail rarely contains a graphic element, and when it does, it's usually encased in a dreary little box at the bottom of the message in the form of an attachment. Even PowerPoint slides are usually words instead of pictures. Most meetings have no visual component to them other than a few graphs or charts. In business, we're visually starved.

Jim Haudan, President of RootLearning® Inc., a company specializing in learning systems for communication of strategy, says that strong visuals in communication are important for three reasons:

1. Visualization helps to give a holistic picture of an idea rather than a piece of it.
2. It is a language everyone can grasp and understand.

3. It allows people to understand concepts at different rates, because visual information isn't linear.

"Visual presentation allows you to convey a lot of information. It's a great vehicle for information movement, communication, and knowledge," says Haudan.

One of the reasons we don't see more graphics is because it is often expensive to do them well. Software packages provide an inexpensive way to add visual elements, but they're often difficult to learn. They're even more difficult to use well. (You know what I mean if you've ever been subjected to the work of an overzealous amateur.) It's usually well worth the investment to use experts when the graphics are complex. It's also important not to make the mistake of emphasizing form over function. Graphics should be used where they add value, not as a distraction from weak content.

With those caveats aside, let's consider some practical ways to make information visual.

Mental Models

In a knowledge-based economy, David Sibbet, one of the world's leading authorities on the use of graphics in group settings, says shared mental models will be critical to success. When working at a distance or across organizational boundaries, it is essential that we develop shared mental models in order to be able to communicate clearly and work together effectively. And visual information is at the core of a shared mental model. Sibbet explains: "A shared mental model allows you to have much more robust communication at a distance than if you don't share a mental model." Sibbet then (visually!) illustrated his point in the following conversation with me during our interview:

SIBBET: Have you ever played chess?

BOONE: Yes, a few times.

SIBBET: Okay. I'm gonna be the blacks and you're gonna be the whites. So I'm moving pawn to Queen 4, get that?

BOONE: Okay.

SIBBET: You've gotta move it on your mental board. Can you make a move?

BOONE: I can see the board in my mind, and I know the different pieces, but I don't know the names for the squares.

SIBBET: So we can't communicate.

Sibbet points out that our "virtual chess game" would be much easier if we were both excellent chess players, sharing a mental model of the chessboard: "The more familiar we were with a common language for the location of each of those little squares, the more we could get to the point of playing chess mentally." Sibbet says that the same thing is true in business, when people share mental models, when they can "see" the same things, then they can share knowledge and work together more efficiently and effectively.

Drawing on his decades of knowledge of group facilitation, in combination with his encyclopedic understanding of graphics, Sibbet has developed an approach to creating mental models for groups in meetings. For example, at National Semiconductor, Sibbet facilitated a workshop on the company's vision by taking a 35-page white paper and turning it into a 4-by-16-foot mural. This mural formed the basis for a week-long managerial workshop that enabled them to quickly and completely grasp the company's very complex long-term strategy and vision and make important contributions to it. Sibbet also captures the mental model of groups while meetings are in process, drawing as the group talks. (See Figure 7-1.)

Visual Grammar.   Sibbet developed a "visual grammar"—an important concept for interactive managers to understand because it can help you develop and add visual elements to your own communication. Sibbet describes seven simple patterns that lie at the base of all graphic representation. They are presented as a Group Graphics® Keyboard in the The Grove Consultants' graphic facilitation work. Sibbet says, "Once you understand these patterns, you've got the key to the entire field of visual expression. They function like chords in a musician's repertoire." (See Figure 7-2.)

1. An *icon*, a single image, is the simplest format for displaying information, according to Sibbet. Think of a logo. Or think of simply making a scribble on a blank page. Your eye will naturally be drawn to any simple mark on a white field. "So if you've got a

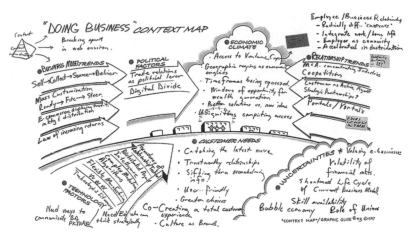

Figure 7-1   Example of a Shared Mental Model
Source: © 1997 The Grove Consultants International

    bunch of writing and one little picture in there, it will attract your
eye," explains Sibbet. "So I call it the poster effect. It's basically one
thing differentiated."

2. The next element is a *list*. This is simply a flow of items arranged
   in a linear fashion. According to Sibbet, lists move the eye and a
   point attracts the eye.

3. The third pattern is the *cluster*. A cluster is several things near
   each other in space. "It's impossible to look at three sticky notes
   on a white board and not compare them," says Sibbet. So clusters
   cause comparison.

4. Element number four is a *grid,* and grids build combinations. The
   process of making a grid is more complex than a cluster because
   you have to combine the ideas by crossing categories.

5. A *diagram,* the fifth element, is a display that branches, allowing
   relationships that are more organized than a cluster and more
   complex than a grid.

6. The big leap comes between elements five and six, because element six, a *drawing,* allows you to animate meaning by projecting
   a metaphor, or graphic analogy, into some simple lines, like those
   that might suggest a landscape, for instance.

7. Element seven, the *mandala,* a Sanskrit name for a circular drawing, shows unity and is centered on a focal point.

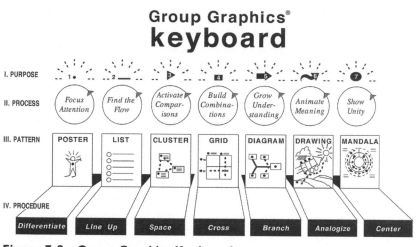

Figure 7-2   Group Graphics Keyboard
Source: © 1994 The Grove Consultants International

Understanding this visual grammar can help interactive managers express concepts visually in a meeting or in a document. If you want to capture someone's attention quickly, use an icon. If you want to activate comparisons, use a cluster. Sibbet's basic grammar can be taught, and he runs workshops to help people learn how to use graphics more effectively, particularly in group meetings.

Using Metaphors.   Presenting information in a visual way doesn't necessarily mean you have to use pictures or drawings. You can also use words to create visual images. As we saw in Chapter 6, in our discussion of high variety language, the use of analogies and metaphor can help make information visual. Steve Kerr, Chief Learning Officer at GE, says Jack Welch's mastery of metaphor is one of the things that makes him such a superb communicator:

> I could give you a thousand examples of how he uses metaphor. Once he told us, "Put on six sweaters, then go outside. Now you don't even know if it's cold out. Every time you take off a sweater you get more in touch with the environment. It's the same thing with an organizational layer. You have all these layers between you and what's happening, you don't even know what's going on. Every time you get rid of a layer, you get more in touch with your

environment." And then he said, "I want no more than five layers between the newest hire and me in any business you're in. Some companies have a system that has 12 layers; I want us down to 5. I want the sweaters coming off, because I want you to know if it's cold out, I want you to know if the customer's upset or an employee's upset, and if you're too insulated, you won't know that." It's just a rich way to describe things. He does it all the time.

As powerful as metaphorical language may be, it's important to use it with care. Peg Neuhauser, a consultant on storytelling and corporate culture, explains that not everyone interprets metaphor in the same way. She has a couple of videos that she uses in sessions on creativity, and these videos are very metaphorical: "I learned the hard way that I had to explain why I was using them and what the point of them was. Because people who are more linear and factual would come up to me afterward and say, 'Well, I love that video, it was really beautiful, but what was the point?' And to me it was glaringly obvious what the point was, but it isn't to everybody. That doesn't mean these people aren't smart. They may be incredibly bright, they just think in a different way and draw a different conclusion, or no conclusion."

David Sibbet echoes the idea of taking care when using metaphor: "The danger of using systematic metaphors of any sort is that you can get stuck in the metaphor. Metaphor eliminates some things and obscures other things—always. Because they're models. They're little prototypes. A metaphor is just a mental simplification. It allows you to grasp something in an essential way and play with it."

Using Technology for Visual Representation

Technology can be used to help make information visual. Billie Alban, a large group event consultant, says the U.S. Forest Service used video streaming to send images from a large group meeting to people who were unable to attend. More important, the meeting required follow-up, and this follow-up was captured in action shots of people out in the field implementing the ideas that had been developed at the meeting. These were distributed to participants. For example, one of the follow-up items was to develop community projects. Following the meeting, these projects were initiated, and then pictures of Forest Service people working in elementary schools and other community-based settings were sent out to people throughout the organization. This visual representation gave tangible evidence of the importance of the work that people had done at the meeting itself.

At Buzzsaw.com, a number of the services they provide are visually based. Owners and other stakeholders who are working together on a construction project can receive hourly (or even more frequent) updates on construction sites through digital cameras that send still shots over the Internet at desired time intervals. "The photos are all archived on the site. That way, if there's an accident on the site, if something gets stolen, or if weather delays start to mount, you can easily see what's going on and why it occurred. This is something that's never been possible before," says Jason Pratt, Director of Product Marketing for the company. Buzzsaw.com also provides drawing tools so that architects, engineers, and others can draw in the same on-line space in a web-based application. This shared drawing application can be in real time or asynchronous. It also hosts web-based meetings in which people can simultaneously see the same thing on their computers via an Internet link, as well as connect in an audio conference.

As Anne Bonaparte, cofounder of Buzzsaw.com, points out: "Construction is a very visual industry, whether it's a drawing, a photograph, a sketch, or an engineering calculation. Sometimes you might need to take a photograph of something unexpected: 'How the heck are we going to deal with that?' Or, 'Look, those two walls don't join like we thought.' You're always wanting to point to something, and our customers are always drawing or sketching. So we needed to create ways for them to share these on-line."

Perhaps of all the people in the construction industry, architects are the most visual. Mike Rosen of Mike Rosen & Associates, an architecture firm specializing in the use of virtual reality, explains how VR can help people visualize construction projects and improve communication among buyers, sellers, architects, and others associated with a project. His typical client might be a developer who is opening up a new housing community. The traditional way to do this is to first build three sample homes and furnish them. Once the homes are completed, their sales team is trained on how to sell those homes. Rosen says this process takes about eight months. "With virtual reality," he says, "the minute the architectural plans are done, we can build a virtual home. So they can do what's called a virtual grand opening, eight months earlier than they would with the real homes."

Rosen says the virtual homes can also help developers communicate with governmental and community entities by giving a much more vivid visual picture of their projects for purposes of approvals. Subcontractors can also use the model to make changes and recommendations. Also, potential customers can use the model to customize their kitchens, see what their furniture would look like, make changes to the construction, etc.

Rosen says that having a clear visual picture can help people before an expensive construction project is started. For example, his company was asked by another architectural firm to work on a virtual reality model of the New Jersey Convention Center in Atlantic City. (See Figure 7-3.) Rosen's company showed how the $70 million project would look upon completion. "They could see how it would be set up for Miss America, as a hockey rink, a boxing format, or a concert. We could literally show it in a lot of different scenarios," he says. In the process of building the model, they came across issues architecturally that wouldn't have been seen by the original architect working in two dimensions. For example, soffit

Figure 7-3   Virtual Reality View of the New Jersey Convention Center, Atlantic City
Source: Courtesy of Philadelphia Virtual Reality Center

detailing that needed to fit into the ceiling and incorporate lighting was revised after seeing the model and before construction began.

Visual representation can help people understand buildings, but it can also help people understand each other. Brad Meyer of Collaboration Ltd., a communication consulting firm, tells a terrific story about the value of a video link between people in different places. He once worked with a company that had sites in two different cities. Each week, the people at the two sites would meet on an audio conference to, as Meyer puts it, "thrash through the 100-odd items that were on the list to thrash through. At least that's what the people at Site A thought was happening." What the people at Site A didn't realize was that the people at Site B were getting up, leaving the room, going for coffee, checking out. Then they got video conferencing between the two sites in order to be able to share engineering specifications.

Meyer says it was a real wake-up call (literally, in one case): "They began to see each other for the first time, and put a face to the name and the voice. People [on Site B], were sitting at the table drumming their hands. One person actually fell asleep and woke up. It was alarming and astonishing to the [Site A] group, who thought, 'Hey, we're sharing all this information every week, we're doing great, we're team-playing.' What they realized is, the majority of the time, there was not a lot of interaction actually happening."

Meyer followed up with the people at Site B to see what could be done to make the meetings more valuable to them. They asked for a reprioritization of issues and elimination of unimportant issues. When this was done, attendance at the meetings improved. "Those changes to the meeting wouldn't even have been considered if this group hadn't seen these guys falling asleep," says Meyer.

The groups also started to do more document sharing through the system, which both sides found useful:

Folks on one end would scan specifications into the computer, the picture would come up on a white board, and the folks on the other side would come over and draw circles over parts and say, "See, that's an issue right there." And the other guys, the engineers, would say, "Well, I don't see what's an issue there. The requirements say this wire is supposed to be exactly this far away from the wall." And the people on the other side would say,

"Right. We'll be back in five minutes, carry on with another agenda item." And one of these guys would go off to the site with a video camera, photograph or video what was happening with a physical wire on the actual site in proximity to the wall, bring that back in and share it in the middle of the video conference. And the guys on the other side, the engineers who had designed it to spec and for all the official parameters, would say, **"Oh, you're right. Obviously you can't have it there; even though it looks right on flat paper, it doesn't work in reality."** So they began to come to an understanding of each other and to develop a respect for each other, based on skills and circumstances. The end result of all of that was that what might have taken three weeks of going back and forth before they would come to an agreement to do something differently, they could take care of within one meeting.

Meyer says that as a result of the video link, a real sense of team-work developed between the two groups: "They began to interact. Rather than have the one meeting, they began to have two meetings, and rather than have two meetings a week, they got to a point where they just kept the systems on in the open office and work areas [in the two different cities].... And the general effect was that you could come up to the window on this end and practically knock on the screen and say, 'Hey, is Joe there?' And someone on the other side would say, 'Oh yes, I'll go get him.' It was like an extended room."

By making information visual, interactive managers can improve the clarity, consistency, and effectiveness of their communication. Another way to capture people's attention is to specifically tailor infor-mation—not an easy task in a diverse world.

Tailor Information for Different Stakeholders

"How do you grab someone's attention in an overloaded environment?" asks Bill Jensen, President and CEO of The Jensen Group and author of *Simplicity.* "You create something that is user-centered, that's personalized, that's mass-customized. It's focused on the individual's need.... That's the better mousetrap."

Creating user-centered communication isn't always easy, but it has high payoffs. The use of intranets to customize and personalize information is truly an exciting area of development in communication. Unfortunately, as Jon Iwata, Vice President of Corporate Communications at IBM, pointed out earlier in this chapter, many organizations still view intranets as a broadcast medium—an information dumping ground for all the things they used to print and distribute. But other organizations are doing really exciting things to personalize information on their internal portals. Iwata says that one of the most popular applications on the IBM intranet is called "MyNews."

MyNews works in the following way: You fill out an on-line form that asks you about your profession, where you work, what your interests are, what customers you call on, etc. Then you can select from more than 300 categories of news and information from both external and internal sources. Once that's done, the MyNews engine scours news sources against your profile, pulls all of the relevant headlines and news stories and aggregates them. It then pushes the information to you either as a personalized web page, or as an e-mail.

Betsy Pasley, Communications Planner at USAA, a large insurance and financial services provider to the U.S. military, says they are instituting a similar approach. She says one of the big benefits of providing information based on profiles is that they can cut down on a great deal of superfluous information being sent to people on e-mail—such as information about blood drives, volunteer opportunities, etc. Some senders of information initially resist this approach, says Pasley: "It's funny, the clients at first resist because they say everybody's not going to see it. But we tell them that the people who want to see it will be more likely to respond, and they won't irritate those people who *didn't* want to see it."

The real value of intranets is that they allow people to tailor their own information. Trying to guess what someone in Indonesia or Indiana wants to see is really difficult. With intranets, people can target what's crucial.

Often, companies find that while they *think* they're targeting their audiences, they're actually missing the mark. Anthony Goodman, CEO of Smythe Dorward Lambert Inc., a change management consulting firm, says that one of his clients decided to have them put together a communications map to track the *actual* communication flows in the organization as opposed to the *perceived* ones, for purposes of communicating during a change management effort. To create the map, they tracked who talks to whom and what they talk about. Goodman says that it is a simple concept, but complex in execution. "What they discovered was that the traditional way they communicated, top-down in the organization, actually made no sense. Most people didn't get things, or got the wrong things. Once they had the communication map, they could really get messages out very quickly to the right people. They could pinpoint exactly how to get a message to the entire organization within 24 hours."

Don Tapscott, coauthor of *Digital Capital*, points out that communication is going to become increasingly tailored by consumers—whether the "senders" like it or not. He uses television as an example: "There will be 50 million options, and the viewer or listener will become the person who makes the decisions. They will do the 'casting,' not ABC. There won't be any such thing as 'Prime Time.' Instead it will be, 'It's 8:27, give me 'Law and Order.' Or, 'It's 8:27, give me David Bowie's latest hit.' "

This same wave of customization of information is happening in business-to-business situations. Effective senders of information will make available the pieces people might need, and provide a context or architecture that makes it easy for receivers to pull together the relevant pieces.

Structure Improves Clarity

Remember when your seventh grade teacher tried to teach you how to create outlines? Structure is critical to understanding. When people have trouble making sense of information it is usually because the information isn't structured properly.

Structuring information requires discipline, persistence, and the right tools. Quite frankly, structuring has never come easily to me. My writing and speaking got a huge boost when I discovered outlining software over 15 years ago. Dr. Douglas Engelbart, the inventor of the mouse and hypertext, invented remarkable software called Augment when he was working at SRI in the 1960s. This software was reconstituted on a PC platform around 1987 by my former business partner, N. Dean Meyer, who worked with Engelbart's group. It has been the single most important tool

I have ever used on a computer, in terms of expanding my thinking capacity. The reason it is so powerful is that it allows me to look at textual information prismatically, revealing the underlying structure and forcing me to place ideas into a structured format.

The structuring of information is not restricted to outlines. David Sibbet, the inventor of visual grammar, has shown us in this chapter how the arrangement of information into a visual format can create structure. Charts, lists, grids, diagrams, etc., all provide ways of structuring information so we can make sense of it.

Mike Zisman, Executive Vice President of Strategy at Lotus Development Corporation, says that structuring is a critical, and often overlooked, component of knowledge management. He makes the distinction between clustering and classifying information in order to impose structure. With classification, you have a predetermined structure that is imposed on the data. So, you have a set of buckets and you sort your information into those buckets. With clustering, the structure is *discovered* in the data. Zisman gives an example: "With clustering, I might send you two million documents, and you could use clustering software to discover a structure—that is, it might find that these two million documents are really about 42 basic topics."

Lack of structure can create confusion in the workplace. Laura Rothman, technical controller for an IBM, Toshiba, and Infineon chip alliance, says that a couple of years ago a lack of structure to their online "team rooms" made it virtually impossible to find information: "About two years ago we were at the point where we had so many team rooms nobody really knew where to go to get information or where to put things... We were creating each little [separate] area. Depending upon the product and what you were working on in the process area, you might have had to visit three or four different places to get the information you needed... It was just becoming a deluge of information, and we really needed some restructuring."

Rothman worked with a consultant to create a better structure for all the team rooms. They improved the overall team room template and created what Rothman calls an "interconnected architecture" for it. With the new structure, Rothman says that now people only have to visit one place to find what they're looking for.

Structure is critical to communication because without it, it's hard to develop shared understanding.

At General Electric, when Chief Learning Officer Steve Kerr talks about "creating line of sight," what he is really referring to is using structure to improve communication. He modestly calls it "dumbing everything down into its simplest element," which is extraordinarily challenging to do. Creating a simple structure for information without losing its richness is an art. He provides an example:

> **We teach at Crotonville [GE's educational center] how to take 30 or 70 new initiatives, or whatever number you have, and integrate them so your people can handle them. So here comes reengineering and Six Sigma and e-business and mass customization and customer initiative and diversity and globalization. . . . Your people are paralyzed and none of it takes. So we teach integration. All we're doing in GE is being a boundaryless company. That's all we do. And there are only three types of boundaries: horizontal boundaries between functions, departments, and territories; vertical boundaries between levels in the organization; and boundaries between the organization and outside entities such as customers and suppliers. The object in everything we do is to permeate these boundaries. So every time a new idea comes in, if it can't be jimmied into these three categories, we don't do it. This is our filter. So, for example, we do all these things, but we don't present them as new. Broadbanding moves money down to lower levels. Stock options move money down to lower levels. Workout moves ideas down to lower levels. Etcetera. So it's one of the tools we have for managing. We teach line of sight. We teach people how to make information and ideas actionable.**

As an interactive manager, whether you are writing a speech, creating a host of new on-line discussions, or trying to involve people in a change management effort, remember to consider *structure* when you communicate.

Attacking Overload

Far too much responsibility has been placed on *receivers* of information in an e-business era. They're expected to sift through mounds of information and make sense of it. They're called upon to act on the information that is sent to them, even if it's sent in a form they can't understand. It's high time that *senders* took on more responsibility for what they're shoving at people.

"I think it's a myth to say that information overload has been caused by technology," says Anthony Goodman, CEO of Smythe Dorward Lambert Inc. "It's caused by people not thinking about communication very deeply. And technology has just given them a massive boost. It's accelerated the process. Instead of somebody's secretary standing by the photocopier running off 300 memos, it can now be done with the push of a button on e-mail. . . . People aren't thinking about who their audience is, what they want to hear, and how they want to hear it. . . . These senders are saying, 'I've always done it like this, and if they know what's good for them, they'll enjoy it.' "

Betsy Pasley, Communication Planner at USAA, agrees with Goodman: "The bottom line on information overload is that people who are sending information aren't thinking: 'Am I really sending responsibly?' " Pasley's guidelines for sending information include the following key points: "First, do you have an objective for this communication? Second, understand your audience. If you're sending information, are you targeting the right group? Third, are you packaging the information correctly? For example, are you sending really large files? Should you instead link people to that information on a website? Finally, are you putting the good stuff up front? Don't make them read through everything to get to the bottom, where you've buried the call to action."

"I'm just in the process of dealing with this problem of sending information in the last few weeks," says Sarah Fasey, Internal Communications Manager at Microsoft Ltd., United Kingdom and Ireland. "Product managers want to evangelize for their products, to get people powered up about them. They want everyone to wear the T-shirt, wear the hat. Traditionally what happens for a product launch is that they get creative agents in here to put together a launch for them, and we'd have balloons, stuff in the atrium downstairs, posters, voice mail, e-mail, stickers on the cars, tray mats in the canteen. They'd have this whole campaign of noisemaking, with really inventive ideas, to make sure they got your attention. I'm actually trying to put a stop to it, because yes you might get my attention, but actually I'm exhausted by the effort you've made to get my attention!"

To address this problem, Fasey is building "resource kits" for distribution to everyone once a month. The kits contain both on-line information plus materials and collateral, and Fasey says she is filtering what goes in the kits: "I'm going to be ruthless about what goes in that box, because unless you can really genuinely prove to me that there is a benefit to me knowing what you want me to know, you're not really communicating anything. If I just think it's adding to the noise levels, it's not going to happen. Because the one who ultimately loses in this equation is the customer. People haven't got time to listen to the customer because they've got all this other stuff they have to listen to internally."

Tray mats and stickers don't even come close to the noise levels e-mail creates in organizations. One of the biggest complaints I heard about e-mail in my interviews was the number of broadcast e-mails people receive. Getting on some clueless sender's distribution list is a nightmare. At Tacit Knowledge Systems, David Gilmour, CEO, says they address this problem with technology: "We intervene with the mail on the sender side, rather than the receiver side. By the time a whole bunch of junk mail gets to your inbox, the genie's out of the bottle. It's already too late. Most programs allow you to sift through and sort it. We're trying to make senders smarter, to make them think about the appetite people may or may not have for reading what they're sending."

Tacit's software provides the distribution list sender with profiles as to the level of interest a potential receiver might have on that particular topic. Gilmour gives an example:

> **Suppose you'd like to send an article to some people in your company. Let's say you put together the e-mail with the attachment and you click on "Westport Office." The system will say to itself, "That's a mailing list." And what it will automatically do is explode that into a list of the individuals you'll be sending to along with information about how good a match there is between the topic of your e-mail and the interests of the people you're sending it to. And you know what? They're all terrible matches. You're a very bad guesser. Collin, Craig, and Liz have nothing to do with any topic you covered in this message, so we'll send this to Collin just cause he's a buddy, but we'll delete Craig and Liz, and now right there we've saved two people spam who otherwise would have gotten it. So right away you can see how interesting your message is to your community.**

Electronic media are not the only media calling for more responsible sending. Even in face-to-face interactions we need to give more thought to *why* we're calling meetings, *how* our messages are designed, and how we're using people's *time*. Interactive managers are responsible senders of information who give thought to both the value and relevance of their content and the appropriateness of their media selection, whether they're sending out a piece of mail, holding a formal event, or starting an on-line discussion group.

Key Ideas from Chapter 7

- Knowledge sharing is more about psychology than technology.
- Expertise location software, audio conferences, web conferences, and other interactive technologies can be as effective as databases for sharing tacit knowledge.
- Intranets can be powerful tools for tailoring information and improving organizational performance.
- Icons, lists, clusters, grids, diagrams, drawings, and mandalas can help you present information clearly.
- Information overload isn't caused by technology, it's caused by people.

By making information available, useful, and enticing, interactive managers can improve their abilities to understand and be understood, increase the speed at which their teams work together, and enhance their knowledge management efforts. Chapter 8 explores a time-tested competency for structuring, presenting, enriching, and sharing information: telling a story.

8

Use Stories to Capture and Share Knowledge

One Day a Boy was going Out to Play and ran until he came to a rock. he picked it up and it Called I want you! the boy asked the rock What owned the rock? a elf! a Bad elf. the Boy ran to see that elf! then he saw a hand. it was the elf! they had a fight and the Boy winned the fight and got the rock

This is one of the first stories I ever wrote. Clearly, I was no budding Eudora Welty, but what's amazing to me is that even when we're in pre-school, we have a sense of narrative. This story contains all the basic elements: opening, conflict, climax, and resolution. A conference speaker on storytelling once said that everything we need to know about story-telling was summed up in one cartoon with the following caption: Once Upon a Time, Suddenly, Luckily, Happily Ever After.

Whether child or adult, Korean or African, rich or poor, we respond to stories. And while the craft of storytelling has been practiced and taught for thousands of years, it is only in recent years that we've started to see how storytelling can have a significant business impact. In fact, it's been a very hot, hip subject in management magazines for the last couple of years. And for good reason. Whether you're trying to have an impact on corporate culture, explain a complex concept, encourage innovation, or add to your storehouse of intellectual capital, stories can help in truly surprising ways.

What I hope to do in this chapter is move past the hype about storytelling and give you some real insights into how you can not only *tell* better stories, but also use storytelling to bring about change and knowledge sharing in organizations. Most of us tend to think of storytelling as a way to inform people. It can also be an effective tool for getting others to inform *us*. We'll see in this chapter examples of using stories as a tool for capturing as well as sharing knowledge, and we'll learn about how technology can help with storytelling.

The good news is that the experts tell me that anyone can learn to tell stories effectively. "I don't think you're going to turn a lot of people into Mark Twain," muses Peg Neuhauser, author of *Corporate Legends and Lore*. "But it's a trainable skill, particularly within a work setting."

Dana Atchley, consultant and Digital Storyteller, agrees: "Everybody tells stories. They tell stories in the elevator, they tell stories over drinks, they tell stories at dinner with their family and with their friends. Or to be more accurate, we'll call them anecdotes. Conversation is the basis for mining stories. In that context everybody's a storyteller."

What's interesting is that many people don't see themselves as storytellers, and they don't see business as a place for storytelling. Johnny Harben, Senior Consultant with Smythe Dorward Lambert Ltd., a change management and internal communication consulting firm, says that some people don't take the concept of storytelling seriously: "Storytelling can come across as being rather fanciful, as being little bit 'short-trousered,' as we might say in England. And the response to it is, 'I'm a long-trousered businessman who wants to make real results.' "

"People believe if they don't give just the facts, they're not being businesslike," says Ann Wylie, of Wylie Communications, a company that provides storytelling seminars for writers and communicators. "They think they'll look soft or silly if they use an alternative to just cramming numbers into paragraphs. But they really need to overcome that."

In this chapter we'll look at ways stories have been used to shape and reveal corporate culture, improve articulation and understanding of an organization's brand, and capture and share knowledge. In the second half of the chapter we'll explore some of the specific storytelling skills interactive managers need to develop.

Shaping and Revealing Corporate Culture Through Stories

The e-mails started flying when Grand Metropolitan, a large food and beverage conglomerate, and Guinness, the world-famous brewers, announced the name of their newly merged entity: Diageo. One employee suggested the name should stand for "Don't Imagine Any Great Employment Opportunities." Now that's an anecdote most corporations would not want to advertise. However, Johnny Harben, who at the time was head of communications for Grand Metropolitan, says it was exactly the type of anecdote he loved to uncover for its highly irreverent merger newsletter. That type of anecdote gave the publication a high degree of credibility with its readership. It contributed to an atmosphere of openness, candor, and clarity. During the merger, when asked in a survey if they had heard any rumors about the integration of the company, over 75 percent of the respondents said no. This amazing response was due to the fact that rumors were dealt with openly by the company in media such as the newsletter. Harben's group had a policy of telling the stories that people really wanted to hear, thereby superseding the company grapevine.

By capturing and sharing stories at the outset of a merger, companies can improve the speed and effectiveness with which they come together.

"In most mergers, organizations often do a lot better job of due diligence on legal and financial issues than they do on cultural issues," says Peg Neuhauser, noted authority on storytelling and organizational culture. "They don't know if there's a fit between the cultures. Many mergers get derailed, and in fact fall apart, because of culture clashes. It makes sense legally, financially, but they can never get it to gel, to get the groups to work together. Sharing stories can be a way of understanding where each organization is coming from." Neuhauser notes that if companies have competing cultures, it's often difficult for them to work together well: "If you find that lots of the stories reveal significant differences between the cultures, then you've got a bigger problem than you're going to be able to work out, unless you've got a real clearcut acquisition situation and one culture's just going to be immediately disbanded. An accumulation of stories allows you to see this landscape fairly quickly."

In all forms of alliances, whether partnerships, b-webs, mergers, or acquisitions, stories can provide a means of creating cohesiveness and shared understanding of goals and objectives.

Julie Beedon, of Vista Consulting in the United Kingdom, works with companies to improve their communication before, during, and after mergers. She says mergers require the creation of a common story: "Companies that are about to merge have separate stories. By coming together and telling and commonly interpreting our pasts, we can create a *common* story. Once we've created that common story, we can start to talk about our *future* story, and that allows the newly formed company to stop disagreeing about the *present* story."

Not only does that new story need to be created, but it also needs to be articulated. Johnny Harben explains: "When you put two organizations together, you have to tell the new organization's story with a new voice. Many different forms of dialogue may have created the story, but 'the voice' of the organization has to be seized and molded and owned by a group of leaders." What Harben did in order to "seize" that voice was to create and distribute a series of audiotapes that captured leaders telling stories about what was going on during the Diageo merger. The stories recorded for these tapes had the same level of candor and straight talk that the aforementioned newsletter contained. Harben gives an example:

> So the chairman would talk, and lo and behold, what did he do? Tell stories. Because that was the best way of getting the real message across. He'd say, "I had this extraordinary meeting with the chairman of the other company on Tuesday. We had to meet on a private aircraft parked at an RAF station outside London because the Federal Trade Commission didn't allow us to talk directly to each other, so we had to go on diplomatically neutral ground. Bloody cold night, it was seven o'clock or eight o'clock, sitting on this bloody aircraft." Now that stuff goes out and it's gold dust. By hearing the stories, people felt like they were in the force field, they felt like they were part of the story themselves, just for a magic half hour.

Stories are the best way to encapsulate the essence of a culture in a way that others can understand, says Peg Neuhauser, author of *Corporate Legends and Lore*. She says companies can use these illustrative stories in a number of ways. In a merger, different companies can use them to understand each other's histories and heritage and how they're related. But these stories can also be used in less formal alliances than a merger. Neuhauser gives an example of how she uses stories to pass on her own company's values to the subcontractors she works with, explaining that the story should not only impart what the values are, but also how that plays out in terms of expected behavior:

> **A core value for me is reliability, because it's extremely important in what I do as a speaker and as a consultant that people can count on me to show up. So if I'm subcontracting to somebody who's working with me, one of the things I'll always tell them is, "Do whatever you have to do, but show up." Well, that's just a statement, but if you turn that into a story, it does two things. First, it brings it alive: They're more likely to understand it; also, the story will be instructive. It will tell them what they're supposed to do. So the story I always tell them is about the time I was supposed to be at the Homestead Resort at nine o'clock the next morning, and at midnight I was still sitting stranded at O'Hare Airport. The closest flight I could find was one to Greensboro, North Carolina, that arrived at 3:30 in the morning. And Greensboro is four hours away from the Homestead. I was too tired to drive so I called Yellow Cab and had a cab driver take me to the Homestead. It was a $400 cab fare. I changed clothes in a dirty rest room on the way, and arrived there at five to nine to do the all-day set of presentations. And so I'll tell people that story, and the message is: This is how far you're supposed to go to make sure you get there. And we won't bill the client for the cab fare—it's just the cost of doing business. Many times in companies people go on and on about the goals and what's supposed to be important here, but they don't give us very much of a road map on what's allowable and what's not. Stories provide that road map.**

Branding and Stories

These days, the field of marketing is highly focused on issues pertaining to a company's brand. Not only are marketing people focused on improving brand understanding and recognition with customers, but there is a new movement called "Internal Branding," which is aimed at getting people *inside* organizations to develop a deeper level of understanding of the brand and what it means to their work. Stories can help a company build and promote a brand.

Dana Atchley, who describes himself as Digital Storyteller, has worked with companies such as Coca-Cola and PriceWaterhouseCoopers to help them do what he calls "emotional branding." In essence, Atchley helps companies build a cache of stories about the products and services they offer, and then his clients can use those stories to build understanding of their brands—both inside and outside the firm.

At the Digital Storytelling Theater for the World of Coca-Cola in Las Vegas (created by Atchley), people have an opportunity to both hear stories that convey the essence of the brand as well as contribute their own stories about what Coca-Cola means to them. The middle of the show is centered on an emotional story: "One of these stories is about a guy who carried six bottles of Coca-Cola with him throughout World War II," says Atchley. "He drank all but one bottle, took it home, and saved it all his life. Fifty years later his house burned down, and the one thing that he saved from the house was the half-full bottle of Coca-Cola. He's long gone, but his daughter tells the story about him carrying this little piece of Americana with him during the war." The show closes with a brand-related story. As people leave, they are invited to enter a kiosk outside the theater, where they can record their own stories about Coca-Cola.

Atchley is refreshingly frank about the fact that these stories haven't been mined for as much value as they're capable of providing. While Coca-Cola is saving and filtering through the stories, Atchley thinks it should be using them in a variety of ways, including putting them on its website. He envisions photographs of people that can be clicked on to hear a recorded voice telling a personal story about Coca-Cola.

Brands are about people's emotional connections to the products and services a company provides. Because storytelling is such a powerful medium, because it triggers emotional reactions in people, interactive managers should consider how they can incorporate storytelling into their brand messages, both internally and externally.

Using Stories to Capture Knowledge

"Knowledge is best embedded in a good story," says Digital Storyteller and consultant Dana Atchley. Indeed, many people in the area of knowledge management have found that the best way to capture knowledge is in the form of an anecdote or story.

"Storytelling is a low-cost, self-sustaining means of capturing knowledge in an organization on an ongoing basis," says David Snowden, European Director of IBM's Institute for Knowledge Management. In one multinational sales organization, Snowden and his colleagues used a technique of holding storytelling workshops where sales teams were reassembled to reminisce about their sales experiences on particular projects. "This creates a series of anecdotes, humorous incidents, lessons learned, observations, and plain narrative," says Snowden. As the salespeople were telling stories, trained observers extracted decisions, judgments, problems resolved or unresolved, and then charted these together with information flows. The observers then presented their ideas to the group of salespeople for validation. Then decisions were made by the whole group about what information should be made "explicit" and shared with the larger organization.[1]

Lisa Kimball, founder and VP Professional Services for Caucus Systems, which specializes in hosting and facilitating on-line discussion groups, agrees with Snowden that in knowledge sharing efforts, people are much more inclined to share their stories than they are to write reports:

> **Whether someone is trying to capture best practices or case examples or an after-action report, that information has to be somewhat standardized in order to fit the database, be useful, and be searchable. The problem is that most companies don't really have very good processes for creating those reports, so what happens is it's a big overhead task for the person who had this great project. So it's like, "You've just finished a great project, now go fill out this form." People don't want to do that. It's very important to make that kind of thing a natural by-product of work. The way to do that is to think about how it's usually done: People describe all the cool, important things they've done when they tell stories in the bar or over lunch or around the watercooler. What we're trying to do is create a space like the watercooler on-line.**

> **For example, one very large technology firm we work with held an annual knowledge management conference that was virtual. It had a storytelling space in it. They selected half a dozen people who had best practice knowledge, and they asked them to come**

tell their stories about their projects. We trained some people to be the story elicitors. The storytellers started the stories on-line by putting the first piece of it as an item, and then the elicitors would ask a question and try and draw them out over a couple of days, and then other people in the group could ask more questions like, "How'd you think of doing that?" or, "Why didn't you do this other thing?" and that actually got out some very rich material. Then they could take that material, since it was digital, and harvest it by excerpting it, summarizing it, etc., and _then_ they put it in a database.

To take advantage of the intellectual capital in your organization, you have to find a way to tap into it. Part of people's reluctance to share their knowledge stems from the fact that they don't want to fill out reports or type things into a database. Sharing stories with colleagues is a way of not only making knowledge capture easy, but also making it valuable for the storyteller. In the scenarios described by Snowden and Kimball, the people telling stories benefited from interacting with others.

Armed with these examples of the usefulness of storytelling, let's take a look at some skills that you, as an interactive manager, can develop in order to make good use of stories for communication in your organization.

Storytelling Skills

There's much more to the concept of storytelling than just sitting around the watercooler swapping a few stories or listening to someone's latest customer service legend. While part of this section contains practical suggestions for how to _tell_ a better story, more of it focuses on storytelling as a knowledge sharing tool. The section begins with the distinction between an _anecdote_ and a _story_. This is followed by aspects of story construction, creative approaches to gathering anecdotes, enacting versus telling stories, and storytelling technology.

Anecdote or Story?

Most of us intuitively know the difference between an anecdote and a story. Length is one critical differentiator: Anecdotes tend to be shorter than stories. A less clear-cut distinction is veracity: Anecdotes tend to be about things that really happened, whereas stories can either be real or constructed.

Why is it important to distinguish between the two? It can lead to some very interesting insights in terms of how you use and construct stories. Dave Snowden, an expert on storytelling and European Director of IBM's Institute for Knowledge Management, has, in conjunction with colleagues in the United States and Europe, constructed a model for using stories in organizations that is based on this distinction. While Snowden acknowledges the value of capturing and distributing anecdotes, he and his colleagues have had remarkable results with constructed, fictionalized stories as well: "Actually, fictional story forms are more powerful than factual ones. If you say, 'I'm going to tell you a story,' then people tune in to learn. If you say, 'Let me tell you what happened,' then they tune in to be cynical."

Communicating Values: Corporate Myths and Fables

When interactive managers want to communicate about values, story construction can be a powerful tool, as Dave Snowden explains. Essentially, there are four primary steps to story construction in Snowden's model. (See Figure 8-1.) In Step 1, anecdotes are elicited from people in the organization, and these anecdotes represent the existing organizational values, rules, beliefs, and archetypes. Step 2 involves deconstructing the anecdotes into basic story elements (e.g., the protagonist, the context, or the initiating event) that can be stored and then subsequently mixed and matched to create a new story, containing the desired values, rules, beliefs, and archetypes. There are numerous ways of eliciting anecdotes. Some organizations use social scientists or professional storytellers to gather anecdotes through observation—Snowden's team uses anthropologists. Others use story "elicitors"—people who ask questions in order to gather stories. Elicitors can be professionals or they can be colleagues: "In a merger, for example, you can get the two different groups to capture anecdotes about themselves," says Snowden. Anecdotes can also be collected through the use of technology in kiosks, on-line discussion groups, e-mail, or voice mail. In Step 3 the collected anecdotes are stored in an electronic repository.

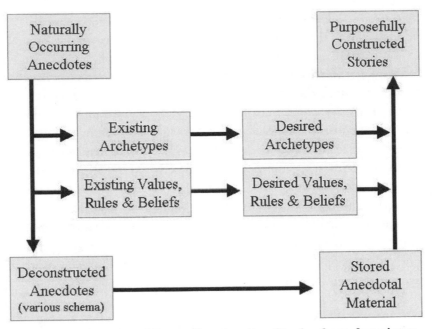

Figure 8-1   Aspects of Story: Constructing Stories from Anecdotes
Source: © Dave Snowden

Once the anecdotes are collected and stored, in Step 4 they can be used to construct two kinds of stories: myths and fables. Myths are simple stories that are easily retold. Fables, on the other hand, are very complex and require the skills of a storyteller or the use of a script. Let's look at an example, provided by Snowden, of how to construct a fable and use it to "interrupt" a myth.

All organizations have what Snowden calls "urban myths." These are stories that have no basis in reality. Snowden explains: "In IBM, there was a story that was a favorite with salesmen who had lost big sales. The story was about a salesman who lost a sale, even though the IBM sales team had done a better job than the competition during the sales process. As the story goes, the client came back a year later because they'd realized that IBM understood them better than the competition. Now, when we went out to validate this story, we couldn't find a single example of this, and it was a dangerous urban myth because it was excusing poor sales behavior." In response, Snowden and his team constructed a fable designed to disrupt the myth, and Snowden delivered it at a large sales conference:

> **We built a story progressively, it started off sounding like a hero story, you know—the IBM team arrived and they appreciated that the client hadn't really understood what they needed, so they went off-site and used all of IBM's expertise and created a better solution. Everybody thinks this is going to be a hero story. Then you gradually transform it. All of a sudden you start to introduce some subtle changes, like, "The competition was taking the client out for lunch and golf, and doing what the client had asked them to. IBM wasn't spending any time with the client because it was too important to produce a good solution for them." Then some of the audience starts to realize what's happening. The story gets worse and worse, and it actually finished up with the client selling his wife and children into slavery, and crawling back across a desert of broken glass wearing a hair shirt, back to the great god IBM, who dispensed the original solution. At which point the clouds parted, water flowed in the streams, lambs gamboled in the field, quite literally, that's how the story ended. And nobody ever dared tell that story again.**

Myths and fables validate or endorse behaviors. Snowden explains that the difference between the two forms is that *myths* are constructed in such a way that they are easily retold, while *fables* are intentionally made complex to ensure consistency in the telling (because only a storyteller can tell them) and also so the storyteller can inject new experiences that make them sound like new stories, but with the same underlying set of principles or values. Snowden says fable is very useful for getting catch phrases or key concepts into a community because it is easier to control the story; the storyteller can reuse the phrases or concepts as many times as they like, whereas with a myth, the person telling the story could leave those elements out.

Communicating principles and values is a crucial part of interactive management. By constructing stories, interactive managers can significantly improve their ability to share information and knowledge in their organizations. But there are things to watch out for when taking this approach.

Anti-Stories

"Anti-Stories" are a hazard in organizational storytelling, according to Snowden. He says an anti-story occurs when you try to "shift too much ground." He gives an example of an anti-story that was so strong that it has survived in the IBM culture for 50 years:

> **Thomas J. Watson was perceived as a dictator. And he got fed up with nobody telling him the truth because they were all scared of him. So he issued a memo that anybody who came into his office and told him the truth would not be punished. And nobody believed him. So, by issuing that memo, what he actually did was to create an anti-story. The anti-story was, "You might want to go and tell him the truth, but have you seen how many heads he's got mounted on the wall of his office?" And that very simple image actually meant that even fewer people told him the truth. If you try and use story to shift the ground too much, it actually has a negative effect, it produces an anti-story, which makes it even more difficult to create change. And the anti-story in this case is still around 50 years later. Basically everybody still retells it.**

Interactive managers should take care to ensure they're telling *believable* stories. Even when a story is true, the culture may not be ready to hear it.

Learning from Mullah Nasrudin

It's one thing to share positive anecdotes, but quite another to communicate about failure. But mistakes often contain the most valuable information. "We created a medium for people to own up to error," says Snowden. "Because we knew that the most valuable learning in an organization is always negative. It's always more important to have a repository of failure than it is to copy best practice." To address this challenge, Snowden and his colleagues created the concept of *extracting archetypes,* which is borrowed from a Sufi storytelling tradition called "Mullah Nasrudin stories":

> **This tradition goes back several thousand years in the Middle East. Mullah Nasrudin is sort of a court jester character. And everybody in the Middle East grows up believing in Mullah Nasrudin stories, which they hear at their mother's knee. And they create their own. In Sufi society they use stories as a means of teaching. If you do something stupid or if you think you might do**

something stupid or if you think somebody else might do something stupid, then you create a Mullah Nasrudin story around the mistake. It's a means not just of passing on your own learning, but of passing on potential learning or warning. There are current Mullah Nasrudin stories such as the one about him trying to get through Heathrow without the right forms.

The way Snowden uses Mullah Nasrudin is to create character sets from the anecdotes he collects, and then he uses those character sets to create stories that can inform and instruct. Snowden gives an example of Mullah Nasrudin stories they constructed from anecdotes collected from the IBM Worldwide Consulting group. The anecdotes were collected in the training classroom environment by participant observers, and archtypes were extracted from those anecdotes. The archetypes were then used in a series of stories that were told in subsequent training sessions. Snowden describes some archetypes:

One was Jason, who graduated from the Harvard Business School eight years ago summa cum laude. Jason believes that only people who graduated summa cum laude from an East Coast business school are worthy of his consideration. He considers the world to be rationally organized and is certain that if he were only paid enough money, he could discover the Newtonian principles that underlie it. Do you recognize Jason? Then there's Linda. She is head of Practice and wants to be a vice president by the time she's 35. And she will kill anybody or anything who gets in the way. And then there's Tom. He has been made redundant three times, was employed by IBM as a favor to a client, doesn't have a business education, doesn't understand the language. But Tom's a guy whom people talk to on consultancy assignments. But nobody ever listens to him inside the company.

Both collecting and using these anecdotes had communication impacts. First, Snowden points out, "the fact that those archetypes came out of that particular practice says an awful lot about that practice. But if you try to drive home that message directly, no one ever listens." By using the stories and presenting them in "soap opera" format, people were able to get the message because it was conveyed in the subtext.

Rather than having to confront their own character flaws head on, they learned from the mistakes of the characters. They also learned the material faster, and Snowden thinks that is because they wanted the reward of hearing what was going to happen to the characters at the beginning of the next module. Another unforeseen benefit, says Snowden, is that it created a *symbolic language* for the community of people being trained: "Anybody who'd been through that course is now using phrases like, 'You're doing a Jason,' and that single phrase references a very large body of learning and causes people to modify their behavior."

Telling Stories Yourself

All of us can benefit from improving our storytelling skills. Here are three aspects of storytelling that interactive managers should attend to: structure, making your point, and practice.

Structure. Structure makes your story understandable and more persuasive. While there are many approaches to structuring a story, Bill Jensen, author of *Simplicity,* has developed a useful model for business stories called a Message Map™. (See Figure 8-2.) By focusing on the four elements in the Message Map as a means of structuring, your business story will come across as focused, clear, and actionable. Of course, this Message Map is not the only means of structuring a story. The structuring tool you use is less important than the fact that you attend to structure.

Making Your Point. Sometimes even if you believe a story is well-structured and clear, people will miss your point. Make sure there is a central purpose to your story, and then drive that purpose home, advises Peg Neuhauser, consultant and author of *Corporate Legends and Lore:*

> One of my clients who is Native American told me that her grandfather was a tribal elder who told lots of stories. And he always ended his stories with the sum-up phrase, "And the reason we still tell that story is. . . ." He made sure they got the point. I think there's a lot of value in doing that. One of the most important ways you can structure a story is to tell people the point of it and not just leave it for them to conclude anything they want from the story. Now leaders may not need to end every story with, "Here's

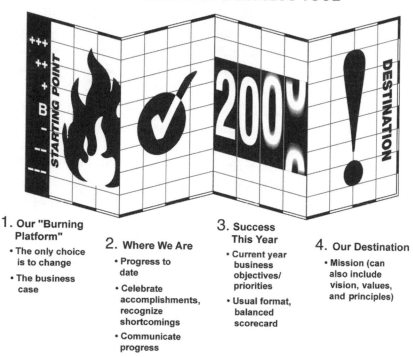

MESSAGE MAP
STORYTELLING AS BUSINESS TOOL

1. Our "Burning Platform"
   - The only choice is to change
   - The business case

2. Where We Are
   - Progress to date
   - Celebrate accomplishments, recognize shortcomings
   - Communicate progress

3. Success This Year
   - Current year business objectives/ priorities
   - Usual format, balanced scorecard

4. Our Destination
   - Mission (can also include vision, values, and principles)

Figure 8-2   The Message Map Tool for Structured Business Storytelling

Source: The Message Map™ tool and Message Mapping™ change management process are trademarks of the Jensen Group, © 2000.

the reason I told you that story." But do whatever it takes to make sure people got the message you meant them to get. And the more metaphorical you are, the more important it is to clarify the point, unless you are being purposefully vague. If you don't want people drawing four or five different meanings from your story, make sure they don't. Tell them what the point is.

Practice.   Neuhauser also notes the importance of practicing a story once you've put it all together. She says that, as a professional speaker and storyteller, she has to tell a story 10 times before she starts to deliver it well. "Good storytelling is a matter of timing, exact word choice and rhythm," says Neuhauser. "You can tell a story and, especially when you get to the punch line or the key point, if you slightly change the wording, or blow the timing on the delivery, it loses its punch, whether it's humor or drama or whatever you're going for. So sometimes it takes a few tellings before you even get the wording and timing right. This is tough even for professional speakers, and so people who are in organizations have an even more difficult situation. You can practice it a lot by yourself, but part of what you're practicing against is the reaction of the audience."

If you're planning to tell a story verbally: practice, practice, practice. And don't use the mirror. Use friends or associates. Also use video and audiotape so you can see and hear yourself. While this may seem like a time-devouring nuisance, it can mean the difference between success and failure. And this is where the difference between an anecdote and a story is once again important. It's much easier to tell anecdotes without a lot of practice because they are conversational in nature. You've probably told them many times in conversation. But a story is different. A story has a structure, certain elements have to be included, and good stories also contain detail. Stories require more practice than anecdotes. And if you think that practicing a story seems forced or staged, forget it. Ironically, a story that isn't practiced will sound less authentic than a story that has been told numerous times.

Enacting Stories

Great leaders know they can tell stories and communicate volumes without ever opening their mouths, and that these stories will be retold countless times by others in their organizations. There's a difference between *telling* a story and *enacting* a story. When leaders enact stories, they carefully orchestrate their behavior to have maximum impact. By doing things in certain ways, they guarantee that others will tell the story throughout an organization and that it will have the intended cultural effects. Johnny Harben, of Smythe Dorward Lambert Ltd., relates how Jack Keenan enacted a story when he moved into a new leadership position at International Distillers and Vintners, a company whose brands include Smirnoff and J&B Whiskey, as well as many others:

> **It's 1996, and Jack Keenan has just been appointed chief execu-
> tive of IDV. There is a lot of excitement at IDV about the new
> chief executive. He's due to join on April 1, and all the way**

through March the big boys are getting together their presentations, to be able to brief him when he arrives. The printers are working overtime producing color overhead transparencies. And among ordinary staff, too, there's quite a lot of excitement, because nobody knows much about him. But rumors begin to get around that he's tough, he's called Jack the Knife, he can be quite ruthless. So there's lots of speculation.

The big day finally arrives and his car pulls up in front of Regent's Park, a very pretty building in London. Word gets around the headquarters, "He's arriving! He's arriving!" Everybody knows his first appointment is with his new P.A. [personal assistant]. All the other P.A.'s are waiting for a debrief; as soon as she's finished with him they're going to be diary planning, of course, all that stuff. And he has his session with his P.A., puts his coat on, and disappears.

And his P.A. reports to her friends, "It's quite extraordinary, he's cancelled all the internal meetings and asked me to arrange for him to meet the head of sales for the West End of London." This is the guy who heads up the sales force whose customers are the style bars, the leading edge places. These are the storm troopers of the drinks business. And Keenan doesn't reappear back in the head office building *for two weeks.* In the meantime, the big boys are gnashing their teeth and looking at their foils and wondering what the hell's going on, you know, what sort of leader is it that spends no time in [the] headquarters of his new business?

Stories begin to filter back of late night carousing sessions in West End bars, not that he's gotten drunk or anything, but he's met a load of salespeople, he's been in a load of clubs, he's said some great things about the brands. And, incidentally, some of the brand managers have been on these drinking expeditions and he's met all these guys and still hasn't met the HR guy or the finance chief. And after two weeks he comes back into the building and resumes a more normal life in terms of people coming and making presentations to him. But this story, which I call "The Absent King," has gotten around the world within those two

weeks, actually probably within the first two days. The story has gotten around to the sales force that this guy is on our side. He doesn't want to spend time with those nerds in Regent's Park. And that sent a message to the organization that was—I think you can only describe it as shattering. It totally changed the way the organization thought about itself.

Harben says this story enactment was a powerful prelude to Keenan's verbal message, which came later, about how important the brands were and how they all had to be closer to the consumer. Keenan had enacted the story by intentionally making himself scarce at headquarters, turning up in clubs with salespeople, and creating a mystery about where he was spending his time. Now some people might say Keenan was simply modeling the behavior he wanted to see from others, but I think *enacting* a story takes modeling a step further in that there is a deliberate introduction of drama and narrative. Keenan set up the story by creating dramatic tension, resolving the conflict, and providing a moral for the story. Having a good sense of theater, knowing how to create dramatic tension, is an invaluable skill for an interactive manager to acquire. Enacting stories is a powerful way to inform people.

Technology and Stories

In addition to knowing how to construct, tell, and enact stories, interactive managers need to incorporate technology into their storytelling repertoire. We've already referred to technologies for collecting anecdotes. There are also other ways in which technology can be used in association with storytelling.

Dana Atchley, an acknowledged expert in the area of digital storytelling, says that technologies such as digital cameras, video streaming, and other visually rich storytelling media are becoming much more accessible and affordable. He notes the development of desktop editing and compositing tools that make it much easier for people to put together more interesting digital stories. Atchley says that while the tools need to be simpler to use, they have certainly improved dramatically over the cost and complexity of high-end, postproduction machines. He's looking forward to the day when brief movies produced by employees themselves on desktop machines will be as prevalent as PowerPoint presentations are today.

Johnny Harben's story of the use of audiotapes during the Diageo merger shows that technology doesn't need to be expensive or complex: "The leaders were quite happy to be taped," says Harben. "It was much easier than writing something themselves or waiting for you to write it and then sending it up for their approval. It had an immediacy to it that they appreciated."

In fact, Harben claims that corporations have missed the boat on what he calls "seizing the radio station":

We used audio during the merger to tell the story of the merger. And the segments we sent out were never very long, no more than 10 or 15 minutes tops. And you hear your boss, you hear a customer, you hear a factory worker telling an extraordinary story, and it's been edited by somebody who's got good interpretive summarizing skills. You might be driving, you might just be at home on a Sunday afternoon, visualizing as you listen. Audio is waiting to be rediscovered as a medium.

Harben's group built an impressive subscription list of well over 1000 people in the organization for these audiotaped sessions.

"We're building a full storytelling technology suite, right down to small devices that people can take into the field to capture stories," says Dave Snowden of IBM. "As consultants in the Knowledge Management group, we use video a lot in meetings with people when we're capturing stories because we found that scribes did too much editing while they were collecting anecdotes. We also use tape recorders and video booths. The video booths are put into stores on a random basis so that people can come off the floor and tell a story in them. There's also a company we're working with in California on a product that will allow us to search digital video for key words without needing to transcribe it first. That's a huge leap forward. We've also done a prototype for something we call the 'Value Miner,' which will allow us to search huge volumes of text to identify words or phrases associated with underlying values of an organization...And we've developed tools to index anecdotes using mind-mapping techniques...And we're also using technology that allows people to change the protagonist in a story so that it can be told from a number of different points of view."

Snowden says they have also adapted an existing technology called "Babble," developed in the IBM labs, that helps people visually understand how others are making contributions in a conversation:

Babble works as a synchronous chat line where people can tell stories. As people bounce anecdotes around, in the corner of the chat room is a circle, and in the circle are colored dots, and if you click on a colored dot, it gives you the name of the person that dot represents. (See Figure 8-3.) If that person stops contributing, [his or her] dot gradually drifts to the outside of the circle. If you want to have a private conversation, then the circle forms around the two of you to say you're having a private conversation, rather like going to an office and closing the door. And that's acceptable, but that smaller circle gradually just drifts outside the larger circle. Now that in its very simplicity is its genius. Because now I have a background visual clue of your participation or non-participation in the group, so it helps induce storytelling. Because you see, there are people who sit on the edge of a chat line and never contribute, but suck benefit out, and that inhibits people's performance. You don't get the social clues you get if you're in an open storytelling environment.

Technology can be employed in an endless variety of ways to help you with storytelling. And it doesn't have to be a complicated proposition. As Dana Atchley points out: "I've seen PowerPoint presentations that just consist of a bunch of bullets. But each bullet was a great story." So don't be fooled into thinking technology will either sink or save you. Despite the promise and allure of technology, in the end it's the *story* that matters.

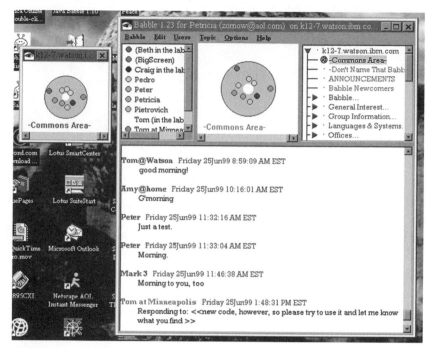

Figure 8-3   Babble Screen Capture: An Example of Software for Storytelling
Source: © Dave Snowden

Key Ideas from Chapter 8

- A range of technologies from audio tapes to proxy software can be used for storytelling.
- Storytelling can play a significant role in knowledge management efforts.
- You can tap into the intellectual capital of your organization through the use of stories.
- Anti-stories arise when stories aren't believable.
- Stories about failure can be as valuable as success stories.

While stories are unquestionably a powerful way of informing people in organizations, they are primarily focused on the *verbal* aspects of communication. Stories are one way to say things in organizations, but as the cliché goes, actions speak louder than words. Chapter 9 explains how to inform people by aligning what you say with what you do.

9

Resolve Hidden Conflicts Between Your Actions and Words

BUILDING TRUST REQUIRES consistency in words and actions. Whether it involves you and your management team, a spouse, or a friend, when actions don't match words, trust is eroded.

Little gets accomplished in organizations without trust. And while almost all the competencies we've talked about in this book will help improve trust, most of them won't make a difference if there's a significant disconnect between what managers say and what they do.

Alignment is a simple concept. But most organizations don't do a good job of it. All over the world, in every conceivable type of business, management communicates conflicting messages to the people who work there. And those conflicting messages come in a variety of forms. Perhaps there's a conflict between what we say inside the organization and what we say to investors. Or there may be a conflict between what a team leader says and what the CEO says. These inconsistencies in message delivery are important. Message misalignment causes confusion that leads to inaction or even contradictory actions.

But perhaps even more serious are the inconsistencies in the way an organization communicates through its actions. For example, we ask for one type of behavior and reward its opposite. Or we tell people that we want them to do something and then we don't give them the resources, such as training, to make that possible. Says John Caroselli, EVP of Corporate Development at the AXA Client Solutions unit of AXA Financial: "You can talk all day. People either believe you or they don't believe you. They get the message or they don't. But once you start aligning your *actions* with the talk, the message really starts to get through."

Interactive managers working in an e-business environment have a heightened sensitivity to the importance of consistent messages and actions. In strategic alliances, b-webs, and other new forms of organizations, there are new complexities and challenges. The fuzzier your boundaries are, the more you need to have consistent, clear communication. Achieving alignment in virtual organizations is perhaps even more difficult than achieving it in a traditional organization. Is what you're saying to one contractor consistent with what you're saying to another? Does your whole b-web share a sense of purpose and direction?

Whether you're in an alliance, a dotcom, or a traditional organization, your messages have to be consistent with your actions, such as reward structures, resources, or training programs.

Simply put, there are three steps to aligning what you say with what you do:

1. Develop a *unifying concept* that is clear and concise. This could be your brand message, your mission statement, your vision for the organization, or your stated purpose for a strategic alliance. The simpler this concept is, the better. People should be able to remember it without consulting any written document.

2. Make sure the things you say (written *and* spoken communication) are consistent with each other and with that unifying concept. Does the information on your website align with your mission? Does your CEO's letter to shareholders align with your brand message? Are the activities of your strategic alliance in accord with its statement of direction?

3. Ensure that what you do (rewards, recognition, training programs, budget, processes, measures) align with the things you say. For example, are your reward structures consistent with your objectives? Are there training programs designed to help people deliver on what you've asked them to do? If you have a project team that crosses organizational boundaries in a b-web, have you checked

whether the measures of success are consistent in the various organizations?

This probably seems mind-numbingly simple to most of you, but if your organization is anything like the diverse organizations I've consulted with in recent years, we'd be able to find dozens of inconsistencies in these three things.

The good news is that inconsistencies present opportunities. In this chapter we'll see how achieving consistency between what you say and do in organizations can have very, very substantial rewards. And we'll also discuss the role technology can play in helping your organization achieve alignment.

Step 1: Develop a Unifying Concept

Quick! Without thinking more than a couple of seconds and without consulting any written materials, tell me in one sentence what your company is primarily focused on this year. If it took you more than two or three seconds, then the communication in your organization is due for some improvement.

Articulating the purpose of a complex organization or alliance in a very concise way is not always an easy thing to do. Encapsulating a purpose or a set of beliefs is a lot like developing a tag line for an ad campaign. It requires talent and skill.

I'm always concerned when I see those little laminated cards that contain mission statements, major strategic objectives, or a list of values. While they may be useful in some instances, they shouldn't be a crutch. If you have to consult a written document (regardless of its size) to understand basic purpose and direction, then, quite frankly, it's too complex. "Until the leadership of an organization makes it clear where they're going and what they stand for, you can't align anyone around anything," says Anthony Goodman, CEO of the change management consulting firm, Smythe Dorward Lambert Inc.

For a number of years now in management theory, we've heard about mission statements, visions, and values. The people interviewed for this book talked about successfully aligning around a variety of different core concepts. They convinced me that it doesn't really matter whether you align around a corporate vision, a mission statement, or a brand strategy. What's important is to have a unifying concept that's easy to understand and easy to explain to others. Unifying concepts are used primarily to tell people two things: what we do and/or how we do it. As a rule of thumb, mission statements, strategic objectives, and strategic plans usually tell people what we do. Values and beliefs usually refer to how and why we do it. Brand and vision statements often refer to both. The point is that these things overlap; therefore, it's all the more important that they be clear and consistent with each other. In this section I provide examples of four different unifying concepts: Brand, Vision, Values, and Purpose.

Of course, an interactive manager recognizes that the *development* of this unifying concept should be an interactive process. All too often executives retreat to the mountaintop to come up with a statement of direction or a strategic plan and then hand the stone tablets to the people for implementation. People *remember* things when they're stated clearly and simply, but they *act* on things when they've participated in developing them. As David Sibbet of The Grove Consultants, an organization that helps with strategic planning and visioning, puts it: "If you don't let people get involved in shaping the vision, they experience it as a done deal and then it just becomes a school lesson.... If you have people who are responsible for implementing a vision integrally involved in helping create it, it's going to have a lot more impact." As you look at each example of a unifying concept, note how people have used interactive approaches to developing them.

Brand as a Unifying Concept

A brand statement can be a powerful unifying concept. Even if other concepts such as mission, vision, and goals are developed, it's critical that they be consistent with the brand message. Organizations are just beginning to focus on "internal branding" as a means of aligning what employees do with the messages that are presented to the marketplace. At AXA Client Solutions, where he is EVP of Corporate Development, John Caroselli says the management team has a process for communicating in which everything the company says and does is driven off the brand message:

> We first bring people together to figure out if we're all agreeing on what the brand positioning strategy is. The way we develop it is very important. It isn't a mandate. We do it with a joint team.

We work through a systematic process with the whole management team so that they own the strategy. Then we make sure that all of the messages are driven off of that strategy. We ask things like, "Well, you ran a major internal meeting, did you use the positioning strategy as a template up front—not after the fact?" or, "You developed this ad campaign, how did you get those brand messages across to people internally and to the customers?" That's been very powerful.

David Reyes-Guerra, Associate Director of Brand Management at Ernst & Young, says internal branding plays a vital role in powerfully and accurately conveying the Ernst & Young brand around the world. The focus on internal branding was spurred by dramatic changes in the business landscape for professional services over the past 12 years.

As the Big Eight has become the Big Five and things have gotten more competitive among them, and as other companies such as IBM and HP have moved into business advisory services, it's become more and more critical to create a strong global brand image. And this isn't easy to do in an entrepreneurial culture of extremely bright, creative thinkers who have independent, original approaches to business. Reyes-Guerra's goal is to create 75,000 "brand ambassadors" who present a consistent, clear, professional image of a global firm.

To that end, his department set up what he calls "The Branding Zone" on the corporate intranet: "We felt that the intranet would be our best tool for establishing a global focus on branding. And we see this as more than simply a distribution channel. We see it as an interactive means to develop a common culture around the brand, as well as a way to encourage dialogue and knowledge sharing of branding and marketing best practices globally."

Brands will become increasingly important in an e-business era, and they will become more interactive, says Don Tapscott, coauthor of *Digital Capital*. This increases the power of the brand as a unifying concept. "The brand is becoming a two-way relationship," says Tapscott. "It's interactive. It's a measure of the degree to which you have relationship capital with your customer as opposed to an image established through one-to-many communications. It's a very different way of looking at the concept of a brand." And this "relationship capital" that Tapscott refers to won't be restricted to customers. Companies will also need to build relationship capital with employees. The brand can define the organization for both customers and employees, and both groups play a role in defining what the brand actually is. Given the increased focus on brands, it will be critical to make sure other messages in the organization are consistent with the brand message.

Vision as a Unifying Concept

Gloria Feldt, President of Planned Parenthood Federation of America, emphasizes the importance of participation in developing a unifying concept:

> **There's enormous pressure for leaders to come up with a vision and then present it to people. I think that's a big mistake. Because then people don't own it and they can take potshots at it. I feel that my role [in developing a vision statement] will be to sit back and do an awful lot of listening, and then give very strong and direct input about what I think. I really believe the best visioning is always both top down and bottom up. I think it is naïve to think that you can just bubble up from the grassroots and come up with this wonderful coherent vision. My job will be to make sure that there's good solid information that goes to people, to give them a clear, unequivocal sense of what I think, to let them know that I'm going to really listen to what they think and that I'm open to changing what I think based on their input.**
>
> **This year's annual meeting was fabulous as a kickoff for the visioning process. Prior to the meeting we brought together 300 top affiliate and national leaders to think about the future by interacting with interesting speakers and each other. Their enthusiasm surprised even me, and my expectations were very high. We are taking this year to enable every affiliate and other groups to participate in their own local visioning process, and then we will adopt and celebrate a shared vision at the annual meeting next year. The latest tally is that 119 of the 129 affiliates are conducting local visioning activities as well as participating in the national visioning work. This is absolutely a first in terms of organizationwide collaboration. It's very exciting, and transformational.**

In an organization such as Feldt's, which is a very loose confederation of highly independent "affiliate" organizations, a unifying concept is crucially important. Feldt and her management team feel a strategic plan isn't really the right vehicle for galvanizing the entire federation. Because the "affiliates" operate so independently, a strategic plan would interject too much detail and come across as too controlling. A vision statement is broader, and yet it gives people a sense of direction for the organization as a whole.

Values as a Unifying Concept

Interactive managers can also align messages around a company's values.

"We spent about a year and a half developing our code of ethics," says Bob Buckman, Chairman of Buckman Industries, a worldwide specialty chemicals company. "We started an organizationwide dialogue to figure out what our values are. And we went back and forth several times, rank ordering them from most important to least important, and we just kept that process going until we came down to the precious few that most people agreed on. Our code of ethics sets the values for the organization, and the values of the organization have a lot to do with a culture of trust. Building trust is absolutely essential if you want a proactive, knowledge-sharing organization. You can't have it without trust. It just won't happen."

Perhaps one of the most famous unifying concepts based around values is the Johnson & Johnson credo. This one-page statement contains the essence of how they do business at J&J. It encapsulates the organization's responsibilities to its customers, employees, community, and shareholders. You'll find the credo on the website, in the annual report, and even etched in stone on a huge structure in the lobby of the Johnson & Johnson headquarters. While the credo was originally developed by a single person in 1943, Chairman Robert Wood Johnson, the implementation of what it stands for has a highly interactive component. Every two years the entire organization is surveyed to evaluate how well managers, executives, and the organization as a whole have lived up to the credo. While this may seem an enormous investment of time and money, J&J has found that it is essential in providing a framework for decision-making. It is well worth the effort in terms of keeping people focused and working in the same direction in a highly decentralized environment.

Purpose as a Unifying Concept

Sandra Gregg, Director of Communications for The Enterprise Foundation, says that when she came to the organization five years ago she asked people to describe how the mission statement of the organization translated into programs and services. "The people who worked here struggled with the question," says Gregg. "They would say, 'Well, we do housing, we provide loans to organizations, we provide technical assistance, we provide consulting services, we provide training'.... They gave me a laundry list of twenty things that Enterprise Foundation does.... Of course when they talked this way to people like reporters or funders, their eyes would just glaze over.... This drove me crazy as the communications person."

In response, Gregg, with the approval of senior management, pulled together a group of smart people from across the entire organization. For about two months they met every other week for about two hours, wordsmithing a core message that would pass what Gregg calls the "Aunt Mary test." "You should be able to describe to your Aunt Mary over Thanksgiving dinner what your organization does," quips Gregg. They finally got their message down to two sentences: "The Enterprise Foundation helps rebuild communities. We work with partners to provide low-income people with affordable housing, safer streets, and access to jobs and child care." Says Gregg, "Employees and others have been thanking us for clarifying things. I guess the best evidence that it's taken hold is that in a senior management retreat a couple of weeks ago, when the strategic goals of the organization were discussed, the discussion immediately centered on those four concepts. Now everyone instinctively knows that our four key program areas are housing, safety, jobs, and child care."

By creating a clear, concise core message about the organization's purpose, Gregg was able to set the foundation for other communication in the organization to be consistent with that message.

Gregg points out the importance of making this an interactive process and including a good cross-section of stakeholders: "I intentionally brought people from different parts of the organization to create this. And we also tested it out on our board members and our partners. We have two primary sets of customers: the people from whom we raise funds, and then the people in the nonprofit organizations and the residents they serve. So we had to come up with something that worked for all those groups."

Articulating a unifying concept is the first step in aligning words with actions in your organization. Next we'll look at some successful examples of how people gain consistency in what they say in organizations.

Step 2: Make Sure the Things You Say Are Consistent with Each Other and with Your Unifying Concept

Speeches, memos, e-mails, brochures, meeting themes, plans, reports, letters, website information, and all other written and verbal communications need to send a consistent message. As an interactive manager, you'll need to carefully attend both to the information you send out yourself as well as how it aligns with other messages sent out in the organization and across your business ecosystem. Sarah Fasey, Internal Communications Manager at Microsoft Ltd., United Kingdom and Ireland, points out how challenging this can be when you're in a worldwide organization:

> There's a general principle that corporate headquarters outlines the message, and the subsidiaries execute on this as they think appropriate for their market. However, when it comes to global projects or announcements, there can be a real challenge in ensuring that, first, the right message gets through, and second, people aren't being overwhelmed by information from various sources—this is particularly a problem with e-mail, where it's so easy for people to add to the information flow.
>
> When it comes to important business news that affects the whole company, the messaging for this clearly has to come from the top of the organization. We can then choose to add to this at the local level. . . . When it comes to campaign, product, and general business news, this approach can sometimes break down. Corporate has to create messaging that works for all—which can mean that it doesn't specifically work in our subsidiary. Sometimes there's a mismatch between what comes out of corporate and what we communicate here at the subsidiary. So we may have to retrofit what we have already communicated. So you find that two things can happen: one is that you overcommunicate, and the other is that the messages are diluted by a bunch of stuff that comes from outside your domain. So you're kind of caught between a rock and

a hard place. Do you create a plan appropriate for your market-place and steam ahead, or do you wait and find out what's coming from headquarters? How much chance do you get to influence corporate in terms of communication? Realistically, not that much, as their priorities are far wider than ours, which I suspect is true of many global players.

There's no easy answer to this dilemma, and interactive managers are often caught in the same spot Fasey describes. However, the simpler and clearer your unifying concept is, the easier this process will be.

In addition to the corporate versus local dilemma, another issue is the development of messages for internal and external audiences. The big challenge here is being able to tailor messages without having them appear to be inconsistent. We've talked about the importance of understanding your different stakeholder groups (Chapter 2), and the need to customize your messages for those groups (Chapter 7). This need for both consistency and tailoring creates something of a paradox. Jon Iwata, Vice President of Corporate Communications at IBM, explains how easy it is to make a mistake in this arena:

The membrane between external and internal communications is now so thin as to be almost irrelevant. From the same screen, employees can move from internal websites to external websites with a single click. You can't have the media relations people trying to shape news stories and coverage of IBM in one way and then have internal communications tell employees something different. For example, let's take some news, like a company announcement to sell off part of its business. Now Wall Street may think this is great. It may be an indication that the company is becoming more focused, spinning off the ancillary parts. But that's not necessarily a great message internally, especially with employees worried about losing their jobs or being absorbed by a different company.

The same is true with customer messages. For example, if you have a product that's struggling in the marketplace and your customers are betting their businesses on this piece of software, you can't tell them that you're absolutely committed to the product and then tell your employees they need to start work on new

software to replace it. It gets out. And it gets out much faster today than it did in the past.

Technology has been a major contributor to creating the "thin membrane" between internal and external information, which in turn creates a stronger need for interactive managers to align their messages. Michael Rudnick, Senior VP of Xceed, Inc., a company specializing in communication and intranet development, agrees with Iwata:

People need to know the company vision and values, they need to know where the company's going. But they now can read that in a number of places. So if management isn't walking the talk, they get caught. There are a bunch of websites like "Company Sleuth," and discussion rooms and other places on the Internet where people can find out what's really going on in a company, where they can find information that doesn't always align with what management's "official" voice is saying.

To deal with the paradox of consistency and tailoring, it's important to coordinate and plan with people across the organization. "You have to design an overall plan and strategy and build a communications program from that, and it needs to be consistent across the board," says Larry Walsh, a principal with communications consultancy Osgood, O'Donnell and Walsh. By pulling together people from a number of areas of an organization, alignment and consistency in messages can be more carefully managed.

Building this type of team requires a cross-disciplinary effort, according to John Caroselli. Before he became EVP of Corporate Development at AXA Client Solutions, Caroselli was head of communications for the retail business at Chemical Bank and then Chase (after the merger). They pulled together a cross-disciplinary team to deal with the communication issues before, during, and after this massive merger:

The communication team was composed of brand management, corporate communications, marketing communications, internal communications, PR, and the human resources function. The group met every three months to do an audit of all our communications. We called it the three-month "oil change." We looked at

our internal and external communication both in terms of message content and also how we delivered messages to each audience. At the beginning it was the usual wall of horrors. When you had it there in front of you, you'd say, "Oh my God, did we do all this stuff?" We could see it wasn't as effective as it could be. There were a lot of inconsistencies, no reinforcement of a common message. So we laid out an integrated communications approach, and engaged all of the various communications professionals in an effort to really look at how to roll out our communications in a more integrated way. So the advertising people, the PR people, the market researchers, the internal communicators, all shared our individual plans. Then we tried to do two things: (1) align all of the messages with the brand positioning strategy, and (2) integrate and coordinate across all of the messages. We looked at all the major initiatives, messages, events, and asked, "How did it work? What did we learn?" And then we'd look at what was coming up in the next three to six months, and figure out what we needed to do to collaborate to more effectively address whatever was happening.

Some people think that you can only get this kind of cooperation and alignment in a crisis situation like a merger. But Caroselli points out that they used what they learned from the merger environment to continue the alignment process:

With a merger you have very definite deadlines to meet, and milestones. You've got Day One, Day Two, Day Three . . . we had to change the signage on the branches, change the names on the products, all those kinds of things. And everybody knew exactly what those dates were, and everybody rallied around that. But when the merger ends, you don't have any dates; there's nothing to rally around. So we created a calendar, a three-year calendar, with major themes each year, and deliverables at the end of the year, and tried to simulate the merger environment in a non-merger environment. We created milestones for people to rally around one component of the positioning strategy, and then we had a set of actions for each area to engage them in working toward that.

It's one thing to get messages aligned with a unifying concept and consistent with each other, but then you have to make sure that those messages match up to what is actually *happening* in the organization. Reward and recognition structures, training programs, resource allocation, processes, and measures all are powerful ways of communicating in an organization. In fact they probably communicate more powerfully than words. Step 3 shows us how to do this.

Step 3: Ensure Actions Align with Words

When Chairman and CEO Lou Gerstner first came to IBM, Jon Iwata, VP of Corporate Communications, was asked to brief him about IBM's internal communications plans. He presented a comprehensive but traditional plan that included the use of internal publications, e-mail, internal television, etc. "Afterward, Lou said it was fine—as far as it went. He wasn't convinced that the workforce could be changed simply by telling them about it in an employee magazine or on TV. These things can help, but they don't do enough. He wanted us to not just communicate that the IBM culture needs to change, but to actually help change the culture. Change the way people think, the speed at which they work. Change their attitudes, change their behaviors," says Iwata. "Of course, Lou was absolutely right. Talking isn't enough, even with a host of different media and very carefully targeted messages."

Let's take a look at how "informal" communication—the things we do—can have an impact on organizations. This section will look at reward structures and training programs, business processes, resource allocation, and finally, leader behavior.

Communicate Through Training and Reward Structures: How to Make $800 Million

Fabulous printed materials and rousing speeches weren't doing a thing for Royal Bank of Canada when it began a program to encourage referrals in its financial services business, says David Moorcroft, Senior VP of Corporate Communications. The bank had bought several other financial companies and was aggressively expanding its product line. It knew that its nine million commercial banking customers were a valuable target market for all of the other services the bank offered. Moorcroft explains:

We talked about this new strategy of referrals, we gave speeches, we wrote it up in employee magazines, we wrote it up in the sales bulletins, we wrote it up in one-off publications, but very little happened for several years. And we said, "Gee whiz, we're producing tons of material talking about business referrals, so it's not our fault in communications. It must be a problem with the business strategy." And the business people would say, "It's a slam dunk strategy. It must be the lousy communications because people aren't doing referrals." And we were both right. The problem was that we were doing the *formal* side of the communication superbly. People were hearing the message. Everyone knew we wanted business referrals; that's what we were saying. But the informal communication, such as training programs, compensation, recognition systems, operational platforms, computer systems, sales programs, advertising, and marketing, did not support what we were saying.

So if you were a branch manager, I was asking you to refer clients to other people, but I gave you no training about the other products and how they would help your client. You have a trusting relationship with your client, and you're being asked to hand that person blindly over to someone else. And as for compensation, you were rewarded on the basis of certain revenue charges for products you had in your branch, so if you were giving these clients away to other members of the financial group, you were likely going to lose some of the deposits they had with you. For example, if your client had $20,000 in a savings account with you and the financial planner you referred him to said, "Look, why don't you diversify your savings? We'll put some into mutual funds, leave some in your savings account, and we'll buy some equities." As a branch manager you would lose a good portion of those deposits. Then you wouldn't make your branch business plan numbers. And of course at the end of the year you would be punished. You would get a bad rating and you wouldn't get much of a bonus. And in terms of measures, we didn't have a way of tracking referrals, so if you did 15 referrals a week and I did none, at the end of the year no one knew the difference. Except that you were probably punished and I wasn't.

Moorcroft's group unearthed these inconsistencies in words and actions by conducting a "say-do" analysis, a survey technique first developed at Towers Perrin, a human resources consulting firm. This survey went out to 1600 employees and it contained two sets of questions, one designed to elicit what the organization was "saying" to employees and the other designed to reveal what the organization was "doing." Moorcroft said the results of the survey revealed "say-do" gaps in each of their four key stakeholder groups. As a result of the survey, personnel from various disciplines all over the company were brought together to exchange ideas and information about closing the gaps. Management instituted training programs and other educational tools to help employees better understand a broad range of products and services offered in other parts of the bank. Compensation systems were revamped to encourage teamwork.

The results of all of these changes to improve message alignment were extremely impressive. In the space of one year, retail referrals quadrupled, resulting in an *$800 million increase in new business.*

Communicating Through Business Processes

Training and reward structures are not the only things that need attending to when you're taking a look at your "informal" communication.[1] The way business processes are structured also communicates messages. When a large software company was working on modifying its value system, one of the key values had to do with a spirit of teamwork. An inconsistency arose when budget time rolled around. The business planning process was all based upon win/lose negotiations for resources. People from different departments were competing for their share of limited resources. The budget process was bloody and antagonistic, and as a result it was hard for people to leave that process and then work together in a spirit of cooperation. Anthony Goodman, CEO of Smythe Dorward Lambert Inc., worked with this company to help remedy the situation: "We had to go in and change that whole business planning and budgeting process because you can't get people to rally around a particular set of beliefs when one of the main processes in the business is completely antithetical to what you're trying to achieve."

Goodman points out that change management processes can also create message inconsistencies. Most change management processes are focused on improving customer service and creating more open, honest, corporate cultures, but then the implementation of the process is counter to the values espoused in the new program. Explains Goodman:

> These companies say, "We want you to be more open and honest and we want you to be better listeners to customers." Then they hire a bunch of consultants who sit in a secret locked room on the 27th floor with darkened windows to plan the "change management program." At the same time that they're asking for more openness from employees, they're also saying, "These consultants aren't going to talk to any of you, and they will send you e-mails telling you what it is you need to do, and we aren't going to get employee opinion, because it's not important right now. We can have employee opinion when we've become the new company that believes in employee opinion. And we're not going to talk to customers because that can wait until we've become the new company that listens to its customers." The whole process by which change is introduced, again, is antithetical to what you say you stand for.

Goodman says change management processes need to reflect the new culture they're trying to bring about. Otherwise employees will become cynical and the desired change will not come about in any kind of timely fashion.

Communicate Through Resource Allocation: Flexibility in Budgets at GE

The ways companies allocate resources is a powerful message that can either reinforce or completely contradict corporate messages. Resource allocation processes are usually about who screams the loudest or who has the most creative accounting system rather than who deserves to receive resources based on the merits of a business idea. As we saw in the previous section, budgets are not always allocated in logical ways.

At GE, one of the primary goals is to create what Jack Welch calls a boundaryless organization. Welch describes this as an organization in which there are no barriers between functions, levels of management, locations, or suppliers. Steve Kerr, Chief Learning Officer at General Electric, says that the verbal messages they send about a boundaryless organization are reinforced by the surprising way they handle resource allocation. Kerr explains with a story. A CEO from a very large consumer products company was on a tour of GE. He was interested in how Welch handled budgets within the context of a boundaryless organization. This CEO felt people at his company were selfishlessly gaming the numbers in order to grab a bigger piece of the pie for themselves, rather than seeing the organization as a whole, boundaryless system. He asked Jack Welch, "How do you handle this problem?" Kerr recalls Welch's response: "Jack said, 'Boy, if we used budgets, we'd be in even more trouble than you have.' This CEO almost almost fell over. He said, 'What do you mean you don't use budgets? It's sacrilegious! Operating without budgets!' "

Kerr says budgets can be an impediment to doing what needs to happen in a "boundaryless" organization:

> **Budgets are just substitutes for good processes. I just hired some people in Japan, it wasn't in my budget. I set my budget in December, it's now May. In December, I didn't know I needed two people in Japan. We didn't have a lot of employees in Japan in December, now we do. So, it's not a prank; if I'd known it in December, I would have put it in the budget. What's the relevance of a budget in that situation? Should companies say, "It's a good idea, but we're not going to let you do it because it wasn't in your budget in December?"**

> **I couldn't tell you within $5 million what my budget is. I've no idea what it is exactly. I've never been asked. When I was a dean at USC [Business School], I knew to the penny what my budget was. If you trust your processes, you don't need budgets. Now it's not easy here [at GE], I'm going to be peppered with good questions. What will it cost? Are there substitutes? Are other companies doing it better? How will you use it? They're great questions. But among the questions will not be, "Is it in your budget?" If you have rigorous processes, you're going to run out of good ideas before you run out of money.**

The point here is not to encourage you to revamp your budgeting process (although Kerr does present a pretty compelling case), but rather to make you aware of whether or not your *budget process reflects the messages being sent about your company's culture.* If they had a very strict budgeting process at GE, it would reinforce the sense of walls and boundaries between departments because they would be competing against each other for resources allocated on a departmental basis rather than resources allocated based on the quality of ideas. Instead, GE has developed processes to provide checks and balances on decision-making that are consistent with the things they are saying to the organization in their communication.

Communicate Through Leader Behavior

"The most powerful communication in any organization consists of the decisions and behaviors of the leaders of the business. Everything else is noise," says Anthony Goodman, CEO of the consulting firm Smythe Dorward Lambert Inc.

We saw in Chapter 8 how Jack Keenan sent a shockwave in terms of a cultural message when he spent his first three weeks as the CEO of IDV with the sales force. The message was, "We need to get close to the customer," and it came across much more powerfully when he made the point with actions rather than words. We also saw examples of Jack Welch's symbolic communication when he preempted the golf game to bring the message of Six Sigma to the organization (Chapter 5), and when he set the tone for others by volunteering for training in presentation skills (Chapter 3). Interactive managers are sensitive to the fact that their behavior is a powerful form of communication.

At United Check Control, Inc., a check verification and collection company based in Houston, Texas, the president made the decision to have every employee spend time in the company's call center on a regular basis. She made this decision in order to communicate the importance of front-line contact with customers: The call center is the area where the most client and check writer contact takes place. And she made no exception for herself in terms of putting in call center time. "From the president on down to the newest employee, customer service—working in that call center is their number one job responsibility," says Scott Schultz, EVP and CFO. "Most people work there about two hours at a time, and so you'll find people from all different departments in there at any point in time. This gives people respect for that position and an understanding of our culture, especially if they're a new employee. Because the new employee will see that they're sitting there next to the president, dealing directly with the customer. She absolutely puts in her time as well."

Another way this president underscored the importance of a customer focus was by her decision about where to place the call center: "When we moved to the new offices two and a half years ago, the architect was walking around the building with the president and said, 'Here's a great view of downtown Houston, we'll make this your office.' And she said, 'No. That's where the call center is going to be because that's where a majority of the work is being done. And that's also where we bring our clients in to see the call center. We want our clients to be able to have that great view. We want the people handling the calls to have that great view.' And so that was her message: the employees and the customers come first," explains Schultz.

Leader behavior can send just as strong a negative, conflicting message as a positive, consistent one. Don Parker, an independent consultant specializing in executive coaching and organizational change, says he worked with an executive who sent an "informal" message that was greatly at odds with other messages being sent in the organization. This executive was head of an advertising agency which was facing significant pressures from the marketplace. It had just lost several key accounts, some top talent had recently departed, and there was significant pressure from the parent company to reduce expenses. A decision had been made in many of the offices to delay all planned salary increases. People were working nights and weekends to try and improve the business. In the midst of these problems, the CEO made the decision to hold a senior leadership meeting for 40 people at a luxurious resort to, as Parker puts it, "philosophize about the future." He says it really sent the wrong message:

New hires at very senior levels were wondering, "Why did I come to this company if this is the way the time's going to be spent during a crisis like this?" People came back from that meeting using words like "disastrous." With that move, this leader completely lost the confidence of his team. That kind of information was fed back to the head of the parent company, and I believe the decision to hold that meeting was a significant catalyst for the parent company to take steps to significantly reduce the level of that CEO's influence.

When leaders make choices about how to behave, even very subtle changes can have huge impacts. A simple decision not to decorate an office can send messages through an organization that a leader is temporary, even when verbal messages are being sent to the contrary. As an interactive manager, you'll need to carefully consider whether the messages you're sending with your behavior are consistent with the messages you're sending in e-mails, speeches, or whatever formal communication medium you choose.

Use Technology to Achieve Alignment

Technology can support both what you say and what you do in an organization. For example, you can use a wide range of technologies to send out formal communications: e-mail, teleconferencing, voice mail, on-line discussion groups, etc. But technology can do more than help you send formal communication, it can also help you *construct* it, and do so in a way that helps ensure message consistency. Let me share an example with you from my own consulting experience.

Once I was on an audioconference with some new clients, discussing a potential consulting engagement I was scheduled to begin with them. Frankly, I was flummoxed by the client's strategic plan, which I had read carefully in preparation for the meeting. There were whole sections of the plan that were incomprehensible to me, and this was not a particularly complex business. So instead of bluffing it, I went right to the heart of the matter and asked, "What does this mean?" Interestingly, I was met with silence on the other end. Finally, the people said, "We don't really know either." Hmmm. This was a problem.

I couldn't work with my clients until the goals and objectives of the overall company were clear. We approached the senior executives of the company with the idea of clarifying the strategic plan in a series of "augmented meetings." In augmented meetings, I use a specialized piece of software that is particularly good at capturing the ideas of a group quickly, structuring the information, and wordsmithing the results. The executives consented (after extended persuasive attempts) to a day-and-a-half augmented meeting.

In the meeting, the software helped me point out conflicting information in the wording of the plan. When these inconsistencies were pinpointed, it surfaced the fact that there were opposing points of view on the executive team, and we discussed those and came to consensus. Where there were hard-to-understand sections, it became clear in some cases that the executives themselves weren't sure what they were advocating, so I questioned them and pushed them until they could word things clearly. The software worked at an executive pace and allowed me to make changes on the fly.

The work was received very favorably by the executives, even though many of them had a reputation for defensiveness and recalcitrance. At the end of two days they asked me to stay for four more days until we finished what we were doing. They cancelled other meetings and we worked an average of 12 hours a day. The resulting strategic plan was much better received by the organization than the original plan. The messages in the plan itself became clearer and more consistent, and we were able to examine other messages in the organization, comparing and contrasting to ensure consistency across different platforms.

Chapter 7 shows how the IBM intranet is used to help employees understand their variable pay scheme. This is a good example of how technology can support alignment in an organization. All too often reward structures are changed and there is no alignment with results. By making specific financial information available to employees on its intranet, IBM uses technology to strongly support the message it sends through its variable pay scheme. Variable pay itself supports the message of accountability for market-driven results. The intranet supports the whole reward structure by giving people feedback on their performance. Both the reward system and the technology are well-aligned with the goal of market-driven results.

However, as always, technology isn't a panacea. In fact, poor alignment between what you say and do can ensure technology's failure. Michael Rudnick Senior VP of Xceed, Inc., and a recognized expert on intranets, gives an example:

For knowledge-sharing technologies to work, you first have to have a culture that's open and accepting of sharing. For example, I did some work for a consumer products company in its R&D facility. It wanted to encourage its scientists to share information by setting up a special website for them. And in particular, it wanted them to share information about their failures, because scientists learn probably as much if not more from their failures

as they do from successes. The problem was, this company had a success-oriented, "good news" culture. This was coupled with the fact that scientists are still rewarded, recognized, and compensated based on what they invent. So setting up a system for sharing failures and in-progress, imperfect work was completely in conflict with the culture and the compensation system. And so the most wonderful website with the most wonderful database behind it and the most wonderful personalization in the world wasn't going to get these scientists to share what they were working on. And sure enough, it failed. The scientists didn't use the system. It just wasn't going to happen.

Getting alignment in an organization isn't easy, but it's essential for good interactive management. Consistency between words and actions is crucial to gaining and sustaining people's engagement in the activities, processes, and purpose of the organization.

Key Ideas from Chapter 9

- Your unifying concept can center on brand, vision, mission, purpose, or values.
- Your actions—budgets, training programs, reward structures, leader behavior, and business processes—communicate louder than words.
- Periodic "oil changes" will strengthen your communication plan.
- Intranets, outline editors, and other technologies can enable alignment efforts in organizations.
- New forms of organization such as b-webs present significant alignment challenges.

This chapter focused on how to create a climate of trust in an organization by aligning actions with words. An environment of trust creates a perfect backdrop for engaging people to not only talk, but also act—the subject of Part III.

Engage

Inspire People to Create, Own, and Act on Ideas

ENGAGEMENT IS ABOUT ownership and action. In Part III you'll discover efficient and effective ways of involving people in developing and executing strategy, beginning with innovative ways of conversing with, and listening to, entire organizations.

It's one thing to have a good conversation with a handful of people, but Chapter 10 also shows you how to create effective dialogue among hundreds or even thousands of people. Part III addresses the issue of how to work effectively across organizational boundaries—an essential competency for interactive managers working in an era of e-business alliances. Special attention will be given to how technology can help you listen and converse in new ways.

10

Listen to Your Whole Organization

Interactive management is about asking more than telling. It's about dialogue instead of monologue. It's about engaging people rather than getting buy-in. In short, you can't be interactive if you're not listening.

In an interactive age, you have to listen to new people, in new places, and in new ways. You need to listen across departmental lines and across different levels in your organization; you need to listen to customers, alliance partners, and contractors; you need to listen to people who work thousands of miles away and who sit in the next cubicle; you need to listen to your leaders, and they need to listen to you. You also need to get people in your organization to listen to each other. The problem is, everyone is strapped for time and already hearing from lots of people.

Dealing with these demands requires listening more *efficiently*. And one of the most efficient and effective ways of listening in organizations is through conversation. Sound simplistic? Don't be deceived.

Good conversation in organizations, like storytelling, is a topic that's been heavily addressed in the popular management literature. However, a recent *Fast Company* magazine cover also proclaims: "Enough Talk! It's Time for Results—Are You Gettin' It Done?" A very reasonable question, because *idle* conversation won't get us anywhere.

In fact, what we'll see in this chapter is that well-conceived, thoughtful conversations are all about getting it done, getting it done at top speed, and getting it done with impressive results. You'll hear from people who've held conversations with thousands of people simultaneously, and you'll hear from people who have suggestions on how to hold better conversations one-on-one. We'll talk about radically new skills for facilitating conversations, and some new ground rules for conversations in the context of what the Organizational Development crowd calls "large scale interventions." We'll also talk about where conversations are being held. Some are held in 7000-square-foot rooms, others are held on-line.

This chapter is full of new ideas for how to listen and converse in new ways—ways that will engage your coworkers. It starts by looking at how to approach a conversation, spends a little extra time on what I call mega-conversations, and then discusses some practical aspects of making conversations go smoothly and productively.

Size Matters in Conversation

Most people think of conversations as being small and intimate. And in fact, size does impact the level of exchange and sharing that goes on between people. In this section we'll look at three different sizes of conversation: personal conversations, dinner-sized conversations, and mega-conversations.

Personal conversations are one-on-one exchanges. These are characterized by a very high level of intimacy between people that is difficult to achieve in a larger group. Phil Harkins, CEO of the human resources consulting firm Linkage Inc., has some very interesting ideas about how to conduct these intimate types of conversations, and you'll see more about them later in this chapter.

Dinner-sized conversations range in size from about three to eight people. I got the idea to term these *dinner* conversations from Jim Haudan, President of RootLearning®, a firm that specializes in creating organizational dialogue around issues of strategy. While Haudan's RootMap™ sessions can involve thousands of people, these large groups are always broken down into smaller "dinner-sized" conversations, as he explains:

> **In groups of six to eight, we find that two things happen—you can't hide and you can't avoid the excitement. In groups that are larger than that, it becomes less intimate . . . . Think of what it's**

like when you go out to dinner. If you go out with a group of about six or seven people, you're able to have one conversation, but once the group gets close to 10, first of all, tables don't support that, and secondly, you end up with more than one conversation going on. You'll either be part of the conversation at the right end of the table, or the left, or maybe in the middle. So when you're talking about bringing together people for a conversation, then the number really is optimally in the six-to-eight range.

If you're going to hold a conversation that involves more than eight to ten people, it's a good idea to think about breaking that group up into smaller conversations, even if it's just for part of the time they are together. In this way, you'll encourage more interaction. Many meetings end up being *broadcasts* rather than opportunities for *interaction*. In some cases this is appropriate, but there is room for a lot more interaction and input in business meetings, and a simple change such as this, even if you only schedule 15 minutes for it, could have a significant impact on the quality of your meetings.

The third size of conversation is what I term a *mega-conversation*, which is related to something very interesting that's been happening over the course of the last 15 to 20 years in the field of Organizational Development. A whole new approach to organizational change has appeared in the form of methods and approaches to involving large groups of people in dialogue. Two pioneers in this area, Barbara Bunker and Billie Alban, have written the definitive book on large group events. Their book, entitled *Large Group Interventions,* is a kind of encyclopedia for large group approaches. Why do we need methods for large-scale conversations? Bunker and Alban explain: "In contemporary organizations, it takes everyone's knowledge to solve complex problems and create the flow of information needed to come to good decisions. [With these methods], the whole system gathers to do this kind of inquiry."[1]

So how in the heck can you involve a whole organization in a conversation? We've already said that you lose a certain level of effectiveness in a conversation once you get over eight people. In the next section we'll explore these "mega-conversations" in more depth and look at some examples of how they've been used successfully to get work accomplished in organizations.

Mega-conversations (aka Large Group Events)

Mega-conversations bring an entire organization (or an extremely good representative sample) into a shared space for the purpose of working together as a group to create opportunities and/or solve problems related to specific topics. Note that I use the word *shared space* instead of *room*. Some large group events are held in physical rooms (See Figure 10-1) and others are connected by teleconferencing or other technologies. But the most important concept to grasp here is the idea of, as Billie Alban puts it, "getting the whole system together."

Bunker and Alban describe 12 methods for "Getting the Whole System in the Room." I highly recommend getting a copy of their book for a detailed description of 12 methods, including examples of their application. Large group methods, or mega-conversations, have an extensive history, and each method takes a different and sometimes very detailed approach. I'm not going to go into this topic in exhaustive detail here, but I will cover one of the methods explored by Bunker and Alban: GE's Workout, which we've already made reference to several times. I'll also give some detail on a method not covered by Bunker and

Figure 10-1   An Example of a Large Group Event
Source: Athenaeum International © 2000

Alban: Jam sessions at IBM. In Appendix 1, I briefly describe additional methods that I discovered in my interviews: Strategic Visioning™, DesignShop events, RootLearning™ sessions, the Circle Process, and Appreciative Inquiry.

GE's Workout Approach to Large Group Conversations

Steve Kerr, Chief Learning Officer at GE, was one of the original collaborators on the design of Workout, but the idea itself came from Jack Welch. Kerr explains that in the early 1980s when Welch first came to GE, he focused on what he called the hardware: buying and selling businesses, reorganizing, restructuring, and downsizing GE. In 1989, Welch turned his attention to the "software": organizational processes. Welch wanted to attack bureaucracy, give employees voice, and take out unnecessary work in the organization. Even though he had earned the name "Neutron Jack," Welch had deep respect for and trust in the people who remained in the organization. He knew that they were smart enough to make decisions without a lot of top-down direction, and he said that what got in the way of that was time and safety. He knew people were capable and desirous of doing a good job, but are usually so busy working that they don't have time to reflect on how to do it better. And Welch also knew that they needed a safe environment where their suggestions and observations would be welcomed rather than rejected.

Out of these convictions, Workout was born. Welch mandated that the sessions last three days and be held off-site, and Kerr says that the structure of the sessions was based around the concept of a New England town meeting: "Welch grew up in New England, and he's got this romantic notion of the elders gathering and the people from the town challenging them and the elders having to respond," says Kerr. "So Workout is based around the town meeting concept. You have people from all levels, mostly lower levels, attending, working on ideas, and then the last part of the session the senior staff come in and receive the ideas."

Workouts have become a popular method for large-scale change efforts not only at GE but in other organizations. Don Parker, an independent consultant specializing in long-term organizational change, tells the story of a Workout session held for ETS (the Educational Testing Service) and the College Board. These two organizations were originally part of the same organization, and together they are responsible for marketing and administering educational exams such as the SAT. Now they have separate presidents, separate staffs, and separate locations, and they function more as a partnership than a single entity. The president of the College Board is Gaston Caperton, the former governor of West Virginia. It was his idea to run a joint session Workout for the two organizations. He felt significant change was necessary in order to help the organizations work more efficiently and effectively together. He also wanted them to build relationships that would carry over after the Workout session ended.

A cross-section of 55 people drawn from both organizations were brought together for a two-and-a-half-day session to work on what they identified as the most important issues facing the two organizations as they tried to work together. The 55 participants were divided into small teams of approximately 10 people each. Related issues were clustered in groups, and the groups defined the issues, set related objectives, explained how they would meet the objectives, spelled out the benefits of taking those steps, and developed detailed action plans.

The small groups worked on these plans for two days, and on the final day they presented their suggestions to a decision-making panel made up of the top leadership from both organizations. Two of the issues they identified were the need for a strategic plan and the need to get rid of legacy computer systems that prevented the kind of responsiveness management was seeking. The change to the computer systems had major implications, not the least of which was cost: "The systems suggestion had a price tag of over $900,000," says Parker. "And it was approved right there on the spot." Seeing that management really was going to listen and take action had a profound impact, he says. "When that was approved, all 55 people sat there for a moment in a sort of state of shock. Then they ended the session by bursting into loud applause."

Parker says mega-conversations have great applicability and impact in an interactive, e-business environment: "Everyone's so busy now, with lean staffs and lots of work. Two and a half days may seem like a lot of time, but it's really not when you compare it with how things normally get done in organizations. If one person had had that idea in a department, it would have had to go through the hierarchy of that organization and then on to the other organization, and we all know what happens then. You'll lose two months just sending papers back and forth."

And not only is time saved in doing large group work, but these conversations ensure that people are really being heard. Parker points out that ideas are usually killed by the hierarchy. "We put people in situations over and over again where we appoint task forces, they bust their tails doing their homework, and they come back with great ideas, only to be thwarted. Whether it's hidden agendas or problems with leadership, nine times out of ten we say to them, 'Thanks very much for your work, we'll take your recommendations and get back to you.' Then one of two things happens: the leadership never says another word, or they say, 'Well, we thought it was a good idea, but here's why we can't do it.' " Good ideas have a much better chance of seeing the light of day when mega-conversations are part of a company's culture.

Jam Sessions

The competition for talent these days is fierce. Jon Iwata, VP of Corporate Communications at IBM, says that its use of a large group method arose out of a desire to improve its college recruiting efforts. "Human Resources did thorough research and analysis to do a better job of recruiting talent from college campuses," he says. "Most people assumed that candidates turned us down in favor of start-ups because they wanted to become bazillionaires. But the research showed that a big impediment wasn't money or stock options. It was our own image. They told us that although they believed we're a fantastic company with great benefits, ultimately they thought they would suffocate in IBM's bureaucracy. They saw us as slow and stodgy. No matter how much we chanted, 'We're not like that! We're not like that!' it didn't change their perceptions of the company. So we asked ourselves, 'How do we change this?' " Iwata says that the initial approaches were the tried and true— brochures and videotapes that portrayed IBM as a cool company—but they quickly realized those tactics weren't enough.

Then the team composed of both Communications and HR people had a terrific idea. "It occurred to us that we had a great opportunity staring us in the face. We had more than 12,000 college and high school students who had chosen to be interns at IBM for the summer, but aside from a few picnics, we weren't bringing them together or doing anything special with them."

The team came up with a concept for an event called Summer Jam, based upon the ideas in John Kao's book, *Jamming*.[2] In a Jam session, a group of people are given a scenario or problem to explore, and the mega-conversation is structured in a way that draws out a series of intellectual "riffs"—raw ideas, theories, and interesting connections that don't always surface in traditional meetings. For Summer Jam, the interns at each of IBM's eight research labs participated in a day-long Jam session with their fellow students to explore the topic, "What Will Life Be Like in the 21st Century?" Says Iwata, "The whole purpose of the day was to think big about where technology is going. We captured their ideas, videotaped the event, sent in industrial artists to sketch the ideas out, and we put all of that output in videos and print materials and gave it to the students. We also told them, 'By the way, all these ideas are going to go to senior management.' " (And as you can see in Figure 10-2, there were lots of ideas to send!)

"In the summer of 1998, when we started this program, 1400 of our summer interns attended," says Iwata. "The next year there were 6000.

Figure 10-2   A Wealth of Ideas Produced by a Large Group Event
Source: Photograph reproduced courtesy of IBM

The 'jam' exercises were facilitated by senior research scientists, some of whom the interns had only read about in textbooks. These were people they ordinarily would never meet in their summer jobs."

When IBM asked its distinguished researchers and scientists to facilitate these Jam sessions, they told them about the students' perceptions. "We said, 'Look, these brilliant young minds perceive you as stodgy, bureaucratic, old world thinkers. We want you to facilitate these sessions and show them they're wrong,' " recalls Iwata. "They said, 'Sign me up!' "

> All the videos, written materials, posters, pens, T-shirts, we produced to document the event worked as we'd hoped. The students went back to their campuses, hung up the stuff in their dorms, left the brochures out where others could see them. And when people said, "What did you do this summer?" They answered them with, "Well, I had a good summer, but there was one really cool day where we just thought about the next century and new technologies." "IBM did that?" "Yeah, IBM did that. Here's the videotape, and I'm in it. See, look, I'm over there in the corner talking to that guy we've been reading about in class."

Iwata says the recruitment win rate has gone up since the sessions began and that the concept of jamming is being adopted in many other areas of IBM to help spark the creation of new ideas: "Our head of Human Resources believes this is a powerful tool, and it's being incorporated into our management training curriculum. All of our managers will be taught how to create and use Jam sessions."

Other Methods of Listening on a Large Scale

Mega-conversations are not the only way for organizations to listen across boundaries and levels. Surveys, feedback forms, focus groups, town meetings, customer events, and a number of other more traditional mechanisms for gaining input are also valid ways of listening. The listening teams at British Airways discussed in Chapter 5 are yet another form of creative listening. And in Chapter 8, Dave Snowden of IBM explained how you can use stories to listen to an organization.

While large group meetings provide an innovative and powerful means of listening as well as fully engaging people in an organization, some organizations may not be ready to take that step. Some of these other mechanisms may provide a more comfortable means of getting started. But however you do it, creative organizational listening is an essential element of interactive management, and even if you're doing some of it now, do more!

Ground Rules for Good Mega-conversations

Each large group method has its own approach and its own philosophy. However, there are some commonalities. There are some things you'll need to keep in mind as you begin to implement them:

Rule 1: Decide what you want as a result
Rule 2: Make it safe
Rule 3: Make it equal
Rule 4: Invite a good cross-section of people
Rule 5: Break into small discussion groups for at least a portion of the meeting
Rule 6: Change your perceptions about what facilitation means
Rule 7: Give the conversation structure without being controlling
Rule 8: Hold the conversation in a flexible physical environment
Rule 9: Give yourself enough time to produce real results

Let's take a quick look at each one of these rules.

Rule 1: Decide What You Want as a Result

If you're going to hold a large group event, make sure you know why you're holding it. Simply holding it for the purpose of "improving relationships" is a laudable goal, but you're more likely to achieve that objective if you use the session as a means of actually getting some work done. Some of these methods are designed to get input on issues; others take the conversation all the way through to an action plan. Being clear on your purpose for the event is essential to its success and to your credibility as an interactive manager. But regardless of your purpose, do NOT hold one of these events if you don't really plan to listen to and act on what people generate. If you ask people to contribute their time and ideas and then do nothing, you will destroy your credibility and end up generating cynicism instead of results.

Rule 2: Make It Safe

One thing common to all forms of large group events is candor and openness. If people are punished in any way for their candor, whether in the context of the meeting or after the meeting, it will have enormous negative consequences both during and after the meeting. Having facilitated large group events myself, I've been amazed at the power they have to impact an organization's culture, even after only a few days. Once people learn to speak up in a large group meeting, they gain confidence about speaking up in all sorts of other venues. But if they are chastised or punished for their candor, those benefits will evaporate.

Rule 3: Make It Equal

This gets back to our original notion in Chapter 3, where we talk about sharing power. Large group events are an excellent way to demonstrate power-sharing in action. For the duration of a mega-conversation, it doesn't matter where you come from in the organization, or what your role is. Everyone has an equal voice, and everyone's contribution is important. If this rule isn't observed, you might as well pack up your sticky pads and colored markers and go home, because you're not going to get good input from people if they don't feel they're being treated with respect by coworkers at all levels.

Rule 4: Invite a Good Cross-Section of People

The concept of stakeholders comes to life in large group events. People really start to see the stake they have in issues when they are allowed to discuss and contribute to their development. Because of this phenomenon, it's really important to get a good cross-section of people involved in these events.

"In these types of conversations, everybody from the janitor, the secretary, and the elevator operator to the CEO has something to say about the company," says Scott Gassman, Director of Organizational Development at Empire Health Care and a frequent facilitator for large group events. "If you create a platform or an opportunity for them to engage, to care, to be heard, to share their ideas, to ask their questions, then you're talking about a whole new paradigm for working in an organization."

Throughout this book I've tried to stay away from the concept of buy-in. Interactive managers do not look for buy-in to their ideas.

Instead they look for ways to get people involved in *shaping ideas,* which naturally builds a sense of ownership. This is ownership through *involvement,* not ownership through *persuasion.* Large group events provide unprecedented opportunities to build ownership across all levels and boundaries of an organization—but only if you invite people to participate.

One of the most exciting potential applications of mega-conversations is with stakeholders who are outside traditional organizational boundaries. Customers, suppliers, contractors, b-web partners, and a host of other external stakeholders could use mega-conversations to forge new relationships and develop all sorts of new creative possibilities. A few of the people I interviewed talked about holding large group events with people outside their organizations. I'll talk more about these examples in Chapter 11, where I discuss how to engage people across boundaries.

Rule 5: Break into Small Discussion Groups for at Least a Portion of the Meeting

Every single one of the large group methods I've ever seen involves breaking the larger group down into smaller discussion groups at some point during the meeting. Some methods do not place a specific limit on the number of people who are in the smaller groups. But the important point is that it is very hard to have an intimate listening and learning experience in a large group if you do not provide opportunities for people to speak with each other in small groups.

Rule 6: Change Your Perceptions about What Facilitation Means

It's hard to overestimate the importance of having facilitators for these meetings who are able to let the group discover things on their own. Much of classical facilitation training has an underlying philosophy that mirrors older management philosophy: "The people need us to manage things so they don't get out of control." In fact, groups often will handle conflict and other situations very nicely themselves. Most of the work a facilitator needs to do in a large group meeting takes place *before* the meeting begins. For example, the facilitation ensures that top leadership understands their role as "equals," sets the context for the meeting with the design team, and makes sure all the right resources are available the day of the meeting. What you don't want is a traffic cop. One of the most important things that happens during this type of meeting is that people begin to take responsibility for themselves and for presenting their points of view. An overzealous facilitator will make it difficult for people to learn this lesson.

Let me give you an example from my own experience.

It was the first time I facilitated an Open Space meeting. Open Space is a large group method developed by Organizational Development specialist Harrison Owen, and it is characterized by a high degree of self-governance. During Open Space events, the group creates a wall that contains all of the issues it wants to discuss during the meeting. People who have raised the issues agree to either hold a small group conversation around that issue or, if two or more issues seem similar to one another, they can together agree to combine them.

As I was walking around the room, I saw a man about six-foot-four leaning over a woman a good foot and a half shorter. He was exhorting her to fold her session in with his. She was resisting, but meekly. I started to go over and facilitate their discussion but caught myself halfway across the room. I waited. And within three minutes I saw this woman stop, look the man in the eye and say, "No, I want to hold a separate session." It would have been very easy for me to rob her of the experience of sharing power in that situation.

Julie Beedon, an independent consultant who specializes in large group work, tells the story of a very seasoned facilitator who not only stayed out of the group's way himself, but also kept a leader from meddling:

> We were working with the head of training at Shell, and part of the whole process was coaching him in the group's ability to manage itself. A whole room full of people had been given a task, and this executive was sitting at the table with my colleague Paul.
>
> At one point one of the tables was doing nothing, absolutely nothing. And this training manager from Shell looks at the table and says, "Paul, they're not doing anything." And Paul replies, "They're doing what they need to." "But Paul, they're not doing anything, they're not going to get the work done." "They're doing what they need to." Suddenly all of them got up and

started drawing on a flip chart—they were *reflecting*. They just weren't using the process that we'd designed. They had decided to use their own process. We let groups know up front that they can choose not to do it the way we've suggested, as long as they achieve the outcome they're meant to achieve. This guy learned that he just had to trust the people in the group. To do this work, you have to trust implicitly the people in the room, and you have to have a deep belief that people can do good work.

Facilitators (and interactive leaders) need to learn to stay out of the way when a group is trying to solve its own problems or come to conclusions or create something new. The primary job of the facilitator is to do what Open Space creator Harrison Owen calls "holding the space," and what physicist David Bohm calls "holding the context" of the dialogue.

"Holding the space" is a little bit like helping a child learn to do something. You have to create a sense of presence so the child senses your support, and at the same time you need to let them learn the new task by doing it on their own. To do this well, you need a good sense of exactly when, and how much, to help.

The best rules for facilitating a large group meeting are to prepare well, coach the leadership, set the stage, ask good questions, set simple, clear ground rules, and then stay out of the way!

Rule 7: Give the Conversation Structure Without Being Controlling

Structure is essential to the success of a large group meeting. When you're holding a meeting with hundreds or thousands of people, it's very easy to have things descend into chaos. Some large group meetings are more structured than others, but all of them are carefully planned. The way props are used, the way rooms are set up, the ground rules that are set for participation, the processes that are put in place, all play a role in ensuring that the experience is useful and productive. If you looked at a materials checklist and preparation guideline for one of these meetings, you'd be impressed with its complexity. What's most amazing is that when you get in the meeting, it feels like it's running itself. And to a large extent, it is. But that type of smoothness and self-governance comes from careful preparation and expert hands-off facilitation.

Rule 8: Hold the Conversation in a Flexible Physical Environment

Chapter 4 discussed the importance of the physical environment to collaboration. Large group meetings present significant challenges in terms of logistics. There's a need for the flexibility to break into small groups, come back together as a larger group, and use a variety of materials to capture thoughts and ideas. With significant expertise in both large group processes as well as design of environments, The knOwhere Store in Palo Alto, California is an environment specifically designed for conversation and learning. It designs all of its own furniture, as we saw in Chapter 4, and it can accommodate all types of groups and a variety of meeting formats. I strongly advise you to take a look at its website (or visit one of their stores) to witness for yourself how environments can influence group process. Using the appropriate tables, having movable furniture, movable walls, etc., can make an amazing difference in the quality of a large group conversation.

Rule 9: Give Yourself Enough Time to Produce Real Results

In the examples of large group events presented in this chapter, we've talked about holding events for a period of time ranging from a day to three days. In their book *Large Group Interventions,* authors Bunker and Alban describe methods that can take even longer.

Many people are shocked at the prospect of taking three days (or even one day) off-site to hold a large group event. However, they've not yet experienced the enormous productivity associated with such events when they're structured properly. In fact, those three days can save weeks or months of time that it would take to communicate with people along traditional channels or for creative ideas to percolate to the surface.

Julie Beedon, a U.K.-based consultant who specializes in conducting large group events, says she's uneasy when clients try to condense the time they've allotted for a large group event because this affects the group's ability to reflect. "There's something about letting people think about things overnight that's incredibly valuable. When clients want to do a one-day event, I'll suggest that we do two half days instead of one long day. I've found that you get double the amount of insight and learning from each other when you work two half days as opposed to one day from ten to five."

When I facilitate large group event sessions for organizations, I often find that convincing executives of the need for time is the hardest part of the sell. Afterward, they uniformly agree with me that it couldn't have been done in less time and that the time was extremely well spent. There's a reason Jack Welch mandated that GE Workout sessions be held over a period of three days. It takes time to do real work in organizations. And the time invested in having a cross-section of an entire organization in one room pays enormous dividends in communication, collaboration, and business results.

Wise Advice for Conversations on a Smaller Scale

In the communication field there are countless books on developing conversational skills. Instead of going into detail in this area, I'd refer you back to Chapter 6 to the personal communication skills we've already discussed, which will serve you well in any type of conversation. But I would suggest reviewing the work of Phil Harkins in his excellent book, *Powerful Conversations*. Harkins provides a host of suggestions for having more powerful conversations, which he defines as "an interaction between two or more people that progresses from shared feelings, beliefs, and ideas to an exchange of wants and needs, to clear action steps and mutual commitments." Harkins says that powerful conversations have three outputs: an advanced agenda, shared learning, and a strengthened relationship.[3]

One of the key models in the book is what Harkins calls the "Tower of Power." This model sets up a simple structure for holding powerful conversations with others. There are four steps to the model:

1. Ask questions to gain understanding of the other person's feelings, beliefs, and ideas ("What's up?")
2. Test people's assertions against the facts ("What's so?")
3. Take time to imagine a variety of alternatives and possible solutions ("What's possible?")
4. Set an action plan ("Let's go!")

In his book, Harkins gives a number of examples of how to apply these principles in conversation. In my interview with him for this book, Harkins summed up the real essence of powerful conversations in one sentence: "The language of powerful conversations is not to respond, but to say, 'Tell me more.' " On a small or large scale, good conversations are ultimately about listening.

How to Approach a Conversation

There's a big buzz in management circles around the work of David Bohm, a quantum physicist who has developed theories and methods for effectively approaching conversations. Bohm says participants in a conversation or dialogue should suspend their assumptions, view each other as colleagues, and use a facilitator who "holds the context" of the dialogue.[4]

This focus on openness and collegiality is terrific, and it is the attitude all of us need to take into our conversations. If you're not willing to have your mind changed, and if you're not willing to share power and treat others as equals, then you're wasting your time in conversation.

However, it's important not to confuse *dialogue* with a state of harmony and perfect agreement. When we're trying hard to accommodate our differences, it's easy to lose sight of the importance of critical thinking skills. The purpose of a conversation is not to *agree* with each other, it's to learn from each other on both an intellectual and emotional level.

In classical rhetorical theory, the Greeks insisted that people enter a debate in a state of mind called *self-risk*, in which the person not only opened him- or herself to *listening*, but to *being changed* as a result of the interaction. So while debaters would argue points, they did so not to win, but rather to come closer to the truth.[5]

Interactive managers need to enter all types of conversation— whether large, small, long, short, debate, or dialogue—with an appreciation for the ideas of others, an attitude of power-sharing, and a well-constructed and well-informed point of view. But it's important to realize that good communication and good conversation is not about agreeing with each other and being nice all the time. Good conversation is about sharing ideas, getting things done, and showing respect for each other in the process.

Virtual Conversations

In this chapter I've primarily talked about conversations that take place in the same place at the same time. But with the advent of a wide range of communication technologies, conversations can take place at the same time but in different places, or in different places at different times. For example, on-line discussion groups contain conversations that people check into at their leisure. When you enter the conversation, the software brings you in where you left off and then allows you to add a comment to the discussion. Such conversations have a surprising feeling of interactivity to them, even though they are taking place "asynchronously."

Some mega-conversations are held simultaneously at a number of different locations, but are hooked together by satellite. Other large-scale events take place in one room or one location.

Audio conferences can be used to host regular conversations, and good audio conferencing services will allow you to create breakout groups or dinner conversations just as you'd do in a face-to-face meeting. The same is true of on-line meetings. Interviewees for this book told me about using interactive voice response systems to get feedback from thousands of people on a variety of topics, and one person described the use of desktop voting systems that afford his company the opportunity to do real-time opinion polling with employees.

Technology enables us to remove the constraints of time and place in order to hold conversations with, and listen to, people. As an interactive manager, think more broadly about all of your stakeholders. Consider how you and they could benefit from holding conversations on a more regular basis, whether face-to-face or through other means.

Key Ideas from Chapter 10

- Mega-conversations allow whole companies and b-webs to cut through bureaucracy and do real-time decision-making.
- Large group meetings completely rewrite traditional rules of meeting facilitation.
- Effective conversation and listening is not about agreeing with each other and being nice.
- Powerful small group conversations have three outputs: an advanced agenda, shared learning, and a strengthened relationship.

Fresh approaches to conversation and listening in organizations are critical to managing interactively. Getting people to talk to and listen to each other in new ways engages them in cocreating the direction and strategy for an organization. The examples we've presented here primarily focus on listening and conversing in the same organization. There are some special considerations for how to engage people in this new world of contractors, alliances, and business webs. New business models call for new models of engagement. Chapter 11 looks at the competency of engaging people across organizational boundaries.

CHAPTER

Engage People Who Don't Report to You— Crossing Organizational Boundaries

I'LL NEVER FORGET the first time I saw a picture of North America taken from space. I was momentarily jarred by the fact that the pictures didn't have the lines drawn in to designate the state boundaries. Even though intellectually I knew state boundaries were conceptual, there was something about the visual experience which made a big impression on me. As I think about boundaries with relationship to organizations, the image of those space photographs return to my mind.

As an interactive manager you need to recognize the importance of both views: the picture with the lines and the picture without the lines. You need to think about your company from both perspectives, recognizing that there's a boundaryless view as well as a view where boundaries make sense. What we need are boundaries that are flexible enough to allow us to cooperate, and clear enough to help us avoid conflicts and misunderstandings.

Within organizations, boundaries exist between levels of the organization and across departmental and geographic lines. While there are some good reasons for structuring organizations this way, strict adherence to boundaries can inhibit collaboration and have profound impacts on an organization's success or failure. As we've seen, it's hard to engage people unless you share information across departments, divisions, and levels. Interactive management has to take place both inside the firm as well as across organizational boundaries.

Between organizations, before the advent of networking technologies and the web, stronger boundaries existed. Even when companies *wanted* to collaborate with each other to produce products or services or to contract out work, it was harder to do so because affordable interconnectivity didn't exist. New networking technologies have changed all that.

Cisco, a well-known provider of telecommunications solutions, is an extreme example. Cisco started out as a manufacturing company. But now, much of what Cisco produces is made by its network of suppliers. In short, it shifted its focus from manufacturing equipment to managing relationships. Now partners do the manufacturing and Cisco sticks to creating software and managing its network of organizational relationships. Cisco connects customers, partners, suppliers, and employees in a global supply network that gives all of the players immediate access to information about one another's demand, supply, manufacturing, design, finance, and a host of other areas.

Because of this connectivity, Cisco has dramatically decreased its costs of doing business. But don't think that this is accomplished simply by farming out work. Cisco has carefully nurtured its relationships by sharing information and adopting a mentality that led the former worldwide VP of strategic alliances, Steve Behm, to say, "We employ 32,000 people. Seventeen thousand of them work for Cisco and the rest work for our suppliers."[1] In a recent *Wall Street Journal* article, CEO John Chambers listed "forming an ecosystem of partnerships in a horizontal business model" as being an essential component of managing growth in an e-business economy.[2]

When people at Cisco think about management, they recognize that they need to include *all of their stakeholders*. They know firsthand the importance of communication. This is precisely the type of attitude that interactive managers need to adopt. Interactive managers recognize that their stakeholders can be found in different departments and even different companies, and they manage and communicate accordingly.

As technology allows us to connect people more closely both inside and outside organizations, the boundaries of those organizations become less clear. And the more we bring down the walls between departments and the more we partner with other organizations to comarket, co-develop, and cocreate, ironically, the more we need to think about boundaries. We need to clearly define our relationships with others, consciously decide how we will work together, understand our differences and our similarities, and recognize how we can share information in ways that allow us to work well together without undue risk in terms of competitive advantage.

Cocreating and codeveloping ideas and products with other entities requires superb communication and collaboration. In this chapter we'll look at some ways to manage interactively across borders.

First, we'll look at different types of alliances. Then we'll talk about six key suggestions for interactive relationship management in alliances:

1. Continually clarify your purpose
2. Attend to roles and rules
3. Designate relationship managers
4. Create shared space
5. Address cultural issues
6. Agree up front on how to share knowledge across boundaries— both within and between organizations

This chapter contains specific ways of creating a sense of shared space between separate entities, examines how culture enhances or disrupts partnerships, and addresses the very important issue of how to share information both inside and outside your organization—including how to deal with sticky issues such as the cocreation of intellectual capital.

Types of Alliances

Alliances are increasing at record rates. According to Andersen Consulting, alliances between companies will represent $25 to $40 trillion in value within the next five years, and the average large company, which had no alliances a decade ago, now has in excess of 30. And these figures only represent what I call *strategic alliances*—excluding other types of partnerships such as joint ventures and acquisitions.[3]

Clearly, alliances are important to all types of businesses, and they create significant new challenges for interactive managers. Whether it's a b-web, a strategic alliance, or a joint venture, all alliances create situations where people must cooperate and coordinate efforts despite the absence of formal reporting structures across the boundaries. This calls for very clear roles and responsibilities, understanding of shared interests, a strong sense of purpose and direction, and ongoing, well-designed, interactive communication.

There are many different types of alliances, and people use a number of different terms to describe them. This section will begin with a definition of terms and then discuss examples.

In a *merger,* two companies or organizations join forces on relatively equal footing in which there's no dominant shareholder. A merger implies that two separate entities will now become one entity. In an *acquisition,* one company buys control of another company by purchasing greater than 50 percent ownership.

A *strategic alliance* is a contractual agreement (either verbal or written) between two organizations that doesn't involve creating a new organizational entity, whereas a *joint venture* involves setting up a new organization that is co-owned. An *outsourcing* relationship is one in which the work that a function (or part of a function) provides is contracted to an outside firm that specializes in performing that function. Usually, outsourcing relationships are based on long-term contracts. *Contractors* and *consultants* operate under temporary agreements with a company to perform project work. *Coalitions* are noncontractual relationships between organizations in which they band together to accomplish a shared objective. In the not-for-profit world, coalitions often substitute for strategic alliances.

Business webs, or *b-webs,* as they are called in the book *Digital Capital,* are a new type of organizational alliance enabled by the web.[4] These are new and important enough that I'd like to take a moment to explain them separately in a little more detail.

The authors, Tapscott, Ticoll, and Lowy, define a b-web as "a network of suppliers, distributors, commerce services providers, and customers that conduct business communications and transactions on the Internet and other electronic media in order to produce value for end-customers and for one another." They describe five types of b-webs: agora, aggregation, alliance, value chain, and distributive network.

- An *agora* is an open market that allows buyers and sellers to find each other on-line; an example is eBay.

- An *aggregation* provides goods and services from a range of suppliers all under one "roof"; an example would be Amazon.com.
- An *alliance*, (according to the very specific definition in *Digital Capital*) provides a context for people to come together in communities to design things, create knowledge, or provide experiences; an example is America Online.
- A *value chain* brings together a specific set of players for the purpose of designing and delivering an integrated product or service; an example is Cisco.
- A *distributive network* exists primarily for the purpose of distribution of products and/or services; an example is Federal Express.

Interactive managers need to be aware of these new types of business models and start to understand their implications for interactive management. If companies are going to band together in wholly new ways in an Internet economy, then interactive managers need to be thinking about how to communicate and collaborate in these new environments.

What's interesting is that despite the fact that trillions of dollars are invested in alliances, most of the people who are experts in this area readily admit that over half of them don't succeed.[5] And while you might think that the primary reason for failure is faulty strategy or inadequate due diligence, that's probably not the case. In fact, there is some evidence that problems with alliances and failures of partnerships are often due in large measure to lack of coordination and communication. "The fiction is that it's the hard issues that matter," says Dan Fitz, General Counsel of Cable and Wireless, a global telecommunications firm. Fitz is a seasoned negotiator—in the past 15 months he has overseen mergers, acquisitions, and alliances on three continents worth almost 60 billion pounds (about $90 billion). "Of course the hard issues matter, but the reality is that it's the soft issues, the human resource and communication issues, that trip you up," continues Fitz. "The soft issues include, 'Who's going to run this thing once we've got it? What happens to employees affected by the deal? How will the corporate cultures interact?' The least amount of time is spent on these issues, but they're the most important things. All these issues are rife in joint ventures, acquisitions, mergers, and strategic alliances."

Smooth sailing in both internal and external alliances is largely dependent upon an environment of trust, and that starts at the very beginning of a relationship. The way a team comes together—whether it's a team of people inside an organization or a massive joint venture— the opening agreements and ways of working together early on will set the stage for that relationship.

Certainly all of the skills and competencies we've described in this book so far will relate to better alliance relationship management; however, there are some particular aspects to managing across boundaries that are worth considering on their own, and that's the focus of the remainder of this chapter.

Suggestion 1: Continually Clarify Your Purpose

What holds alliances together is a sense of purpose. All of the parties to an alliance must have a clear sense of how they will benefit from working together before they'll be willing to invest the time and energy it takes to make an alliance work. This is often a challenge because people don't have a clear shared vision of what the alliance will accomplish. Dan Fitz of Cable and Wireless explains how this confusion can occur:

> **Many companies rush headlong into very high-stakes negotiations without being clear where it fits within their own strategic objectives and without necessarily understanding thoroughly what it is they're wanting to acquire or develop. This lack of clarity can lead to bad deals for both sides. Particularly for a joint venture, you need alignment, you need a meeting of the minds, to make a true joint venture work. Most joint ventures fail within three to five years, and it's probably due to lack of clarity at the beginning and a lack of communication even where there is clarity.**

We've discussed the importance of creating a common language across diverse groups of people in Chapter 6. In developing the purpose for an alliance, this becomes particularly important. When companies are putting together b-webs or vertical strategic alliances, they will often be working with companies outside their own industries. This can cause confusion and misunderstanding in the process of putting things together because people are speaking the languages of their own industries or disciplines.

Jim Haudan, President of RootLearning, came across this challenge while working with a research and development alliance. The team, which was made up of people from different divisions, external suppliers, and other outside partners, experienced significant communication challenges. "They were having a difficulty just agreeing on what it was they were talking about," Haudan explains. "They spent the better part of a year convinced that they still weren't talking about the same thing. And since there was no common reference, no mental picture of what they were working on, they couldn't come together on how to build it. They were spending all of their time trying to codefine it."

Remember the shared mental models discussed in Chapter 7? In this case, Haudan and his team listened to all of the members of the group and built one in the form of a graphic representation. This, combined with dialogue, accelerated clarity, says Haudan.

Developing a sense of purpose for an alliance is very similar to developing a unifying concept for an organization, which we discussed in Chapter 9. A clear purpose for the alliance needs to be built by a number of different stakeholders from all of the parties to the alliance. "You've got to figure out what constitutes a win for everyone involved in an alliance," says Larry Walsh, of Osgood, O'Donnell and Walsh, a communications consulting firm that works with clients to help communicate during mergers, acquisitions, and strategic alliances. "I think one plus one has to equal three. You've got to be able to demonstrate how combining research, databases, sales organizations, or whatever you're combining, is going to benefit all the parties. Everyone has to feel like they got a little bit more than the other guy."

And the shared vision or purpose for the alliance must continually be communicated throughout the life of the alliance. The need for alignment in alliances is similar to the need for alignment in individual organizations.

Suggestion 2: Attend to Roles and Rules

"You can't get very far down the path with an alliance without getting serious about who's going to run what, who's responsible for what," says Steve Kerr, Chief Learning Officer at General Electric. "You have to manage issues of role clarity, role conflict, and role ambiguity in order to make it clear who has what responsibilities. Companies that don't do that up front are going to have problems."

Jeff Weiss, Founding Partner of Vantage Partners, a spin-off of the Harvard Negotiation Project, agrees: "When you begin to implement an alliance, you need to figure out the roles in terms of communication and decision-making. For example, who should be informed versus consulted about key decisions?"

Communicating about roles up front can pay off handsomely in the long run by avoiding conflicts, misunderstandings, and subsequent lack of communication. If all of the parties to an alliance are not clear about who is going to take responsibility for different aspects of communication and project management, it is unlikely the alliance will flourish.

In addition to clarifying roles, all of the parties to an alliance also need to agree on some rules of operation. For instance, up front they need to ask questions such as: What will our process for conflict resolution be? How will we share information? What are the rules for exiting the alliance? Communicating about these issues beforehand will lead to better communication throughout the life of the alliance. For example, if you know what the rules are for leaving the alliance, it's less likely that there will be conflicts when the time comes to end the relationship. Interactive communication in these instances is essential. Through inclusive conversations with stakeholders—perhaps in a large group event—rules can be set that encourage better collaboration and understanding.

Surprisingly, even some very large alliances are formed on the strength of a handshake. One interviewee made the observation that when alliances are negotiated with a handshake at the executive level at her company, a lack of explicit communication leads to unwanted results:

> **I can say with complete certainty that we have not had a bullet-proof alliance agreement in the last ten years. . . . What used to be pretty common was that these deals would be made on the basis of a handshake, with nothing in writing. We've tried to get away from that, deals aren't *finalized* that way anymore. But the problem is that the deal still starts that way, and it will usually reach a crisis when they're working out the details in a contract and there are no written notes from that initial meeting between the executives and one of them will say, "I distinctly remember him telling me they would do that."**

This same interviewee says that another part of the problem is that the senior executives make these agreements without consulting people in the field who have a better understanding of how things play out on a day-to-day basis. She says that in these cases, fulfillment becomes an issue: "The executives are promising things to the other side without knowing what it will take on our part to meet those promises." Capturing roles and rules in writing can have significant benefits.

Part of establishing the rules means also communicating about enforcement of those rules. Rules don't have meaning without enforcement. Enforcement could be as formal as legal action, or it could be accomplished within the alliance itself. Once again, an inclusive communication process is a good way to develop these rules.

Communicating clearly regarding a set of rules and roles, writing them down and then putting them in a place where people can share access to them, will help establish clear boundaries and clear lines of accountability for an alliance. Why is it important to do this? Because things will change as time goes on, says Jeff Weiss, founding partner of Vantage Partners, a consulting firm that assists clients with relationship building in alliances:

> **The amount of change can be enormous—the context around the partnership changes, the people that are part of the partnership and what they want changes, the very strategy and goals of the partnership may change. If at the outset the partners haven't discussed what might change and agreed on how they'll handle those changes, you can bet they'll face surprise and conflict and have trouble coping when change inevitably crops up. Companies are usually very formal about partner selection, due diligence, and the like, but what they tend to frequently ignore is planning how they will work together—how they "get on the same page" and how they'll manage their relationship over time. They often fail to define even the simplest things, such as roles and authorities, never mind things like management processes or mechanisms for communicating, problem-spotting, or conflict resolution. Focusing on such things can make a huge difference in ensuring the success of an alliance.**

Of course, roles and rules may need to be adapted over time. However, it's much easier to renegotiate existing rules than it is to start creating rules late in the process.

All of the competencies we've talked about in this book so far can help with the job of communicating clearly regarding roles and rules, but some of the most critical are the competencies of accessibility, alignment, listening, and conversing. Setting up an alliance will call for putting people in touch with each other across organizational boundaries (accessibility), gaining alignment among all the parties to the alliance, and developing mechanisms, such as large group events, for people to share ideas about how the alliance should be set up.

Suggestion 3: Designate Relationship Managers

Successful alliances almost always have a relationship manager designated to make sure the alliance is running smoothly and that information is being communicated well across boundaries. Several people in b-webs that I spoke to were particularly clear about the importance of relationship managers.

According to Jeff Weiss of Vantage Partners, relationship managers are critical to success. "The concept of having a relationship manager is not uncommon, but the term is used extraordinarily loosely," he says. "The alliances that we have seen work well have someone who truly manages the relationship and makes sure the partners are working well together on all levels. The relationship manager should not be an executive who oversees the alliance, receiving status reports and meeting with some other CEO or EVP a few times a year. Rather, it should be a fairly senior, experienced person who plays the role of day-to-day point person, focused on assessing how well people work together; spotting potential problems and opportunities, working through issues and conflicts, and ensuring that value is being captured, created, and shared. This person addresses the kinds of relationship and communication challenges that arise in, and often seriously threaten, ongoing alliances."

Weiss explains that senior executives are better in the role of executive sponsor, rather than relationship manager: "Ordinarily it works out better when there is an experienced mid-level person assigned as relationship manager. When the relationship manager is too senior, they are usually too removed from the day-to-day workings of the partnership to be effective in the role. They don't have enough contact with how the alliance is operating and how the partners are actually working together. No matter how wise or experienced any given senior executives might be, they're apt to not have the time or bandwidth to truly manage the relationship."

Relationship managers are different from "alliance" managers. Weiss explains:

> **If you really look at what most alliance managers do, you'll see they're mainly focused on issues of strategy, contract management, and the like. They are necessarily focused on the substance of the deal. Yet there is also a need for someone to ensure that the partners are working well together—the relationship part of the deal. Too often, when I come in and ask about the *relationship* manager, I am pointed to someone who is concerned with the substance, not the relationship. A true relationship manager is required. If the relationship is left to chance, there is a very good chance that the alliance will fail.**

In addition to needing all of the interpersonal skills and competencies for interactive managers mentioned in this book, qualities of a good relationship manager also include excellent analytical skills, an ability to put the needs of the alliance before parochial interests, an ability to see situations from multiple perspectives, the ability to think systemically, and a high level of credibility in their own organizations.[6]

Examples of Companies Using Relationship Managers

At GE Capital, "integration managers" manage the process of integrating new acquisitions. They create communication strategies, develop education programs for the new management team, help new managers understand GE Capital's corporate culture, and educate GE Capital management on what they need to know about the new business they've just acquired, among other activities. What's important to note is that these integration managers are focused on *relationship activities*, not running the new business.[7]

Crimson Consulting is a b-web that provides marketing consulting services. When a client comes to them for marketing consulting, Crimson pulls together a consulting team from a number of independent consultants and part-time employees who work through them. A relationship manager is crucial at two steps in this process. First, there is a relationship manager from "Consultant Services" who establishes the relationship with the consultant before he or she is actually engaged to do an assignment. Then a relationship manager from their "Consulting Management Team" takes over. This person is responsible for brokering the relationship between the client and that consultant. They are available to both the consultant and the client throughout the assignment.

Silicon.com, a b-web based in the United Kingdom, provides up-to-date news and job information to the information technology community. Silicon partners with a number of entities, including the British Computing Society, to bring professional development information to their community. Anna Russell, Marketing Director, points out that a relationship manager is critical to maintaining these relationships with their partners: "We have two people employed full-time who work with all of our partners...these are people who are dedicating their time to making sure the relationships work. Our partners are really interested in creating an on-line presence and working with us, but it's not always at the top of their agenda. They have full-time jobs and other things that are demanding their attention. So we think it's very important to have somebody working on maintaining those relationships. That's vital."

A relationship manager can help implement all of the suggestions mentioned in this chapter, including helping to create a sense of shared space.

Suggestion 4: Create Shared Space

In order to build a sense of unity, alliances need a home base. This can be accomplished through the establishment of a shared space. Whether it's a shared website for merger partners or an on-line discussion group for a cross-boundary team, having a place to go is critical to building alignment and esprit de corps. These spaces can be virtual or they can be physical. Mega-conversations or large group events can be excellent shared spaces for newly formed entities.

Virtual Shared Space

Buzzsaw.com is a b-web that has made a whole business around providing a shared space on-line for people who work on large construction projects. Architects, contractors, owners, and all other parties to a project can use the Buzzsaw website as a home base for the project. In this space they're able to share documents, hold conversations, view pictures of the construction site, and capture lessons learned, all in one spot.

Interviewees told me about using a variety of technologies to create shared spaces, including team rooms and video conferences for joint venture partners, on-line discussion groups for strategic alliances, databases as a shared space for a sales alliance, and extranets with potential outsourcing partners.

On-line Discussion Groups for an Alliance

Lisa Kimball, founder and VP Professional Services for Caucus Systems, says she has found that it is critically important to create shared space for the alliances in which her company is involved: "People very much identify with space when they're working together. By setting up a site with on-line discussion groups, you give a 'homeroom' to the alliance. If we don't share an office, we need a place that we all identify with. We can also use the space as a common repository for any agreements, norms, and role definitions we've developed. It's all there in one place, and we know that we all have access to the same information, the same versions. We're looking at the same things.... It provides a real sense of continuity. So the first thing that we do when we become part of an alliance is to create shared space on-line with the other entities."

Extranets for Outsourcing Partners

Extranets, which are private and secure portals to a company's internal website, can provide a shared space for potential alliance partners to get to know each other better, particularly in outsourcing situations. Jon Iwata, VP of Corporate Communications at IBM, gives a good example of how IBM uses extranets to connect to the employees of customers who may potentially outsource their entire IT department with IBM.

Companies outsourcing their IT departments not only transfer their computing infrastructure to IBM, but also the people who work there. Companies are concerned about how outsourcing partners will take care of their employees. Before a deal is closed, as customers evaluate different outsourcing partners, IBM sets up a tailored extranet site for its employees. Says Iwata:

Until you're part of a company, it's hard to know what it will be like. So we give them access to IBM. Imagine that you're in the IT department of a bank. IBM is in negotiations to win your bank's outsourcing contract. A thousand of you may become IBMers

overnight. So we offer you this extranet site, and when you log on, you receive a message designed for you and your fellow employees saying, "We know you have a lot of questions and concerns, we want to help you answer those questions. We want to help you get to know IBM, the people here, and learn about what our practices are."

The extranet gives those potential employees customized access to a huge portion of IBM's intranet. "We create a place for them to go find answers to their questions about what IBM is like, how we manage people, what kind of training and benefits programs we have, etc.," says Iwata. "We even give them access to discussion sessions and chat sessions with IBMers. So they feel as though they are *at* IBM. No boring presentations. Instead they get to discover IBM for themselves."

This approach of creating shared space has been enormously successful for IBM's services business, says Iwata: "Many times for multi-billion dollar deals, our customers have told us that the extranet really made a difference in their decision to choose us. It was an important decision factor because their employees came back to them saying that IBM looked like a company where they could be really happy."

Face-to-face Shared Space

We discussed mega-conversations in Chapter 10. Quite often these large group events are held with internal stakeholders, but very effective working relationships can be quickly established by holding these events with stakeholders from alliances. Some of the interviewees I spoke with are just starting to experiment with this idea and they're having very good results.

For example, Empire Health Care held a very successful large group event that brought together representatives from different health care entities partnering with them in a new e-business alliance. During the session, key discussion topics included: resources for the new venture, roles and responsibilities, training sessions for new alliance partners, conflict resolution, and cultural differences between the different companies. The meeting was so successful that they have decided to hold one large group event per month as they develop the new business together. "One of the alliance partners from the other company said he was really surprised by the amount of openness and risk-taking in terms of the comments that were shared in this initial meeting," says Scott Gassman, Director of Organizational Development at Empire. "That's what the leaders want to see because they know it takes that kind of openness to achieve the speed to market that's necessary to make a business like this work."

Many companies hold mega-conversations with customers and new merger partners. GE regularly conducts Workout sessions with customers and other outside entities, and they are just beginning to hold sessions with acquisition partners. When I asked Steve Kerr, Chief Learning Officer at GE, about Workout sessions for acquisitions, he said, "It's funny you mention it, because six days ago [Jack] Welch, said, 'We really should make Workout part of the acquisition integration and have everybody do one.' We have done some, it's unusual—not rare, but unusual—but looking forward, we may be doing it regularly now."

By bringing alliance partners together for these large group events, the process of learning how to work together and developing a shared focus is greatly accelerated. All of the benefits people experience when they hold these mega-conversations internally are benefits they can also share across boundaries. Particularly as customers and other external stakeholders start to participate more in the process of helping to shape brands, design products, and get work done, large group events can provide a shared space for the alliance not only at the beginning of the relationship, but also throughout its duration.

As an interactive manager involved in any type of alliance, you should create shared space with all of your stakeholders—whether it's on-line or face-to-face. By creating shared space, you'll also create shared opportunities, shared insights, and shared understanding.

Suggestion 5: Address Cultural Issues

In Chapter 6, we talked about corporate cultures as well as national cultures. Cultural differences between alliance partners can create some interesting communication challenges. These differences can be handled in a variety of ways, based upon the type of alliance you're involved in. When ties between the organizations do not have to be particularly strong, differing corporate cultures may not matter, because there may not be a need for much communication. But in alliances such as mergers and acquisitions, or even joint ventures, clear decisions need to be made about whether corporate cultures can coexist, or whether communication will become so difficult that a new culture will have to be built.

Dan Fitz, of Cable & Wireless, says differing cultures aren't necessarily an alliance show-stopper, but that care must be taken in paying attention to these issues when building alliances or communicating with acquired companies:

> We're a 125-year-old company that has been in the telecommunications business for that whole period of time. Two years ago we jumped with both feet into the Internet world, which as you know has a much faster corporate culture . . . . There are big cultural differences between a traditional major corporation and your typical Internet company in terms of the way people like to interact and the way people like to work.
>
> For example, we've recently bought an Internet service provider in Germany. We want them because of who they are, an innovative, creative, fast-paced company. So there's a conscious decision not to integrate them into our more conservative corporate culture until we have evolved ourselves. We try to quarantine certain cultures where we think it's better for us and better for them if they continue to develop in their own way.
>
> This has obvious implications for how we communicate with those companies. So for senior management in a place like Cable & Wireless, when you're addressing an issue about a business, you first have to step back and think, "Which business is it that I'm addressing?"

Interactive managers who are communicating with alliance partners, whether they're part of an acquisition or a b-web, need to take the culture of the partner into account and tailor their communication accordingly.

While some companies want their acquisition partners to retain their separate cultures, other companies are more interested in assimilating those cultures. "We don't merge, we acquire. We're so big that we take over things," says Steve Kerr of General Electric. However, even though GE "takes over," they often do so with a sense of understanding of the importance of culture. GE has acquisition integration screens that assist in cultural assimilation of new acquisitions. Surveys are conducted to determine differences in culture between the two companies on a number of different dimensions. The results of these surveys are used in facilitated discussions with the new companies. During the discussions of the survey results, they talk about the history and folklore of the two companies, allowing them to understand the differences in their cultures, and the implications those differences have for doing business together. In some instances three-day Workout sessions are held with acquisition partners to focus on cultural issues.[8]

Facilitated conversations about differing cultures is not only useful in acquisitions, but also in mergers. Peg Neuhauser, a consultant to companies on cultural issues, says many mergers get derailed because of culture clashes: "The merger may make sense legally and financially, but the groups never gel because of the cultural differences. So to avoid that problem on the front end, since it's an extremely expensive problem, take the time to get to know each other's history and heritage. You need to understand both companies' key values and key goals." (As Neuhauser points out in Chapter 8, one of the best ways to learn about values is through sharing stories.)

The formation of alliances or b-webs may or may not require cultural changes, based upon the nature of the alliance. However, regardless of the type of alliance, Jeff Weiss points out that at the very least, people will need to discuss cultural issues:

> **Over time, an alliance may or may not develop some kind of common culture. In any alliance, you will see aspects of each partner's culture bubbling up. Likely some conflict—often significant ones—will occur as two or more value systems come together. For an entity that's only going to be intact for a limited period of time, it may not make sense to develop a fundamentally new set of operating assumptions and ways of working. However, it's critical for the partners to develop some common understanding of how each thinks and acts, and how they will jointly bridge those gaps. Without this, the alliance won't work. In my experience, the most successful alliances address those issues explicitly.**

By using any of a number of methods, such as large group conversations, and by keeping people informed through the use of extranets and other technologies, interactive managers can help ease cultural transitions when they are communicating across organizational boundaries. I anticipate that the use of large-scale events to bring together b-web, strategic alliance, and joint venture partners will rise as companies begin to understand the value of up-front interactive communication in helping partners to communicate cross-culturally.

As you consider your company's current and potential alliances, consider cultural compatibility and how you can use interactive communication to take advantage of opportunities and alleviate problems.

Suggestion 6: Agree on How to Share Knowledge Across Boundaries—Both Within and Between Organizations

Long before the concept of knowledge management became popular, people in IT departments were dealing with what they called "the politics of data." As soon as we started capturing data in information systems, people started worrying about who was going to own it and who was going to have access to it. Managers didn't like the idea of people below them in the organizational hierarchy having access to information. Nor did they relish the idea of people in other parts of the organization having access to the information they controlled. But the fact is, sharing information is a strategic imperative. If you don't give people access to information, you make it more difficult for them to do their work and help your company be competitive.

Ten years ago I wrote a story about how information sharing at Phillips Petroleum helped rescue the company from hostile takeover attempts by T. Boone Pickens and Carl Icahn.[9] Bob Wallace, who was president of Phillips at the time, said that the only chance for survival as a company was to effect change in how they managed the business. They needed to rid themselves of bureaucracy and get information flowing throughout the organization in order to dramatically improve performance. But Wallace had a heck of a time convincing managers that they needed to share information with people working on oil rigs and all levels in between. He knew that without that information, the company wouldn't stand a chance in hell of getting out of its predicament. He knew they needed the smarts of every single person in that organization, armed with up-to-the-minute information, in order for the company to regain its footing. By getting managers to loosen their grip on information and recognize that they needed to share across levels and across departments, Wallace was able to bring the company back to life.

Ten years later, companies are still often struggling to get people to share information across different parts of an organization. Fred Schoeps, Program Director of Knowledge Management at IBM, says that this is natural: "Unless you explicitly create an environment to encourage knowledge sharing across boundaries, there's much less likelihood that it's going to happen." Technology can certainly assist in encouraging cross-boundary sharing, because if it's easier to do, people are more likely to do it, but technology alone is no guarantee.

Now we're just beginning to grapple with these same kinds of issues *between different organizations.* As I did the interviews for this book, I asked people how they were handling situations where they shared knowledge or cocreated intellectual capital with outside stakeholders. It quickly became apparent that few solid answers are available and many people are just starting to find ways of approaching the challenge. You'll find more questions than answers in this section, but this will give you a foundation for asking some of the right questions as you deal with partnerships and alliances at your own organization.

There are many issues and complexities associated with communicating and sharing knowledge between companies. In the course of my interviews, four basic themes arose. However, I recognize that this is only the tip of the iceberg in terms of the issues that need to be explored.

The four issues we'll cover in this section include:

- Giving people background information for the purposes of working together
- Protecting existing intellectual capital
- Providing for ownership of joint intellectual capital
- Enabling customers to share information with each other

Informing People. The need to communicate and share information with outsourcing partners, contractors, alliance partners, and customers is often overlooked or not well managed.

Sarah Fasey, Internal Communications Manager at the United Kingdom and Ireland subsidiary of Microsoft, says they make a point of sharing information with their outsourced call center and other partners. "The people in the call center receive our in-house magazine, our executive team goes up and talks to them at their location in Glasgow, and they can access our intranet. We have whole groups of people who manage partner relationships and they will tend to make the call themselves around what it is those people need to know." But Fasey adds that people don't always make the right decisions about what to share:

> I felt this very keenly when I first joined the relationship marketing team. One of the things we do is manage all our relationships with our marketing, advertising, and PR agencies, and I was really surprised at the lack of information those guys had. Really surprised. I think we all assume if somebody's managing a relationship with an external party, that they take the trouble to communicate to them what's important to the organization: the vision, the values, the objectives, where you're heading. That's a dangerous assumption because the reality is that many people are very focused on getting the specifics of their particular project or campaign completed, and they don't make the time to complete the bigger picture for people. When you do, outsourced partners are far more able to take on a real partnership with you.

Even in a successful partnership like the DRAM Development Alliance (DDA) between IBM, Siemens, and Toshiba, where communication is a top priority, knowledge sharing across boundaries is challenging. "When we did a communications assessment, we found that everybody who needed to know about certain decisions didn't always find out about them in a timely way. They'd find out indirectly. So they might be proceeding down a path that they didn't know had changed," says Sheri Feinzig, Senior Consultant for Internal Transformation Consulting and Services at IBM, who assisted the alliance with a knowledge management effort.

Keeping customers informed presents another cross-boundary challenge. How much do customers want or need to know? You might be surprised. The Director of Sales Alliances at a financial software company describes a situation in which very close communication with customers is causing some interesting problems. Years ago, this company started a customer steering committee for the purpose of getting input on software product enhancements. Over the years, the steering committee became so involved that they developed very strong expectations around what information should be shared with them. The Director explains: "It's really been shocking for me. The stuff that they're demanding is amazing. When one of our general managers was terminated, the steering committee felt they should have been notified before the general public. And they wanted to know why the decision was made, and they wanted to know how we would handle the message in the marketplace."

The steering committee wants information across the board, all the way from high level personnel changes to product enhancement information. They even want to participate in management decisions, says the director: "When they're not happy with how a manager is performing, they've created their own vehicle to deliver that information to the executive team."

I asked where expectations for this kind of information came from. "The steering committee was formed when this was a privately held, family-owned company that made a practice of sharing this type of information," she says. "But now they're part of a much bigger company." They've beefed up product-related communications, but they are reluctant to provide the kind of detailed organizational information the committee wants: "I think the decision not to share that information has arisen more from legal concerns that we're going to say the wrong thing, or the wrong information's going to get to the wrong person and put us in a compromised position."

While there are very practical reasons for being careful with the information they share, the director says the decision to withhold information has compromised the relationship to a certain extent: "We're losing a lot by changing the way we communicate with them. This steering committee consists of the largest corporations in America, and they serve as wonderful references for us. They have helped us penetrate the market. While I don't agree that they should have this level of information, unfortunately because we're not giving it to them, they're detaching themselves from us and their loyalty to us is waning. We're not getting as many referrals from them as we did in the past, and that's because we're shutting them out in terms of sharing information." This example illustrates how important it is to set proper expectations for information sharing up front.

There are no simple answers regarding how much information people need in order to work together across organizational boundaries. However, interactive managers need to examine all of their external relationships and explicitly discuss these issues with external stakeholders.

Protecting Existing Intellectual Capital. This is an issue when companies form alliances such as b-webs, particularly when one partner is more powerful than another. "You've got to share enough to negotiate the deal, but you've got to protect yourself in case the deal doesn't go through or unravels in six months," says Jeff Weiss, founding partner of Vantage Partners and an expert in building alliance relationships. "This is a challenge that is part of the whole phenomenon of 'co-opetition.' Our clients are frequently faced with the question of what and how you share in order to negotiate a valuable deal and build a strong relationship in the context of being fierce competitors in other areas."

Existing ownership of intellectual capital is not just an issue when you're forming a strategic alliance or considering a merger. As more and more companies outsource larger and larger portions of their businesses, Mike Zisman, EVP of Strategy at Lotus Development Corporation, says that the outsourcing companies themselves will have to take on the responsibility of protecting the intellectual capital of their customers, because many of their customers will be competitors with each other. "These outsourcers are going to have to build infrastructures to know where the fences are, what can be shared and what cannot," he says. "One of the impacts of business process outsourcing is that you are going to see your key outsourcing partners providing the same service to your competitor."

I asked George Polzer of Reveal.net, a company that provides outsourcing capabilities for sales to high technology companies, how he deals with this issue. "Most companies that we work with see a high enough value proposition to take the risk that competitors may be working with us as well," he explains. "We also develop exclusive relationships with some companies if they're willing to share the risk financially with us."

Again, there are no hard and fast rules or guarantees in terms of protecting your intellectual capital. Interactive managers will have to balance risk with reward when they're deciding what to share with potential partners. But this decision process should include up-front communication with stakeholders.

Up-Front Provisions for Ownership of Joint Intellectual Capital. External alliances often create joint intellectual capital, not only in the form of a product or service, but also in the *way* that product or service is created. For example, an alliance may discover a new way of approaching a business process or they might together develop an innovative HR or communication method as part of creating a new product. Who owns it? Unless such discoveries are provided for in up-front communication, disputes are likely to arise.

In formal alliances, often there are contractual provisions for ownership of intellectual capital and provisions for how knowledge will be shared. In the chip alliance between IBM, Infineon, and Toshiba, explicit provisions exist for shared intellectual capital, explains Laura Rothman, Technical Controller for the alliance. The contract explicitly points out how technical content will be shared and with which parties. It also provides for other types of knowledge that are captured in the process of working together, such as lessons learned or process knowledge. This type of knowledge is termed "residuals" in the contract. Rothman says that careful communication around details such as these have helped contribute to the success of the 10-year alliance.

But alliance partners have to avoid slowing themselves down or creating difficulties because of too-stringent restrictions on communication. Jeff Weiss of Vantage Partners recalls the example of a major technology alliance that experienced significant problems with information sharing and communication: "The companies had very strict rules about what got shared by whom and with whom. While there were some very good reasons for the partners to be careful, the particular ways they set up the rules made it extremely difficult for the codevelopment teams to work effectively together."

Alliance partners aren't the only people you'll be codeveloping intellectual capital with. The Internet is enabling unprecedented new relationships between customers and businesses. Through their participation on websites, customers are now helping companies create information and knowledge which the companies then sell or use to attract other customers. For example, at Consumerreview.com, customers provide reviews of products that the company then repackages in a structured format and resells to other websites. This raises an interesting question: When customers communicate and share knowledge with you through your website, who owns it?

Many companies that have interactive websites automatically make the assumption that the information customers share on their sites belongs to the company that owns the website. Bill Machrone, VP of Technology at Ziff Davis Media, says that ZDM owns the pages for its website, so any ideas that are shared on the website belong to it.

We try to get readers to talk to us and among themselves as much as possible so that almost every story that we write, every column, has a talk-back that allows them to post their responses. It's very heavily used in some areas. For example, some columnists like John C. Dvorak are intentionally provocative, and they get a tremendous amount of talk-back . . . . What the readers post publicly on our site belongs to us because we own copyright on all the pages.

Machrone readily admits that customers are generating a product through their participation on-line: "By putting their comments on-line, and because of the fact that other readers take the time to read their comments, they are creating a portion of our product. Is it ancillary, is it secondary, is it tertiary? Yes. But they're still creating a product."

I'm intrigued to see how long it will take before customers start becoming more hip to the fact that they're doing product creation. Along those lines, I asked Greg Lee, VP of Marketing at Consumer review.com, how they reward customers for their participation. Essentially their customers generate their product: consumer reviews of a variety of products for home and outdoors. Lee responded, "All these guys feel rewarded in the sense that we're providing them with a forum to share their experiences as well as gain valuable knowledge from others, whether it's in the review forums, the discussion groups, or the marketplace [where enthusiasts can buy and sell their used equipment]. The neat thing about having highly passionate people is that they're always looking to sell their old stuff to get new stuff, and so we have quite a vibrant marketplace. This is of value to them."

I also pushed Bill Machrone to speculate about what they'd do in a case where someone gave them valuable information in an on-line forum. He quipped, "Well, if someone gave us a business idea and we built a new $250 million business on it, I'd definitely send the guy a fruit basket." We both had a good laugh over this comment, but it started me thinking. For now, participation in on-line forums is relatively novel. Therefore, issues of ownership or rewards for participation haven't been frequently raised. However, I think companies should consider these issues before they become problems, by being vocal and explicit in their agreements with customers about who owns the information on their sites, and by think–ing through how they will reward customers for their role in product development.

Enabling Customers to Share Information with Each Other.   Suppliermarket. com is a company that provides an on-line marketplace for people who buy and sell manufactured parts. Bill Sheehan, Vice President of Busi-ness Development at Suppliermarket.com, explains that sometimes cus-tomers on the buy side are reluctant to share drawings for parts they want manufactured. Usually these drawings contain engineering specifics, and they think of these as their intellectual capital. Supplier market.com deals with this issue by having suppliers sign a nondisclo-sure agreement when they register, and they also allow buyers to select specific companies to make bids, so they know precisely who the draw-ings are going to. But there's a tradeoff to the latter decision because the buyers may not get the best price bid from suppliers when they restrict the bidding process to companies they know instead of opening the market to new companies that may provide a better deal.

Buzzsaw.com also makes a business out of providing a forum and a vehicle for knowledge sharing across organizational boundaries. Con-struction project teams use Buzzsaw.com's website and software to share project information. "A construction project is one big set of interrelated tasks that you have to try to manage as a group. Adding to the complex-ity of that is the fact that none of these people work in the same company, and they don't typically work together for long periods of time. So there's just a lot of forces that are acting against them having a really good com-munication infrastructure. We provide that infrastructure for them," says Jason Pratt, Director of Product Marketing for the company.

Anne Bonaparte, cofounder of Buzzsaw.com, says the idea of shared intellectual capital in the construction industry is raising some inter-esting issues:

The question of knowledge management is really an interesting one. Typically, at the end of a building project a lot of the knowl-

edge goes away and the owner's sort of left with just the building. They get a set of drawings, but it's really uneven, even with that. Sometimes there's even a debate over those drawings. You would think that because the owners paid for those drawings, they could expect to have ownership of them. The architects want to own the drawings because they want the owner to come back to them to do the modifications for the next remodel. Some owners want the drawings so they have the flexibility to go to another architect. I think in the end the owner owns the information, but often the drawings aren't archived electronically. Sometimes owners have to hire other architects just to get floor plans done because they're not kept anywhere . . . New knowledge sharing technologies are going to open a bunch of questions for this industry.

Managers in dotcoms and b-webs need to be particularly careful not to get caught in the middle of knowledge sharing disputes among their customers. By proactively helping customers to think through issues of knowledge sharing and by facilitating productive, up-front discussions, companies can add tremendous value to customer relationships.

Taking Risks.   There's no getting around the fact that there's a risk to sharing information, but what it boils down to is how much you trust the party you're dealing with, and what the rewards are to taking the risk.

Phil Harkins, CEO of Linkage Inc., says that many of the problems related to intellectual property and intellectual capital have to do with the fact that both parties aren't being completely honest about what they want and need in the up-front negotiation of an alliance. If they have concerns about intellectual capital, often they won't say anything for fear of blowing a deal. Says Harkins: "They think, I don't want to screw things up, so we'll solve that later, we'll get to it."

Dan Fitz of Cable & Wireless says that it's not only that people are afraid to ask for what they want, but also that sometimes they don't even *know* what they want: "When people are in a situation where too little information is being shared, it's often because they aren't clear about what they want out of the alliance. Because unless you're clear about what you want, you can't be sure what information is relevant to the negotiation and what's irrelevant."

In the vast majority of cases, companies focus on the risks of sharing too much information rather than thinking about the problems of sharing too little. As we've seen throughout this book, sharing information with all of your relevant stakeholders can bring huge benefits, and a lack of information can often ensure failure. As interactive managers begin to work more with companies outside their normal boundaries, much more serious consideration needs to be given to sharing instead of protecting. As Phil Harkins notes, paranoia about information sharing is a dated way of thinking:

> **In the old days, you put guards around your company, and you weren't willing to share anything because someone would steal your ideas. Now companies recognize that their real value is in their ability to execute ideas. So in a way, it doesn't matter so much about what you share about your strategies, it's whether or not you can innovate and execute. And I think that the organizations that have learned how to innovate are the ones that have learned how to share and trust.**

Interactive managers will increasingly need to develop this competency of engaging people across boundaries. It's all too easy to think of the people in just your department, your division, or your company, when it comes to communicating. When you're putting together a cross-boundary project team, or working in a b-web, or forming a strategic alliance, give special consideration to engaging all the people who have a stake in the outcome.

Key Ideas from Chapter 11

- Mergers, acquisitions, joint ventures, strategic alliances, and outsourcing present significant challenges in terms of communication and knowledge sharing.
- The b-web is an emerging form of organization that raises new issues with regard to cross-boundary communication.
- Relationship managers can add value to all forms of alliances.
- Extranets, web conferencing, and mega-conversations can be helpful in managing across boundaries.

Engaging people across boundaries is the last of the ten competencies for managing interactively. As you face the challenges of managing in a new business era, developing skills in each of these ten areas will help you to connect, inform, and engage people in your company and across your business ecosystem.

Practical Strategies for
Smart Communication

THROUGHOUT THIS BOOK, we've looked at competencies for communicating and managing your organization more effectively. In Chapter 12 we'll see how these concepts apply at the top of an organization. Several executives, including Bill Esrey, the Chairman and CEO of Sprint, and Gerry Laybourne, the CEO of Oxygen Media, share their insights. Their stories reflect a number of the principles set forth in Parts I through III.

The book closes with practical ideas on how to start managing interactively tomorrow.

Interactive Leadership: Insights from Four Top Executives

YOU CAN MANAGE interactively whether you're a department supervisor, a division president, or a CEO. The competencies and skills in this book apply at all levels of an organization. However, special challenges face the top executive who needs to interact with hundreds or even thousands of people. This chapter reveals how the following four executives manage interactively in their organizations:

Bill Esrey, Chairman and CEO of Sprint, is a highly interactive, well-respected leader who understands the difference between ordering versus engaging and who has a fascinating perspective on how to stay connected to 78,000 people at Sprint.

Gerry Laybourne is the CEO of Oxygen Media, a new venture aimed at bridging two media: the Internet and cable television. Oxygen's content is aimed primarily at women, and the goal of this venture is to build an interactive community of women around the issues and ideas that they care about. Laybourne, the creator of Nickelodeon, and a former Disney executive, truly understands the concept of interactivity, and not only applies it in her style of management, but also in the way she is building the business at Oxygen.

Ed Miller, CEO, and Mike Hegarty, Senior Vice Chairman and COO, of AXA Financial, have worked as an interactive top executive team for years. First they worked together at Manufacturer's Hanover, then Chemical Bank, then Chase. Now they are heading up AXA Financial, which owns Equitable Insurance among a number of other entities. You'll hear from Miller and Hegarty about the challenges of interactively building a brand and building alignment across a massive international organization.

What all of these leaders share is a deep appreciation for the creativity and intelligence of the people they work with, a willingness to listen and interact with those people in innovative ways, and a strong focus on candor in their communication.

In this chapter, they talk about the challenges of managing interactively at top levels, how they find ways of listening and encouraging dialogue, how they gain alignment through interactive processes in their organizations, and what they consider to be some of the most important personal characteristics of an interactive leader.

Ordering Versus Engaging

One of the most difficult aspects of managing interactively at top levels is that people expect CEOs to tell others what to do. It's hard for some people to realize that a top executive doesn't have all the answers, and that they're not there to simply issue orders. Bill Esrey tells the story of how some community leaders had a hard time understanding his interactive approach regarding affirmative action at Sprint:

> **A couple of years ago when we were first building our new campus, Reverend Wallace Hartsfield, who is the Chairman of the Congress of National Black Churches, came to us and challenged us on our numbers with regards to employment of African Americans. When we looked into it, he was right. We were, of course, hiring African Americans, but there were some issues around the positions they were hired for, etc. So we wanted to take action on this, and we have.**
>
> **Our dialogue with the African American community has been going on for about a year and a half, and all along the way they've been concerned about the rate of change. For example, the com-**

munity brought in Jesse Jackson to put some pressure on us to get the numbers up. What I keep saying is, "Well, we're not going to operate that way. We're going to do what we think is right. We'd like to work with you because you have good ideas and you can show us some things that we could do better. And we're going to get these numbers up because it's the right thing to do. But I'm not just going to issue the order to hire a specific number of African Americans for specific positions. I don't believe in that as a style of management. I don't think it works." This was frustrating to Hartsfield and the other leaders because they couldn't understand why I wouldn't simply *order* people to start hiring.

You see, the thing is, I can't just tell people to do this. What we've done instead is create training programs, change policies, hold discussions with people, and try to weave it into the way we work. We want to change the culture. And it's starting to happen. Recently I sat down with Hartsfield and we pulled out the numbers. Frankly, it's startling what's happened in just a year and a half in terms of how many total African Americans we have and how many African American managers we now have. So I asked Hartsfield, "If we had sat here a year and a half ago and agreed together on objectives, would you have imagined setting them anywhere near this high?" And he said no. His original idea was: It's a big company, you're the big boss, tell them to do it. That's just not how you get real change in a company.

Gerry Laybourne says people at different levels of an organization are often uncomfortable with the concept of an interactive CEO: "A lot of people just want you to tell them their job. But if you're managing interactively, you have to let people figure out their jobs for themselves within the context you've created. It's messy and a bit chaotic at times. Remember, most people grew up in a pretty hierarchical family situation, where Mom and Dad said what was what. It's not easy to get people to break out of that mold and take responsibility for their contribution to setting direction. Interactive management is way harder than hierarchical management, but you don't have a choice in this new business environment. Any traditional hierarchical manager is a goner."

It took time for employees at AXA Financial to adjust to Ed Miller and Mike Hegarty's interactive style of management when they first arrived at the company, then known as The Equitable Companies Inc. Hegarty explains:

> **When we first came here, people wouldn't ask questions when we opened things up for discussion. Or if they did ask questions, it would be about things like benefits and pensions and stuff like that. So we started telling people, "We're going to come up with some questions we think you might want answered, but after we address those, we expect *you* to ask some questions." And we made certain that the questions we started out with were really tough questions, things we thought they were really wondering about. After a while we didn't have to do any staged questions, they started asking more penetrating questions themselves. But it took some time to convince them that we wanted real interaction, not just the easy lay-up questions.**

Getting people in an organization to make the shift to accepting an interactive style of management isn't always easy, but these executives all insist that it's the only way to go in a fluid, fast-paced business world. And getting people to accept an interactive approach on the part of top executives is just the first step in the process. These executives want to encourage the development of an interactive management environment at all levels of the organization by modeling the style they want others to adopt. To that end, Bill Esrey says he and his management team hold interactive sessions to try and encourage people to adopt a similar approach:

> **What we're really trying to do is let people know that there's no question that's out of bounds, there's no question that's inappropriate, there are no ideas we want to throw out before we've had a chance to consider them. This is the message we're trying to deliver. And what you hope is that they then do the same thing with the people they work with, and that this attitude will spread throughout the company.**

Interactive Listening

Whether you're trying to listen to 600 or 60,000 people, it's difficult to do when you're at the top of an organization. A variety of things make it hard to interact with a good cross-section of people: time constraints, people's reluctance to cross hierarchical lines, isolation because of travel schedules, etc. But effective interactive executives know they have to find creative ways to listen and learn from people in all parts of the organization.

Bill Esrey explains the obvious problem in very large organizations:

Any leader of a large company today has a huge challenge in communicating. I remember an employee once said to me, "Gee Mr. Esrey, we've never seen you. How come you haven't gotten out to my workplace before?" And his question prompted me to sit down and figure out the answer. I did a rough calculation and concluded that if I went to every workplace and I went to five a day, it would take me something like four years doing nothing but that full-time to get around to every site. It's physically impossible in a large company that's spread out like ours to go around and visit everyone. It doesn't take a rocket scientist to figure out that it's difficult to interact with 78,000 people; what's more challenging is to figure out what you're going to do about it.

Esrey attacks his listening challenge through a variety of media and techniques. He says one of the most effective approaches he uses involves holding a series of meetings with 50 to 70 people at a time. He finds this to be a good number for encouraging a high level of interaction in the sessions: "When we first announced the merger with MCI WorldComm, Ron LeMay, our President and Chief Operating Officer, and I realized that we needed to get out and interact with lots of people. So everywhere we went, we scheduled employee meetings. I like meetings of 50 to 70 people because you can connect better."

Esrey admits he can only hit a small sample of people with these interactive meetings but notes that the word then spreads. "You have to be interactive, though," he warns. "You can't just broadcast a message. Because when you interact with people, when you listen to them and answer them thoughtfully, then they internalize what you discuss. Then when someone you haven't reached is saying something that's not on target, what happens is that a person who attended one of the meetings will say, 'Well, listen, I was at a meeting with Esrey two weeks ago, and I don't believe what you're saying, because this is what *I* heard him say.' You have to establish your credibility as a messenger and you can only do that through a lot of interaction, not through broadcasts."

One of the more innovative approaches to encouraging interaction and interactive listening is what Esrey refers to as a "catalyst conference." As part of an effort to introduce some new concepts around changes in organizational structure, and resulting personnel shifts, Esrey and Sprint President Ron LeMay held a series of four meetings with the top 1000 people in the company, with 250 people attending each session. Small groups of attendees each had PCs that were hooked to a large screen at the front of the room. The technology allowed people to ask anonymous questions. Esrey says it was a way of opening up an interactive listening channel with a large number of people all at once: "We asked them what was on their minds, what we should be doing differently. We got really great questions, provocative questions, and we also used interactive voting technology to poll them for their opinions on different topics." (See Figure 12-1.)

The interactive nature of the sessions was what really made a difference, says Esrey: "We made the sessions completely interactive. We

Figure 12-1   Sprint Chairman and CEO Bill Esrey at a Catalyst Conference
Source: Photo courtesy of Sprint

purposefully created an environment with no barriers. Ron and I sat on stools in the middle of the room. We didn't want to sit in chairs behind a table or stand behind a lectern. It was real time and it was participatory, not canned."

Esrey also uses video conferencing to reach people in interactive meetings. And sometimes he uses a more basic technology: the telephone. "I don't do nearly enough of this, but I really try to," he says. "When I read something about an employee, I'll just pick up the phone and call them. When you connect with one person like that, you can learn a lot, and also the word really spreads."

Use a variety of techniques and approaches, says Esrey. "The one thing you can't do is use one medium and do it top down," he warns. "Because no message really gets through that way."

While Gerry Laybourne's organization is significantly smaller in size, she still faces challenges knowing what the 700 people in her organization are thinking. Laybourne found a novel way of listening to them when she and her husband Kit started Oxygen: "We did something really smart when we started this company. We hired five kids straight out of college who were really bright. And we put them in a windowless conference room and had them map the web for us. It was this giant room covered with maps, and every Friday, they taught us about what they had learned. It was really a reversal of the listening process. You know, we're the 50-year-olds and they're the 23-year-olds. And it was exciting. We learned a tremendous amount from them."

A mentoring program for high potential employees at Sprint affords Bill Esrey an opportunity to listen. "One of the good things about this program is that you get to see the organization through a different person's eyes really closely, because we work together every day, all day, and you do that over a year's time. You begin to see things that you don't normally see. As an executive you get a lot of people saying, 'Yes, Mr. Esrey, everything you do is wonderful.' After you've worked with someone awhile, that kind of formality drops away."

Esrey says that working with someone less experienced in business is helpful to developing your sensitivity as a listener and a leader. He explains:

Sometimes Mark [Kenyon, Esrey's executive assistant] will ask a question, and I'll think to myself, "That's a stupid question." Of

course, I'm smart enough not to *say* this. And then as I ponder it for a moment, I realize it's not really stupid coming from that person's point of view. The problem is that I haven't explained something very well, not that the question is wrong. Over the decades of working, something becomes secondhand to me, but it's new for that person. By working with a variety of types of people at different levels of the organization, you start to understand the type of things other people are wrestling with. You try to put yourself in the other person's position and listen from their point of view, not from your point of view. There's a big difference.

It's important to develop this listening sensitivity in order to stay in touch with an organization. "I'll give you an example," says Esrey. "You know, most CEOs are financially independent. They forget about all those years when they weren't. They forget that people have financial worries. And yet it is a *huge* consideration for a majority of people who are working for you. It's important to get out there and be reminded of what people are experiencing, and having your eyes and mind opened. It keeps you in touch. Because, let me tell you, it's really easy to get out of touch with your organization."

Interactive listening involves creating a physical environment that encourages it, as we discussed in Chapter 4. Mike Hegarty explains that when they hold meetings to listen to people at AXA Financial, it's critically important to put them in the right physical environment: "Instead of having people sit in audience rows, we group people at tables of eight—like a luncheon. And then we say to people, 'Okay, you're the team captain for your table, and during lunch I want your table to come up with two questions.' It really works for changing the nature of the interaction."

Gerry Laybourne has carried this concept of an interactive listening environment into Oxygen's headquarters, right down to her office: "I majored in art history with a strong concentration in architecture history. I originally wanted to be an architect.... I believe that places communicate to people." Laybourne's office has a glass window that opens into the interior of the building, so she can have both an interactive view and a way of physically opening up part of the wall of her office to interact with people. Originally, she wanted to have an entire wall that would open and retract—a kind of garage door that would open her office up into the center of the building, but allow for privacy when she needed it. The garage door was an extremely expensive prospect, so she settled for the interior window. "I like to be in the open," says Laybourne. "I don't like to be shut away."

Aligning and Engaging People

We've discussed the centrality of alignment and engagement to interactive management in Parts II and III. Interactive executives struggle with these same issues at their level of the organization.

At AXA Financial, Miller and Hegarty have an interesting approach. They believe in aligning around their brand positioning strategy, as we saw in Chapter 9 in our discussion of unifying concepts. "When we say 'brand positioning' around here, most people think we're talking advertising, but we're really talking about reengineering and realigning the company around what the experience of AXA is from a client point of view," says Hegarty. "The brand is the essence of who the company is and what the company does. We try to get everything in the company, all of the internal and external activities, aligned around that." Miller concurs: "I see myself as keeper of the brand, but I partner with Mike [Hegarty] to handle brand issues. We have to make sure that the customer's experience is consistent with the message we're sending them, and on the internal side we have to make sure that people are doing things that will allow customers to *have* that experience."

This is a highly interactive, iterative process. Miller and Hegarty are the "facilitators." They constantly seek the input of the organization in constructing and evolving the brand message, and in making sure the message is articulated in a way that allows the activities of the organization to be easily aligned around it.

"What we've done differently from many companies, and I think it's very important, is that we've *engaged* the organization," says Miller. "Ultimately, I had 230 people who were involved in one way or another in the strategic planning process and the definition of the key initiatives. Then when it came time to execute the strategy, these were people who believed in it. They'd been part of the process of creating it, they had credibility with other people in the organization, and they were committed to communicating it to others. Ninety percent of strategy is in the execution."

As part of executing the strategy, Miller and Hegarty also use an interactive business review meeting to sit down with people and hear how they are performing against their objectives and how what they're doing aligns with the overall company strategy. "When people come to these meetings, they'll bring a whole team of people who work for them to deal with those issues," says Miller. "So it brings a larger number of people in the room, and that helps with communicating the message because it means that fewer people have to hear the message second-hand. The key group of people who are really responsible for making something happen are in the room."

Like interactive managers, interactive executives also struggle with the problems of gaining alignment across boundaries. Bill Esrey notes that it's particularly difficult to get alignment in alliances and joint ventures: "Getting alignment in these looser confederations of organizations is an enormous challenge. And many times they're not effective in the end. We have as much experience with these kinds of alliances as anybody, and we find them to be very, very difficult." Esrey did not have any easy answers to the problems posed by engaging people in an alliance, but he did refer to the importance of shared purpose and relationship managers, two concepts we mentioned in Chapter 11: "Most alliances don't work unless there's a real need for the parties to work together. Without a very clear purpose, it doesn't work. And even when that purpose is clear up front, things can change. You have to continue to need each other.... And you need to have a core group of people who are responsible for communicating across the joint venture or the alliance. You have to have people who make sure the companies responsible for creating the alliance or joint venture are well-aligned and clear in their communication. Otherwise the messages get confused."

Getting Over Yourself as an Executive

It's a challenge to develop the ability to get over yourself as a manager. This is even more difficult when you've reached the pinnacle of an organization. The executives I spoke with mentioned several key characteristics that interactive executives need in order to succeed: candor, respect, self-knowledge, and humility. These characteristics correspond directly to the skills discussed in Chapter 6.

Candor

All of the executives mentioned candor as being crucial to credibility and building effective organizations. Esrey says his father instilled the importance of candor and honesty in him many years ago:

> **My dad talked a lot about integrity. He said people can take a lot of things away from you, but they can't take away your honesty. Only *you* can lose that. And he said if you ever once distort the truth or lie, then people will never be sure whether or not you're going to do that again. He was right. Honesty is critically important to a leader because when everybody can't get to know you personally, they're going to know you through your reputation. And there's a lot of things we can't control as leaders, but we can control whether we're honest and straightforward. You can't focus on creating an "image." You have to let people see you as yourself and make their own judgments.**

Esrey also says it's important to encourage candor in others: "I know we're really going to get somewhere when I say something and someone says, 'Bill, that's the craziest thing I've ever heard.' I love that! Then we're engaged in a dialogue. You have to work hard to instill that because people are often afraid you're going to jump down their throats."

Laybourne says encouraging people to be candid in replaying their mistakes can be extremely helpful to a learning organization: "We've got a weekly executive meeting that's an open dialogue. Two of the top people on my team told me at this meeting that they are instituting what they call a 'deal process learning session.' They bring together all the people who work on putting together deals for us. What really makes those sessions valuable is when people are willing to replay their mistakes. One juicy mistake, if you talk about it in the right way, can have learning value across your entire business."

Laybourne also says that candor is critical when an interactive executive is preparing people for bad news:

We took a big risk when we launched this company. We launched it when it wasn't really cooked. A conventional media company would have waited another eight months. A lot of people, including the press, want things to be perfect when you launch, but I knew we needed to do it this way in order to learn some valuable lessons. So the night before our television launch, I called the staff to the center hall here and said, "Look, so far we've gotten nothing but great press. We've been the darlings of the media, and tomorrow that is going to change. We are going to get hit from all sides, but we're going to get through it." You have to put it all right out there. This is the hardest management I've ever done, it's messy. But throughout the process, you've got to let people know what's really going on.

Respect

In addition to candor, interactive executives have to model a high level of respect for others. Ed Miller points out that this can sometimes be a difficult issue when you're working across cultures. The parent company for AXA Financial is based in France, and Miller noted that this initially required individuals from each country to develop respect for, and understanding of, their colleagues. "It's really easy for people to gain a mistaken impression or interpretation due to different cultural business practices," says Miller. "For example, in France their business meetings tend to be more formal and there's very little brainstorming. In the United States we're more informal at our meetings and we brainstorm. The French talk to each other during meetings, some people call them 'concurrent minimeetings.' Americans tend to oversimplify things. So you have to have respect for each other and how you work; otherwise you'll have a hard time encouraging interaction."

Miller gives another example of the importance of respect for different types of backgrounds: "I knew this guy, years ago, who ran a branch banking division right before I came in to take it over. He was always asking people out in the branches where they went to college. He had no idea it was intimidating to them. He thought he was just being friendly and getting to know them. But most of those people in the branches didn't go to college, so if you asked them what college they went to, you're on the wrong foot to begin with. I come from Brooklyn, and I knew the boroughs, and I think that's been really useful to me in terms of being able to respect people from a variety of different backgrounds. That's very important to establishing a rapport and interacting with people."

Self-knowledge

I mentioned earlier that self-knowledge is critical to interactive management. Gerry Laybourne says it is important to understand your strengths and weaknesses as a leader. "I learned a tremendous amount from an executive coach I worked with for a number of years," she says. "For example, one of my gifts is that I'm able to go into a room without my mind made up, which is very hard for most executives, because many of them are very targeted and directed and just want to make things happen. I'm naturally a good listener, but I had to discipline myself about being more forceful in presenting ideas to people, and I have to surround myself with people who are targeted and results-driven."

"If you want people to be engaged," says Mike Hegarty, "you have to have inclusive, participative processes for decision-making, and you have to lead people through a process of self-discovery. It's not that Ed Miller has the answers or Mike Hegarty has the answers; it's the energy of a whole lot of people coming to a collective answer. And they have to discover that answer for themselves."

Humility

Another important quality mentioned by interactive executives that is closely connected to self-knowledge is humility. Ed Miller says he learned humility in the military:

> When I was in basic training, I was selected as a potential candidate to go for pilot training. Of course, this was a big honor and I was very excited about it. But upon returning to our barracks after receiving that news, the basic training instructor said to the five of us who had just been selected, "So you think you're going to be officers and pilots in *my* Marine Corps? You think you're *intelligent* because you got selected for pilot school? Well, let me tell you something. Because of your high level of intelligence, I have a special job for all of you for the next four weeks."

And you know what we did? We changed the lightbulbs and cleaned the ceilings. For four weeks. Ultimately, I flunked the eye test and never attended pilot training. I learned humility in the Marines. I learned to avoid developing a sense of arrogance.

Mike Hegarty learned a lesson in humility after passing judgment on two other executives: "I was in a meeting once listening to two executives get peppered with questions about their strategy. They were very tense and their attitude was, 'It's in the annual report, you can read it.' And I shook my head thinking, 'Wow, they just don't get it.' A month or two later I was at a cocktail reception for about 300 people in my new organization and this young woman came up to me and proceeded to tell me there was a real lack of communication and organization and process improvement in her area. She had come over from Citibank six months ago and she said they had it there, but it was lacking here. Well. She was talking about *my* area now. And I thought back to my position as an outsider observing those other executives and thinking I understood it all, and suddenly I realized, 'Gee, maybe I better make sure that *I* get it.' "

Humility is important because leading without it can make it difficult to manage interactively. Bill Esrey tells a story of discovering how disconnected people had gotten in one division of his organization and the likely impact on the organization:

I don't remember where exactly we were going, but I was riding somewhere with a group of executives from one division of the company for a meeting. We had to stop for gas and so I jumped out of the car and started filling up the tank. When I got back in the car, they all looked at me, astonished. I couldn't figure out why they were looking at me so funny. It turns out they were amazed that I would get out and pump the gas because I was the CEO. Can you believe that? Well, that told me right away, "Boy, have we got a problem in *that* division," because from their perspective, the boss was better than everyone else. Now how are you going to encourage an interactive approach in that kind of organization? How can someone feel a sense of equality and know that their ideas are respected if you have things like that going on? I recognize the importance of a hierarchy to decision-making and that somebody's got to be responsible for making a decision in the end,

but how you get there is very, very important. And if you try to get there by waiting for someone else to fill the gas tank, you're not going about it the right way. You're not going to get the interaction from people that you need for making the *right* decisions.

While executives face special challenges, certain things are the same when you attempt to manage interactively, regardless of your level of management. Engaging people requires an atmosphere of equality, clarity of purpose, and creative approaches to bring it all together.

What Should You Do Tomorrow?

Today's INTERNET-ENABLED business environment requires a change in management style. How is this environment different?

- You're often managing people who don't report to you—in virtual teams, b-webs, alliances, and outsourcing relationships.
- Attitudes toward power and authority in organizations are changing—people are no longer willing to be passive recipients of directives or messages.
- Scarcity of attention makes it harder to engage people.
- It's increasingly difficult to tailor information for diverse audiences.
- Increased focus on intellectual capital highlights the value of knowledge sharing, and knowledge sharing is more about people than databases.
- New technologies require the development of new on-line communication skills.

In an interactive world, you need to manage interactively. And managing interactively is about communication—connecting, informing, and engaging people. You need to give as much attention to your ability to communicate as you give to your balance sheet or budget.

Some managers seek compliance with memos and speeches and inch-thick strategic plans. How often have you heard the words, "Well, we already told them that"? Telling isn't enough. Corporate cheerleading campaigns are usually greeted with skepticism or even cynicism. Broadcast e-mails get lost in the noise. Managers and executives need new skills and competencies to cope with a new environment.

Whatever business you're in or the position you hold, communication is more important than ever to your success. Communication in an interactive world must move beyond persuasion. Effective communication engages people in a dialogue to help develop and execute strategy in an organization. It's about moving beyond buy-in to *ownership* of innovative ideas and strategies. And it can have multimillion dollar results—as seen in the stories from this book.

Communication Competencies for Managing Interactively

Interactive managers consciously work to connect, inform, and engage people. They apply specific methods and technologies to make the greatest use of the intellectual capital in their organizations.

Interactive managers are able to:

- Make people and their knowledge accessible throughout an organization or business web
- Share power with people at all levels of an organization
- Design on-line and physical environments that enhance collaboration
- Create effective rituals and experiences that build cultures
- Actively use key interpersonal skills
- Make information available, useful, and enticing to a variety of stakeholders
- Use stories in innovative ways to both share and capture knowledge
- Resolve hidden conflicts between actions and words
- Listen to a whole organization
- Engage people across organizational boundaries

How and Where to Start

This book presents a range of ideas, methods, and technologies for immediately improving your ability to manage interactively. Some methods are as simple as changing the way you construct your e-mails. Others require a larger investment of time and effort—like holding a mega-conversation or implementing a new interactive technology.

To determine where to start, consider the following approach:

1. Identify your key business goals and consider them from a communication perspective.
2. Review the methods and technologies for interactive management.
3. Focus on the options most relevant to your business objectives and start with a manageable project.

Identify Your Key Business Goals and Consider Them from a Communication Perspective

Interactive management incorporates effective communication approaches into the practice of management. In much the same way that you might examine your business processes, you also need to take into account how effective communication will help you get things done.

Develop a list of your most pressing business goals—your critical success factors. For each, consider how you need to connect, inform, and engage people in order to make them happen. Are you trying to promote an innovation in your company's business model? Do you need to encourage people to share their ideas with others? Is there a concept that needs explaining where a visual approach will help? Is it important to include your b-web partners in formulating or implementing your strategy? Once you have a clear picture of how communication plays a role in making the strategy happen, you will be able to match an appropriate method or technology to the communication challenge.

Review the Methods and Technologies for Interactive Management

Technologies and methods are seductive. People often adopt a particular method simply because it's the latest fad or because it worked in another company. This is particularly true for technology, where people often make decisions about what they want based on an airline magazine article.

Target your business priorities and then match them to a method or technology. For example, if you're in the midst of a merger or acquisition, you'll need to connect people in the newly merged organization who don't know each other, inform people about how the merger is progressing, and engage them in working together to make the merger successful. Next, analyze the techniques and technologies associated with connecting, informing, and engaging people. (Figure 13-1 provides some examples.)

To *connect* people you may want to use expertise location software. To *inform* people you may want to hold meetings where a graphics facilitator creates mental models of a shared vision for the newly merged companies. To *engage* people, mega-conversations held throughout the merger process could help get people to work and communicate more effectively as a newly formed team. Depending upon your priorities, select a technique or technology.

Focus on the Options that Seem Most Relevant and Start with a Manageable Project

When I see people successfully implement new ideas, they've almost always done a good job of scoping the project. There are a lot of ideas in this book. Implementing any of them could probably improve your management effectiveness, but it's important to think through what's most important to your business. Whatever methods or technologies you choose, be sure they're attached to a clear business priority.

Here's an example of how this process might work. Suppose your three most important critical success factors are to build your company's brand, complete an acquisition, and develop an e-business strategy. The first step is to decide which of these three things is most important. You choose building your company's brand.

The next step would be to determine the critical steps involved in building the brand—in other words, get more specific. For example, you might need to develop an advertising campaign, host focus groups, or initiate a program to create internal brand awareness. Once again you'll need to set priorities. Assuming you choose an advertising campaign, think next about how you'll need to connect, inform, or engage people to put together a great campaign. Brainstorm this with your coworkers and determine once again what your priorities are. Do you need to connect internal people with an external advertising agency? Perhaps an on-line discussion group would be helpful. Do you need to collect customer stories? You may want to consider using storytelling technologies like the ones described in Chapter 8. Could you possibly

TECHNOLOGIES

-Web Conferencing
-Chatrooms and On-line Discussion Groups
-Augmented Meetings
-Expertise Locations
-Video and Audio Conferencing
-E-mail, Voice Mail, and Instant
 Messaging

CONNECT

TECHNIQUES

-Conduct a stakeholder analysis
-Develop an internal consultancy to leverage expertise
-Initiate and nurture communities of practice, purpose,
 interest, learning or support
-Alter your physical environment to be flexible,
 purposeful, stimulating, and comfortable

TECHNOLOGIES

-E-mail   -Outline Editors
-Proxy Software   -Pattern Recognition Software
-Intranets   -Augmented Meetings
-Digital Mini-films   -Video and Audio Conferencing
-Web Conferencing

INFORM

TECHNIQUES

-Create a "911" location for knowlege sharing
-Conduct a media match exercise
-Create mental models with visual language techniques
-Structure information carefully
-Gather anecdotes and construct stories to share
 values, shape culture, and build your brand
-Develop clear and simple unifying concepts based on
 brand, values, vision, and purpose
-Conduct an analysis to ensure alignment between
 actions and words
-Compile and review knowledge using an After Action
 Learning approach.

TECHNOLOGIES

-Extranets
-Audio and Video Conferencing
-On-line Discussion Groups
-E-mail and Voice Mail
-Web Conferencing

ENGAGE

TECHNIQUES

-Conduct large group events
-Designate relationship managers
-Create shared space
-Clarify alliance ground rules, roles, and responsibilities
-Co-develop approaches to sharing information across
 organizational boundaries

Figure 13-1   Techniques and Technologies to Connect, Inform, and Engage

Source: Boone Associates © 2001

engage customers in helping you think through the ad campaign? Perhaps a mega-conversation with a variety of external stakeholders would be useful. Establish where you need to start and then look at the techniques and technologies associated with connecting, informing, and engaging people.

You may have the resources and capabilities to implement more than one idea at once, but I'd suggest starting with the most exciting possibility. It's critical to choose a project that's manageable. Don't try to bring in new technology, hold a mega-conversation, and work on your personal communication skills all at once. Start small and then add to your repertoire.

Be Interactive

You can start tomorrow by simply remembering one concept: be interactive.

At its core, interactive management is about listening and being heard. If you're in a position of power, chances are you'll need to focus more on listening. If you're not in a position of formal power, you'll probably need to think more about speaking up.

Remember, interactive management is not about putting things up for a vote or postponing decisions for extensive discussions. Interactive management is about communicating effectively and leveraging the intellectual capital in your organization.

When you're at work, consider *all* of your stakeholders and find innovative ways to include them in your management process. When you make presentations, write memos, begin change management efforts, send e-mail, or attend meetings, make all of these forms of communication more interactive. Encourage your coworkers to become interactive first by setting the tone yourself and then rewarding them for interactive approaches.

As you start to manage interactively, it will become instinctive. You'll naturally share power. You'll ask more than tell. Technologies you haven't used before will come to mind when you're putting together a project. You'll catch yourself when you're too focused on sending messages instead of harnessing the power of lateral communication among your employees.

In the end, you'll obviously still make your own decisions, but you won't overlook the tremendous contributions that others have to make to that process. You also won't overlook the fact that quite often, even if you're at the top of an organization, there are new things to learn from just about everyone you meet. You'll talk with them, and you'll listen to them.

The business world will always be complex and fast-paced. To keep up, you'll need to take advantage of interactive technologies, tap into the wellspring of creativity and knowledge in your organizations and partnerships, and find new ways of absorbing and acting on an ever-increasing amount of information. If you can "be interactive," you'll gain the support you need for meeting your management challenges.

And I mean what I say about interacting. The book in your hand is only a beginning. You're invited to visit my company's website at *www.maryboone.com* to share your thoughts and get an update on these ideas from other managers and executives.

Additional Large Group Approaches

IN CHAPTER 10, I mentioned that there are numerous large group methods, and that the book *Large Group Interventions* is the best place to go to get a good overview. However, in the course of interviewing people for this book, I came across some additional approaches worth investigating. Here is a brief explanation of these approaches.

Strategic Visioning™.   This is a large group method designed by David Sibbet, a group graphics consultant and the inventor of visual grammar. It draws on four change management methodologies: strategic planning, visioning, large-scale change processes, and graphic facilitation. There are seven stages to the Strategic Visioning process, and each step in the process involves a series of conversations that are augmented by the use of group graphics to capture the ideas of the group on a large mural, which are fed back to the group in the form of a "map."

Sibbet has used this method to start mega-conversations in a variety of organizations, including Levi-Strauss and Netscape. (To view examples of the maps of these types of conversations, go to *www.thegrove.com.*)

DesignShop™ Events.   Developed by Gail and Matt Taylor, consultants and specialists in group working environments and group processes, the DesignShop model for a large group event is based on three phases:

Scan, Focus, and Act.[1] In the Scan phase, participants explore a whole range of ideas, many of which are outside the realm of their expertise, in order to stimulate creative thinking. In the Focus stage, the participants begin to link the results of what they've found in the Scan phase to the problem or opportunity that they came to explore in the first place. Often in the Focus phase, the problem or opportunity will be redefined, which underscores the importance of creativity in the Scan phase. Act happens very quickly at the end of the entire process. In this phase, practical considerations, including action items and due dates, are formed for implementing the ideas. The Scan, Focus, Act model is recursive. While the entire DesignShop process can be modeled on Scan, Focus, Act, so too are each of the modules within an event. Each DesignShop™ event is a major production designed specifically to the needs of the client. The knOwhere team that stages these events is drawn from both inside and outside the knOwhere organization and includes writers, artists, educators, actors, engineers, executives, lawyers, accountants, etc., who provide a multidisciplinary approach to their large group events. (For additional information on how DesignShop™ events work, go to *www.knowherestore.com* and click on Methods.)

RootMap™ Sessions. These center around a company's strategy or any complex concept that needs exploration by a large cross-section of people in an organization. The sessions are held either simultaneously or over a series of weeks or months in workshop settings where participants are given a visual that presents the basic issues accompanied by a series of questions to help them explore the concepts. Large groups are broken down into tables of up to eight people and facilitators assist the group in exploring the visual metaphor and answering the questions associated with it. (For additional information on RootMap™ sessions and their application, go to *www.rootlearning.com.*)

Circle Process. David Specht, an experienced mediator and CEO of Seeing Things Whole, says that while it has not been widely implemented in business settings, the Circle Process has great potential as a large group method, particularly where conflict situations exist. This is a method based on tribal practices in dealing with conflict resolution among indigenous tribes in northern Canada. Essentially, the Circle Process consists of a series of small preparatory meetings and then a large meeting to bring together people who are party to a dispute. An important element of the process is the involvement of a cross-section of the local community. Not only are offenders and victims brought together, but other members of the community become involved in committing to work with the offender, with the goal of helping them to become reintegrated into the community. This type of intervention allows the *whole group* to deal with a conflict rather than leaving it to a judicial or administrative system.

Appreciative Inquiry. This method, originally developed by David Cooperrider of Case Western Reserve University, is a thought process that can be applied in large group settings. The fundamental underlying principle of Appreciative Inquiry is that many change-management approaches focus on what's *wrong* in an organization instead of what's going well. In Appreciative Inquiry, questions center on what's going *right* in a group or organization. The result of an appreciative inquiry process is a series of statements that describe where the organization wants to be, based on the successful experiences it has already had.[2]

Interactive Technologies: Available Tools and How to Use Them Wisely

"Forty-nine years ago, I, in some wild moment, committed my career to helping mankind's collective ability for coping with complex, urgent problems—getting the picture, even in 1951, of interactively using a computer." This quotation, from Dr. Douglas C. Engelbart, inventor of the mouse, windows, and hypertext, reveals his remarkable insight.

Doug Engelbart knew, long before the rest of us, that interactive use of computers would have a profound impact. And by being a huge part of making the computer revolution happen, he's changed the way we work together forever.

One of Engelbart's most important contributions was the idea of computers as intellectual and collaborative tools. When others simply saw them as huge calculators or information storage mechanisms, Engelbart knew they could do much more. He knew that if people could *interact* with computers, we could expand our intellect and our capacity to collaborate in unprecedented ways.

Today we have a host of interactive technologies at our disposal. But as I noted at the outset of this book, a great deal of this interactive technology capacity isn't used well. Certainly we're using interactive tools more than we used to, but an interactive *philosophy* is what really leads to excellent use of interactive *technology* in business, and we've still got some room for improvement on that score. We've focused primarily on how to develop an interactive approach to management. This appendix describes *tools* that are available to interactive managers. We'll define some of the common interactive tools, talk about how they've been applied in business settings, share tips on how to use them effectively, and examine some of the key issues associated with incorporating interactive tools into your work.

Tools for Interactive Management

What's really interesting about collaborative technologies is that they haven't changed very much over the past 20 years. Surprised? While it's certainly true that interactive technologies have gotten less expensive, more widely available, easier to use, faster, and better integrated with one another, the basic *functionality* isn't dramatically different. Twenty years ago you could do a video conference, host an on-line discussion group, write something in hypertext, and send e-mail. Of course, the *scope* of how these technologies are used has greatly expanded. Because functionality remains relatively stable, what I've done in this appendix is talk about tools in terms of their basic capabilities.

What you'll find here are technologies you may want to investigate as an interactive manager. I've grouped them into four categories: There are tools to hold meetings, gather and structure input, exchange messages, and share information. (See Figure A2–1.) Of course, many of these tools cross the categories I've constructed. However, categorizing functionality can help you consider how to combine different tools in your own context. "In 20 years it will all be mix and match anyway," says Richard Dalton, expert on interactive technologies and a regular columnist for Byte.com. "So while it's difficult to separate out the tools, it's worthwhile for purposes of understanding the larger picture of what's available."

As you explore these tools in the following sections, you'll want to consider whether a tool allows people to interact asynchronously or synchronously. *Asynchronous* tools can be used without people having to be available at the same time. For example, if I send you an e-mail, I'm messaging you asynchronously because you can pick it up any time you want. *Synchronous* tools are used by two or more people at the same time. For example, an audio conference is often held in order to bring a group

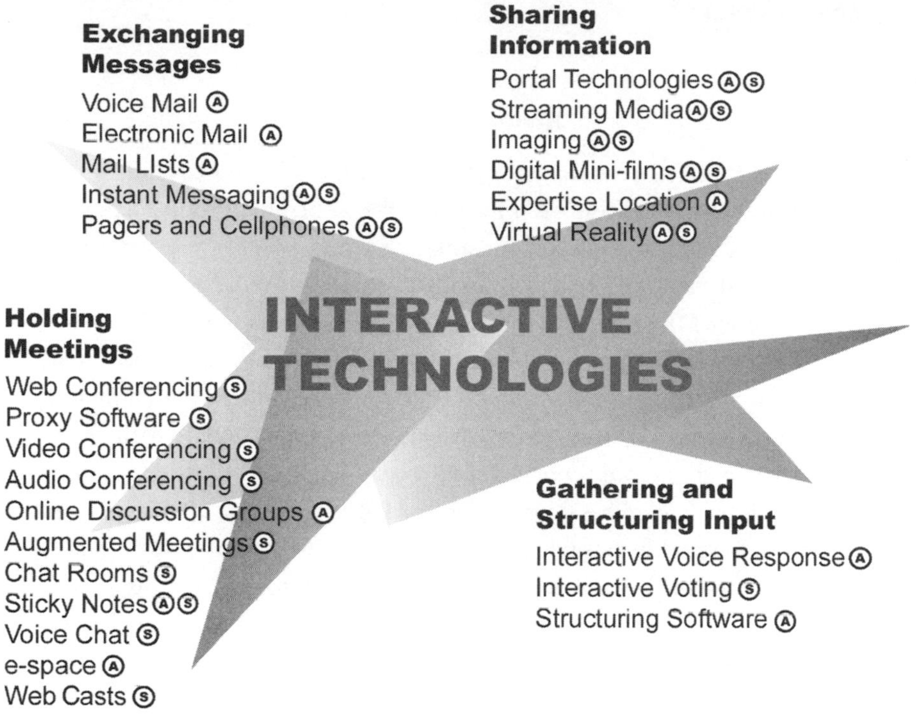

Exchanging Messages

Voice Mail Ⓐ
Electronic Mail Ⓐ
Mail LIsts Ⓐ
Instant Messaging ⒶⓈ
Pagers and Cellphones ⒶⓈ

Sharing Information

Portal Technologies ⒶⓈ
Streaming Media ⒶⓈ
Imaging ⒶⓈ
Digital Mini-films ⒶⓈ
Expertise Location Ⓐ
Virtual Reality ⒶⓈ

INTERACTIVE TECHNOLOGIES

Holding Meetings

Web Conferencing Ⓢ
Proxy Software Ⓢ
Video Conferencing Ⓢ
Audio Conferencing Ⓢ
Online Discussion Groups Ⓐ
Augmented Meetings Ⓢ
Chat Rooms Ⓢ
Sticky Notes ⒶⓈ
Voice Chat Ⓢ
e-space Ⓐ
Web Casts Ⓢ

Gathering and Structuring Input

Interactive Voice Response Ⓐ
Interactive Voting Ⓢ
Structuring Software Ⓐ

Figure A2-1   Technologies for Interactive Communication

Source: Boone Associates © 2001

of people together simultaneously. These distinctions are important when you're selecting technologies. (In Figure A2-1, you'll see synchronous tools marked with an S, asynchronous marked with an A, and tools that can be used either way marked AS.)

You'll see very few references to any specific product names in this section. That's intentional. Products come and go. It's much more important that you focus on what the tools *do*, and I'm not in the business of promoting or evaluating vendor products. If you're curious about how to find more information on these tools, you can do a web search on most (but not all) of the terms I've used and find more specific product information.

If you do decide to explore the use of technologies, experiment with more than one brand, says Professor Martin Elton of New York University's Interactive Telecommunications Program. Nontechnical people often write off a particular technology because they have a bad experience with one product, and Elton says it's important to try a number of products for comparison. You may experience a technology totally differently when you use another company's product, particularly since products vary so much in terms of quality and functionality.

Holding Meetings

This section may tax your definition of what a meeting is. But that's a good thing. All too often we think we have to bring a group of people together in a room to get things done. Not so. There are a variety of ways to hold meetings, and we'll explore some of them here.

Chat rooms: Many people are familiar with the concept of a chat room. *Chat* provides the ability to exchange messages with a group of people in a shared on-line environment. It is a synchronous meeting in that people have to be in the on-line "room" in order for you to "chat" with them. Content in a chat room is not usually stored. (There are some exceptions to this rule we'll explore later.) Therefore, if you enter a chat room you won't know what's been said except for a very short period of time before you entered. Comments are added and responded to in real time.

Elizabeth Churchill, a senior research scientist at Xerox, has been working on an application called *sticky chat*, which combines instant messaging capabilities with other software such as publishing software or word processing software. With sticky chat, someone working on a document or piece of work can stick a chat window anywhere in a document and then invite people to view that document and make comments on it.[1]

On-line discussion groups are more appropriate than chat rooms when you want to encourage an ongoing, structured conversation among a group of people. In an on-line discussion group, when you enter the "room" you have the choice to go back and read all of the comments that have been made before you entered the discussion. Then you can enter a comment of your own after the last comment that has been made. These discussions are often divided into different topics or "threads" that get introduced as a group of people converse. In on-line discussion groups, when a topic starts to shift, a facilitator will see to it that a new thread gets explored in a separate conversation. In this way, the conversation can proceed without getting pulled away from its primary focus, and it makes life much easier for those who come in later and want to get up-to-date with what's been said. These interactions can be very lively, despite the fact that they are asynchronous. Their asynchronous nature lends itself to reflection, and usually what results is a deeper level of discussion than you will normally find in a chat session.

Sticky notes, a sort of hybrid between chat and instant messaging, is somewhat akin to sticky chat (described above). Sticky notes are a form of chat session in which the content is stored, so when you enter a sticky note session, people may be chatting synchronously or asynchronously. Bill Machrone, VP of Ziff Davis Media, explains:

> **When you run software such as uTOK on your machine and you go to a website, if other uTOK users are there or have been there, you "see" them. They kind of pop up in a little chatlike window and you can see messages they left behind. So if you're an e-business, it's kind of like having people standing around outside your store talking about what they see in the window, or, having just come out of the store, chatting about the great bargain they got or the rude salesperson or whatever. So users are having a whole conversation about your site, using your site as the backdrop on-line, but you don't even know what's going on unless you're a uTOK user as well.**

Voice chat operates on the same principle as text-based chat. Instead of connecting via direct phone lines, voice is sent over the Internet itself, using a special protocol called IP. "Voice over the IP is going to happen sometime between last week and never," says technology writer and author Richard Dalton. "It tends to be very clunky in general usage; it's not at all like picking up the phone. The most common use of Internet voice is for call-back systems on websites where frustrated on-line customers can click on a button to talk with a customer service person. But the problem with that is there's always the assumption that you have a convenient microphone hanging around your PC. Some PC users don't even have speakers. It's just one step too many for general usage. People at high-tech companies who are willing to put up with a degradation in quality are willing to use it. Voice chat is still pretty exotic. But it's kind of like the dancing elephant. It's clumsy, but it's amazing you can make it dance at all!"

Professor Martin Elton of NYU says it's important to recognize that voice over IP can operate both on the Internet as well as private networks. And interactive managers need to be aware that there's a significant difference in quality using the Internet versus a private network; otherwise they might be fooled during a demonstration of "voice over IP." "A private network usually provides a higher transmission quality," says Elton. "So voice over IP using a private network may sound fine, while the same system may not sound nearly as good over the public Internet. Unless you know what you are listening to, you may be misled."

Audio conferencing is a much less exotic and much more reliable standby technology for holding virtual meetings. It is essentially the same thing as a conference call, although there are different capabilities when you use different equipment or services. An audio *bridge* links phone lines together, although many telephones have rudimentary capabilities for linking several locations. Interviewees for this book said that they use audio conferences extensively, and many people find them to be a useful way of bringing people together for a meeting—particularly if they're getting into problems communicating via e-mail, where a lack of synchronous contact becomes an issue. Audio conferencing is synchronous, although its content also can be recorded and replayed. However, to participate in an audio conference as opposed to simply listening to it, you obviously have to be there in real time. Bridges can be purchased or professional bridging services can be obtained from special service bureaus or the phone company. Very high quality, specialized bridging services are available for meetings where you want increased functionality, such as the ability to break people into small groups, the ability to play audiotapes during a session, real-time translation services, and expert audio meeting facilitation services.

Video conferencing: If audio alone doesn't fulfill the needs of your meeting, there are a lot of different varieties of video conferencing for you to choose from. We've come a long way from the days when video conferencing was an expensive, limited proposition. It can be two-way, one-way, or multipoint. In two-way video conferencing, people at two locations can both see and hear each other at the same time. With one-way video conferencing, the video signal is sent from one location, the people at other locations receive that video signal and then there is usually a call-in number where questions are taken from remote sites. Increasingly, cameras are being set up at remote locations so the picture can be switched as well. For example, when a video conference is broadcast from San Diego and a person has a question in Brussels, the camera will switch to the Brussels location to show the person asking the question.

There are PC-based video-conferencing products that allow a number of different people to both see and hear each other simultaneously. You've probably seen pictures of PC screens where there are several "talking heads" on the screen all at one time. These multipoint video conferences are improving in terms of capabilities, but they're nowhere near the level of quality in terms of picture resolution and audio quality that you get from a dedicated two-way video-conferencing system. PC-based conferencing is primarily used with small groups of people, based in various locations, for regular business meetings, as opposed to events.

Webcasting: Many people are familiar with the form of video conferencing called a "webcast," where a video signal is sent out over the web and received by people who tune into the webcast by going to a particular website at a preappointed time. Webcasts events are held with varying degrees of interactive capabilities. Usually the speaker on a webcast will take questions via an e-mail link, unless the meeting is simultaneously connected via an audio conference. Interactive voice links over the Internet haven't really developed to the point where an Internet-based interactive voice link is practical for a meeting environment. If you want to hold an interactive webcast, combine it with an audio conference to ensure that the voice portion of the program goes smoothly. Webcasts are often used for messages from a CEO inside a corporation, or a presentation by a famous person on a public webcast. Webcasts are usually held as an event, as opposed to a regular meeting.

Web conferencing is similar in some ways to the concept of a webcast, but there are some very important differences. Here's how a web conference works: A group of people can be instructed to access a website at a preappointed time. When people arrive at the website, they dial a phone number that immediately connects all of the participants via an audio bridge. While they are connected on the audio bridge, participants also see exactly the same thing on all of their PC screens at the same time. Therefore, they can be taken on a "web tour," be shown a slide presentation, or in some cases can take turns literally drawing on the screen with their mouse to illustrate a point. One service provides the capability to share any type of software application—even if all of the participants don't own the same software. So, for example, if I had special engineering software, I could run that software and both of us could use it at the same time for the purposes of communicating during our meeting.

Web-conferencing functionality can be accessed through an intranet or Internet portal. Some companies purchase their own web conferencing software and hardware; others simply use services available over the Internet through a public portal.

Augmented meetings: Web conferencing is one type of augmented meeting, but using shared software in a meeting environment is something that can happen on or off the web. Augmented meetings are simply meetings that are held using some sort of display technology (like a projector) to display what's on one PC to an entire group of people. While this sounds like a simple concept, it can transform a meeting in terms of the level of interaction and activity. In Chapter 12 we saw how Bill Esrey, Chairman and CEO of Sprint, held a meeting where the questions were captured and displayed for the entire audience to see. This is one example of an augmented meeting. Augmented meetings can also make smaller meetings more productive. For example, a budgeting session with live models and spreadsheets displayed for the whole group to see is much more dynamic and interactive than simply having everyone look at a static, printed briefing book. It also allows the whole group to engage in "What if" discussions, and it sparks more interactive conversations.

E-space: The functionality found in what is alternately called team rooms, knowledge rooms, or e-rooms looks an awful lot like "groupware." For our purposes, I'll use the term *e-space.* In essence, e-spaces are on-line places where several types of functionality can be combined. Usually they contain some sort of repository where people who are sharing the "room" can store things such as work, related articles, or a database of best practices. It's important to realize that e-spaces can be small or large. For example, you might want to create an e-space for a thousand people to hold a general session for an on-line conference, or you might want to create a "team room" for a small virtual team. E-spaces usually contain some sort of conversational functionality; for example, many of them incorporate discussion groups or PC-based video conferencing.

Proxy software is a more experimental meeting technology. This software allows people to see a visual representation (a proxy) of people who are participating in an on-line (often text-based) chat group. The visual representation of an individual might be as simple as a dot on the screen, but it represents a person's level of involvement in a group exchange. We saw an example of proxy software in Chapter 8 in our discussion of storytelling. This software can be useful when you're trying to encourage interaction between people. Often when you're working in an on-line environment, people feel uncomfortable contributing to on-line discussion groups because they can't tell who's listening. This software allows you to see when people drift away from the discussion, and you can determine who is integrally involved. Proxy software is not widely used at this point, but it gives a good synchronous picture of the level of interaction and participation of the individuals involved in a meeting.

Gathering and Structuring Input

Interactive managers are always looking for new ways to get feedback from their organizations. But simply getting the feedback doesn't make it useful. Therefore, technologies are needed to both gather *and* structure information.

Interactive voice response (IVR) technology allows an audio message to be played when someone calls into an 800 number. Then the person calling can respond to the message by using the telephone keypad. Paul Sanchez, former Communications Consulting Practice Director at Watson Wyatt Worldwide, says his clients have used this technology effectively to survey their stakeholders: "With IVR, you can put up five or six key questions, and people can dial in and in a few seconds give feedback to the organization on how they feel about important issues. This is a good follow-on to efforts such as the periodic 90-question printed survey. It allows you to get people's feedback both immediately and incrementally."

Interactive voting technology provides another way of taking the pulse of an organization on important issues. This technology can be used in meetings or via PCs, allowing people to vote on issues in real time. We saw an example of the use of this type of technology in Chapter 3, when it was used by a top executive to determine the level of agreement with the company's vision statement at a large group event.

Structuring software: Different types of software can be used to structure people's input, including neural network software and outline editing software. Neural network software takes large amounts of data, draws inferences from it, and recognizes patterns in it that people might not normally detect on their own. For example, you could use it to analyze employee surveys to see if there are patterns in the data that you're missing. Outline editors allow you to put textual information into a hierarchy that you can collapse and expand as you create a structure. Some outline editors also allow you to create links in the text, so your structure not only includes what is in one document, but also looks across documents.

I used two types of structuring software when I wrote this book. The interviews produced over 4000 pages of data. The trick was how to make sense out of all of that input. To do that, I used a piece of qualitative analysis software that allowed me to code the data. Then I could type in a code or a word and the software would pull together all of the examples of that code across the entire 4000 pages. An outline editor helped create a structure for the entire book. This was really useful for moving things around and developing a logical flow to the ideas.

Exchanging Messages

Many of the tools in this category are very familiar. For example, voice mail and e-mail are tools to exchange messages. However, it's worth quickly reviewing some basic technologies.

Mail lists are a special form of broadcast e-mail. Technology expert Richard Dalton says that mail lists were originally designed as a means of sending out ideas for comment in scientific communities. Think of a mail list as a sort of automatic e-mail generator. Mail lists are used primarily for keeping members of a specific community or interest group updated on particular topics. If you subscribe to a mail list, you will automatically be sent messages that contain articles and/or comments of other subscribers.

Instant messaging: When you sign up for instant messaging, you can make yourself continuously available to a select group of people based on a list of names or a topic area. The software provides a window that can be accessed to show you who among your buddy list is on-line, and at the same time it informs others that you are on-line. If you or someone else wants to send an instant message, you can begin a back and forth exchange. If you have instant messaging "turned on" while you are working, a message from the other person will pop up on your screen immediately after the person sends it, regardless of the software you're working in. So, for example, you could be logged into the Internet with instant messaging running in the background while you're working on a spreadsheet. Instant messages immediately appear in a window on your screen.

One interesting aspect of instant messaging is that it falls somewhere between the asynchronous and synchronous category, according to Richard Dalton: "It's kind of hard to say where instant messaging fits between e-mail and a telephone call. It's real clear that when you get an e-mail, you sit down and respond to it. With a telephone you're sitting there and you're both capable of talking at the same time. Instant messaging is somewhere in between."

People using instant messaging are on-line at the same time, but only one message can appear at a time, so there is a very brief delay between the moment you type a message, when it appears to the other person, and when they send you a reply. However, there is a sense of back and forth exchange.

Bill Machrone, VP of Technology for Ziff Davis Media, sees instant messaging being used frequently as an adjunct to face-to-face meetings. NYU Professor Martin Elton expects it to be even more useful in audio conferences. Machrone notes that people will often carry on side discussions through instant messages while a face-to-face meeting is proceeding. This brings up some interesting etiquette issues that we'll explore a little later in this appendix.

Pagers and cell phones are messaging tools as well. Some multifunction pagers and cell phones now provide access to the web and to e-mail. There's likely to be a surge in these multifunction devices, according to Martin Elton. Already he notes heavy usage in Europe and Japan. As of this writing, Richard Dalton adds that most handheld organizers will soon have similar capabilities.

Sharing Information

In Part II we talked about the importance of getting the right information to the right people in the right format. Sharing information is an important part of interactive management. There are a number of ways to share information, and not all of them include information technology. Printed information in the form of brochures, booklets, reports, etc., can be a very effective way of sharing information. Interactive managers need to consider whether they actually *need* communication technologies when they're sharing information. All too often, technologies are simply used to display something that is better left in a printed format. With that said, here are some ways you can use technology to share information with people.

Portal technologies: Let's examine three types of "portal" technologies: websites, intranets, and extranets. Most people by now have seen what a website on the Internet looks like. When you enter a website, you do so through a portal or web page. This window into the web allows you to navigate in a structured way, clicking on links to information. This same type of portal can be set up *inside* a company on an internal network. Information that is stored on internal company networks can be displayed in much the same way that you see information displayed on an Internet website. These internal portals are called intranets. Customized portals can also be created for external stakeholders. Extranets provide controlled access to information on a company's intranet. Jon Iwata of IBM described an example of an extranet in Chapter 11 when he told the story of how potential outsourcing partners were given customized access to IBM's intranet. An extranet is a portal that is set up (on an intranet) for a specific external audience.

All portal technologies can be set up in either dynamic and interactive ways, or they can be static. Unfortunately, many companies simply use intranets and extranets as publishing technologies. That is, they load what has previously been printed information (policies, procedures, annual reports, etc.) onto the intranet. While having access to this type of information can be a good thing, companies often miss out on much more powerful ways of using this technology.

"Intranets, so far, have been very disappointing in terms of what's actually happened in organizations," says Anthony Goodman, CEO of the change management consulting firm of Smythe, Dorward, Lambert Inc. "Far from being a workflow application, far from being the cultural hand grenade that we were predicting it would be two or three years ago, it's actually just turned into a bit of lame-o newsprint that happens to be digital rather than ink."

Jon Iwata, VP of Corporate Communication for IBM, says companies are just starting to make the transition to more powerful Intranet applications: "Most [companies] are still in the brochureware, information-heavy publishing stage. They haven't yet made the transition to providing a business platform where transactions and business can be done on intranets."

By incorporating discussion groups, interactive access to data, and other interactive technologies into the intranet site, interactive managers can make them much more powerful tools for change in their organizations.

While it's important to consider how to make portals more interactive, they are also useful as *repositories* of information to be shared across an organization or between organizations. Databases, shared filing cabinets, and libraries of information on various topics can be useful places to visit on a portal, depending upon your objective as a visitor.

Streaming media: Streaming media is simply a fancy term for distributing digital audio and video information over a network. Audio and video presentations can be recorded and then made available to a much broader audience through websites, intranets, and extranets. Of course, alternatively, *audiotape* and *videotape* can be sent out via mail or courier. In fact, in cases where the quality of the audio or video signal is an issue, you may choose to stick to audio- and videotape. Your budget, timing, and picture quality considerations will influence which of these methods you ultimately choose.

"Streaming's perceived value is very dependent on available bandwidth," says Richard Dalton. "If a network has relatively low bandwidth, or if some people who are in the audience have low-speed access, it's worth testing to see if streaming will provide a useful experience or just add to the viewer/listener's frustration."

Imaging technologies: Imaging, including scanners and digital cameras, can be very effective for information sharing. For example, we saw in Chapter 7 how Buzzsaw.com uses digital cameras at construction sites and then shares the pictures either synchronously or asynchronously in meetings or at individual desktops.

Digital minifilms: Films or short video segments provide another means of sharing information. Dana Atchley, digital storyteller, explains that new PC-based technologies are making film editing much more affordable in organizations. He believes that the minimovies that people can create at their desks will prove to be a powerful form of information sharing in organizations.

Expertise location: While we've already talked about e-mail in the section on messaging, it's important to recognize that e-mail is a means of sharing knowledge as well. David Gilmour, CEO of Tacit Knowledge Systems, Inc., a company that provides expertise location software for knowledge sharing, explained in Chapter 7 that e-mail actually serves as an amazing source for organizational learning because it contains a history of everyone's work focus, interests, and capabilities. By using new filtering mechanisms, expertise location software can contribute to the ability to link and inform people in unprecedented ways. Properly sorted and filtered, with considerable attention given to issues of privacy and user control, information automatically extracted from e-mail (by the software, *not* a person) can connect people who have similar interests. For example, with expertise location software I can type in a subject or topic, and the software will provide me with names of people throughout an organization who are interested in, or have expertise in, that topic.

Virtual reality: Mike Rosen, head of the architectural and virtual reality firm of Mike Rosen & Associates, defines virtual reality as having three aspects: an immersive environment, interactivity, and unlimited navigation.

A virtual reality (VR) environment is immersive. That is, first, you can see the environment all around you when you turn your head in any direction. Second, you can interact with the environment, such as picking things up or turning things on and off. The third test of a VR environment is unlimited navigation capabilities. Rosen explains: "In other words, you can go anywhere you want. You have the freedom to move as you would in the regular environment—so you can go this way, that way, up, down, whatever you want. Whereas in an animation or a fly-through, it's a controlled environment."

Network Virtual Reality allows people in remote parts of the world the flexibility of operating in the same visual space. This existing technology allows people to actually share "objects" that are created in virtual reality. So, for example, in a Network VR system, if we're sitting around the same virtual table and having a conversation, I might pick up a "virtual" cup or book in San Francisco and hand it to you in Somerset, England.

Virtual reality provides a whole new means of interacting with shared information by allowing people to immerse themselves in a three-dimensional representation of the information. As we've seen, VR software is currently being used to help architects communicate with customers by showing them a virtual representation of the building they're designing. As it develops and becomes less expensive, interactive managers should consider ways in which they could apply this technology in their own communication environments. Richard Dalton notes that available bandwidth is even more critical with VR than with streaming technologies.

Other technologies are available and more emerge daily. This appendix provides an overview of what is commonly available today.

Microskills for Using Interactive Technologies

Here are few practical tips on some of the most important skills and things to watch out for when you're using interactive technologies.

Writing Skills

Many of the text-based technologies, such as e-mail and discussion groups, point out the crying need for better writing skills. While these technologies are highly conversational in nature (and we can't expect everyone to be a Hemingway on-line), there are a few basic things people need to remember when they're expressing themselves in writing:

1. Choose your words carefully and read over what you've written at least once before you send it. In cases where the material could easily be misunderstood, send it to someone else for an opinion before you send it to the designated person. Before you say you can't spare the time for this, consider how risky e-mail can be by trying an exercise suggested by Brad Meyer of the communication consulting firm Collaboration Ltd.: "Take just about any sentence out of one of your e-mails, and if there are 12 words in the sentence, read it 12 times, each time emphasizing a different word in the sentence. You'll probably experience six to eight absolutely different meanings of the sentence, depending on where you put the emphasis."

   For example, take the sentence: "Will you please call me and let me know when you really need to see the finished document?" If *call* is emphasized, it could mean you don't want an e-mail. *Me* might mean me directly instead of my assistant. *Really* could refer to an absolute deadline. *See* might mean that you want to actually see something as opposed to talking about it. *Finished* could refer to a final document, or it might be a draft. There's a lot of room for ambiguity in written text, and senders need to be aware of this.

   It's also a good idea to make your subject line extremely explicit. Think of it as a headline in a newspaper. If you don't catch someone's attention immediately, it's unlikely it'll be read further. Also, readers will set priorities as they go through their e-mail, and your explicit subject line will help them.

2. Keep it short. Try to remove at least part of every thing you write when you reread it. Martin Elton, Professor at New York University's Interactive Telecommunications Program, also suggests sending several short e-mails instead of combining different topics into one long one. "This makes it much easier for recipients to deal with filing and forwarding, where appropriate," he says. I also consider this a particularly good suggestion given that people are checking their e-mails on smaller and smaller screens these days (e.g., pagers and cell phones).

3. Elton also warns against sending an attachment without sufficient explanation. "Tell people what's in an attachment," he says. "It can be incredibly time-consuming and irritating when you don't." All of the attachment-related viruses going around these days make this indispensable advice. Also remember that attachments, particularly images, may take a long time to receive if your correspondents have connections that are 56 kbps or less. This ties up the receiver's e-mail until it is completely downloaded.

4. Never, ever send a broadcast e-mail unless you really, really have to. It's an illusion to think that your friends enjoy all those jokes and "inspirational pieces" you send out to them. I assure you that the majority of them are trying to protect your feelings by not saying anything to you, when what they really want to do is ask you to stop sending the stuff. If you don't believe me, keep a tally for a while of how often you get responses to these kinds of messages. If people aren't responding, it's unlikely that they want you to keep sending them. Keep them to a minimum and target your audience. Or better yet, set up your own joke or inspirational website and simply give people a link to it. (But don't be surprised if you don't get a lot of hits.) And absolutely, positively no broadcast e-mails about the Honda you have for sale in the parking lot, thank you.

5. Read (or reread) Strunk and White's book, *The Elements of Style*. It's a tiny book that's an excellent treatise on writing.

Technology-based Listening and Speaking Skills

It's harder to listen when you're using certain interactive technologies. You don't have the nonverbal cues that you normally get in a face-to-face conversation. So, you have to compensate:

1. Pay attention to silence. Whether it's on an audio conference or an on-line discussion group, you won't have the nonverbal visual cues to tell you whether people are bored, unhappy, or distracted. Ask people what they're thinking and feeling when you haven't heard from them in a while.

2. Talk openly about how the technology is altering your perceptions of each other, instead of just being uncomfortably silent. For example, most video-conferencing systems have cameras set up in ways that make it very difficult to make direct eye contact—particularly when you're working on a PC-based system. Instead of pretending this isn't happening, or worse, assuming that the other person is avoiding looking at you, tell them what you're noticing.

3. When you're speaking on an audio conference, *always say who you are* when you're making a comment. People rarely do this, since they're accustomed to speaking on the phone without identifying themselves. It can be very confusing for listeners.

4. Stay on topic. Taking a group away from its focus, particularly in an on-line discussion group or audio conference, is really annoying. Ditto on an e-mail.

5. Don't just jump into the content of a meeting when you're working either on-line or in a teleconference. Remember the importance of setting a *context* for the meeting. People need to feel connected to each other before they're ready to get down to work. Of course, you don't want to overdo this, but don't overlook it, either.

6. When you're working with a group in which people speak different languages, pick a medium that allows you to listen to everyone. For example, audio conferencing is usually not a good medium for cross-cultural groups. Asynchronous technologies seem to be better for accommodating language differences because they give people time to both absorb what others have said and to formulate their replies. If you need to hold a synchronous meeting for a multilingual group, Martin Elton notes that video conferencing seems to work better than audio conferencing when there are language difficulties. "Two common sense reasons probably explain this," he says. "First, the added channel of video provides more information, and second, visual feedback

can be helpful in reducing uncertainty about whether people have understood what one has said."

7. Share your media preferences and ask other people about theirs. Some people are big e-mail users, others prefer voice mail. Some people only check their pagers. Whatever the case may be, tell people how you prefer to receive information and ask them the best way to reach them. It will make you a much better listener and sender of information.

Key Suggestions for Implementing Interactive Technologies

There are some key points you need to consider if you're going to use interactive technologies in your organization. These observations are based on 20 years of experience working with information technology organizations, as well as the information gleaned from the interviews for this book.

Attend to Security Issues

"Many companies spend as much time figuring out security arrangements for various conferencing methods as they do on training or implementation," says Richard Dalton.

Dalton explains that a primary security consideration is whether you are communicating within your own organization or whether you're also including outside entities such as customers, business partners, or suppliers. When you go outside your intranet, you have to find a way to breach the firewall security without giving up the overall security you need. Firewalls allow people to communicate freely within an organization, but they block a great deal of communication with outside entities because sensitive internal data must be protected. One way of getting around the firewall issue is to go to an outside vendor that uses browser-based systems for communication. Such systems can generally be accessed from any direction without worrying about firewalls because all of the data is exchanged through browsers. Companies that construct their own internal communications networks to allow for incorporation of outside parties often find that they have to invest heavily in special security software.

This is an issue for the experts, but as an interactive manager, take the time to ask good questions about security if you're using interactive technologies to exchange sensitive information.

Even Small and Medium-size Companies Can Afford to Use Interactive Technologies

If you're an interactive manager in a small- to medium-size company, you may think you don't have the resources to use interactive technologies. Not so. Much of the equipment and software described in this chapter can be leased or used on an as-needed basis. There are also companies that now provide the necessary bandwidth for interactive technologies, such as video conferencing and streaming media, at prices comparable to those that larger companies have received for years. For example, Teligent, based in Vienna, Virginia, offers small companies such as Mike Rosen and Associates, the architecture and virtual reality firm, the bandwidth they need for their very high-tech applications. "Teligent gives us excellent rates and stable service, uninterrupted, without problems," says Rosen. "We do a lot of fairly sophisticated integration of Internet and telephone lines into our presentations. We will have people calling in or we're dialing out to the Internet while we're making a presentation. So it's very important to us for the communications to function properly.... There are also other ways for smaller companies to justify the entry cost into a more advanced stage of technology use, such as public relations and marketing. If you can use resources from those budgets to offset the acquisition cost, the stuff more than pays for itself."

Installation Does Not Equal Collaboration

"Simply providing access at the desktop to a technology that has the label 'collaborative' attached to it doesn't mean people are going to flock around it and suddenly want to collaborate," says Mike Burtha, Executive Director of Knowledge Networking at Johnson & Johnson.

Whether it's groupware, Knowledge Management databases, intranets, or e-spaces, installing a technology is no guarantee of improved communication and collaboration. Installation of a technology doesn't guarantee results. In order for interactive technology to have an impact, people must see the need for interaction and understand the connection between the technology and their ability to succeed in their work.

There are numerous guidelines for assuring successful technology implementations (I address many of these issues in my previous books, *Leadership and the Computer* and *The Information Edge*). But the two most important prerequisites to effective implementation of technology are the identification of a person and a need.[2] All too often, technologies are installed for a department, division, or even a whole organization. And they're installed with nebulous goals, such as "improve knowledge sharing." In order to be successful, technology efforts need to be focused, and they need to have clear near-term payoffs. The people heading up a technology effort should be in a position to deliver on strategy and should have a clear need for collaboration and interaction. Then, and only then, should they pick an interactive technology to match that need. By following this course of action, interactive managers will find that they've set a good foundation for gaining real results from interactive technologies in their organizations.

Keep It Simple

Sometimes people get caught up in all the bells and whistles and hype of new technologies. Let me assure you that the simplest route is the best route when it comes to technology. One interviewee for this book told me that audio conferences are often more valuable to his company than databases in their Knowledge Management efforts. Another interviewee said a very important community of practice at his organization was built around simple e-mail exchanges. Audiotape can sometimes be more effective than a full-blown video conference.

"Technology's not the issue," says Mike Burtha, Executive Director of Knowledge Networking at Johnson & Johnson. "Technology does not create collaboration. People create collaboration.... Maybe the optimal way to interact and share knowledge is a teleconference every Friday. You need to say to yourself, what's the simplest way to approach this that has the fewest encumbrances on people's work? You want to select something that integrates with, and is reflective of, the way people work."

The point is, there's a technology that's right for your situation and your budget. It's great that new technologies are loaded with functionality and provide vast new opportunities, and in some cases you'll need more complex technologies to accommodate your purpose. But technology doesn't have to be complex to be effective.

It's critical to know what you're setting out to accomplish first. Then you can begin to match the right technology to the right business problem.

There are no simple answers for matching technologies to applications in your company. The connection of technology to communication objectives requires creativity, imagination, and guts. Doing something in a new way is always a challenge. The step-by-step needs assessment approach I outline in my book *Leadership and the Computer* is one way to get started.

Don't Forget the Importance of Face-to-Face Contact

"Frankly, e-mail and teleconferencing are not going to put the airline industry out of business," says Doug Loewe, Vice President of Global Sales for UUNet, a division of MCI Worldcom. "The bottom line is you still need to get your butt on an airplane and get in front of your team, get in front of customers, and get in front of your senior management team."

For the last 20 years people have fantasized about being able to displace travel costs with electronic communication. But in many studies of technologies such as teleconferencing, what they've found is that the use of technology actually *increases* travel because it puts people in touch with a broader array of business colleagues. Technology enables the creation of new relationships that often end up filling airline seats. Certainly some travel can be avoided through the use of technology, but technology will never completely replace the need for face-to-face contact.

However, Martin Elton notes that face-to-face meetings can often be expensive propositions, particularly if you factor in the value of the participants' time both at the meeting and during travel. "So try to get the best value out of this investment," he says. "In doing so, almost certainly there is a place for electronic media in preparing for, and following up after, a face-to-face meeting. It makes sense to ask, 'What is the best mix of media through time (including face-to-face)?' Audio and video conferencing and e-mail can be very important in helping with such tasks as setting an agenda for the face-to-face meeting, ensuring that you've invited the right people, etc."

I see technology as a way of augmenting face-to-face communication. Clearly there are some relationships that will never result in face-to-face contact because of practical considerations, but I believe there is tremendous value in bringing people face-to-face at some point during a project when that's a feasible option.

Regardless of whether you agree with my philosophy on the importance of face-to-face contact, it's hard to argue with the need for considering it as one of a full range of options in the communication process.

Yes, You Can Build Trust On-line

While face-to-face contact is an excellent way to build trust and context for group interaction, it's also possible to establish a sense of intimacy and trust on-line.

"If people can fall in love on-line, they can certainly build business relationships on-line," quips Phil Harkins, CEO of Linkage Inc., a human resources research and consulting firm. "It's amazing to me that people think that electronic communication is going to impact trust in a negative way. In fact, I think there's more opportunities to gain trust using e-mail and voice mail. People have learned to connect on-line in a way they sometimes can't in person. But you have to be very thoughtful about what you say. Authenticity, candor, and commitment are necessary whether you're having a conversation on-line or in person."

Lisa Kimball of Caucus Systems, a company that provides on-line discussion group consultation and services, has participated in an ongoing, on-line discussion group that has established deep levels of intimacy and trust over the last 17 years of its remarkable existence. I heard other examples from interviewees of situations where people had close, effective business relationships that were primarily established via technology.

Trust building on-line comes naturally to some people, but not to others. Particularly in on-line discussion groups, facilitation and coaching skills can help develop the kind of relationships that will promote achievement of shared goals. In this appendix, we've touched on just a few of the personal skills that can help interactive managers use interactive technologies more effectively. There are also numerous websites and books devoted to the topic of "net etiquette" that can be useful in developing on-line personal communication skills.

Develop Rules of the Road

Groups that will be working together via interactive technologies need to establish up-front norms about how the group will operate. By agreeing on how technologies will be applied and what behaviors are acceptable and unacceptable, a great deal of conflict and misunderstanding can be avoided.

For example, group norms should be established around how often people will be expected to pick up and respond to voice mail, e-mail, etc. Groups also need to establish norms around how they'll conduct themselves in on-line meetings. The practice of flaming (aggressively verbally attacking someone in an on-line discussion group or chat room) should obviously be discouraged. But the best way to do this is not by leaving it up to the facilitator to handle, but having a group discussion about it up front. The team or group needs to take responsibility for its own behavior and the rules for that behavior.

Please (and I'm Begging You), Stop Being Rude!

In Chapter 6, I told the story of "George" the cell phone abuser. In my mind, that was a clear-cut case of rudeness, no getting around it.

But some situations are less clear-cut. I talked to several people, including Bill Machrone, VP of Technology at Ziff Davis Media, who noted a rise in the number of people accessing e-mail and instant messaging during face-to-face meetings. This practice presents communicators with an interesting challenge. Some people will consider it rude for attendees to be typing during a meeting; others won't. Richard Dalton explains:

> **I don't know a meeting that's held anymore, at least not in Silicon Valley, where people don't come in and spend half their time checking e-mail and passing instant messages around the table while someone's giving a live presentation. And it's kind of a goofy environment where everybody's time-sharing between the speaker and their screens. But it's become so common that no one's even offended anymore. It's less disruptive than having people whispering to each other.**

What's clear is that we're all going to have different opinions as to what's acceptable behavior. In the same way that different countries and cultures will have different norms and cultural practices, people from different organizations and different environments will have differing opinions regarding the appropriate use of technology.

Another practice that could be misunderstood is noted by Martin Elton, Professor in the Interactive Telecommunications Program at New York University. Elton points out that people often speak in shorthand for e-mail and voice-mail messages, leaving out common courtesies such as saying "Please" and "Thank you." To some people this will seem efficient, to others it will seem rude.

It's best to err on the side of caution. People will rarely be offended by courtesy, but they will most certainly be offended when they perceive a lack of it. If it's not common practice to bring a laptop into a meeting at a company you're visiting, ask the presenter if it will distract him or her. If you don't know someone well, take the time to be courteous in your voice mail and e-mails. Saying please or thank you is not going to absorb all that much of your time.

What this all boils down to is a sensitivity to the way others think and feel. The best advice is to "pay attention." If you're in a restaurant talking on a cell phone, look around you at the faces at nearby tables. Do the natives look friendly or are they staring at you as though they'd like to toss your phone into the lobster tank? When someone walks into your office to speak with you, ask them if it bothers them for you to continue typing as you converse, or better yet, stop typing. When you're in an online discussion group and there's something interesting that you'd like to share outside that group, ask the members if they mind if you share it. In a video or audio conference, make sure to pause to let others speak.

In short, always think about what you'd like the other person to do if the situation were reversed. I recognize that this is simple, age-old advice, but I've seen enough instances where it's been ignored that I don't think it hurts to repeat it here.

Throughout this book I weave people's comments about how they use technology into their stories of managing interactively. We've seen examples of using voting technologies in large group events, audiotapes for distributing stories during a merger, web conferencing for project management meetings, video conferencing for town meetings with top executives, intranets for allowing employees to check progress against organizational goals, and proxy software for storytelling, among many others.

The combination of stories found throughout this book, in conjunction with the description of what's available in this appendix, should help you find innovative approaches to using interactive communication technologies in your organization. You're also invited join us on-line to hear from your colleagues and peers about how they're continuing to use technology by going to my company's website, *www.maryboone.com*.

Endnotes

Introduction

1. Hamel, Gary, *Leading the Revolution* (Boston: Harvard Business School Press, 2000).
2. Tapscott, Don; Ticoll, David; Lowy, Alex, *Digital Capital: Harnessing the Power of Business Webs* (Boston: Harvard Business School Press, 2000).
3. Hamel, Gary, op. cit.

Chapter 1

1. Drucker, Peter, *Post-Capitalist Society* (New York: Harper Business, 1993).
2. Graham, Pauline (ed.), *Mary Parker Follett: Prophet of Management* (Boston: Harvard Business School Press, 1996). (The first article I saw about Follett's work was "Designing for Freedom in a Technical World," Enid Mumford, in *Information Technology and Changes in Organizational Work*, edited by Orlikowski, Wanda J., Walsham, Geoff, Jones, Matthew R., and DeGross, Janice (London: Chapman & Hall, 1995), 425. Enid Mumford was also helpful in directing me to other works by Follett. I also would like to thank David Sibbet for giving me a copy of the management map he codesigned with the *Harvard Business Review* staff, which appeared in HBR in the September–October 1997 issue. This wonderful map is where I first encountered Follett's name.)
3. Zuboff, Shoshana, *In the Age of the Smart Machine* (New York: Basic Books, 1988), 402.
4. After coming up with this term, I did an extensive search through business databases, and the only references I could find to "interactive management" came from prominent systems theorists Russell Ackoff, Jamshid Gharajedaghi, and J.R. Warfield. Ackoff's definition: "...the objective of management and planning should be to create as much of the future as is possible. This is the objective of a new type of management, the interactive.... Our lot is due more to what we do than what is done to us." Ackoff, Russell L., *Re-creating the Corporation* (New York: Oxford University Press, 1999), 55.

In *Systems Thinking: Managing Chaos and Complexity* (Boston: Butterworth Heinemann, 1992), 22, Gharajedaghi describes interactive management as a "design approach" to management. "Design is the operational manifestation of the purposeful systems paradigm developed by Ackoff (1972) in response to the challenge of managing interactions between purposeful members of a highly interdependent social organization.... Ackoff then proposes a design methodology by which stakeholders of a multiminded system participatively design a future they collectively desire and realize it though (*sic*) successive approximation."

Warfield coauthored a book with A. Roxana Cardenas entitled *A Handbook of Interactive Management* (Ames, IA: Iowa State University Press, 1994). Warfield defines interactive management as a process designed to help people cope with complexity and to arrive at designed alternatives from which a choice can be made.

My definition of interactive management embraces the concept of organizations as purposeful systems and, of course, is heavily reliant on a "participative" approach. In placing a strong emphasis on the communication and social construct, I am defining the term differently. Instead of focusing on "managing interactions," I am focused on how people interact based on their roles and communications patterns.

5. "Second-Generation Knowledge Management," Don Cohen, *Knowledge Directions: The Journal of the Institute for Knowledge Management,* Volume 1, Spring 1999, 4.

6. Thanks to Don Tapscott for giving me the idea to organize around competencies.

Chapter 2

1. "Communities of Practice: The Organizational Frontier," Etienne Wenger and Williams Snyder, *Harvard Business Review,* January–February 2000.

2. Davenport, Thomas H. and Prusak, Laurence, *Working Knowledge* (Boston: Harvard Business School Press), 38.

Chapter 3

1. I highly recommend to you the book from which these definitions are taken: *Mary Parker Follett: Prophet of Management,* edited by Pauline Graham (Boston: Harvard Business School Press, 1995).

2. Drucker, Peter, *Post-Capitalist Society* (New York: Harper Business, 1993), 65.

3. Krakauer, Jon, *Into Thin Air* (New York: Villard, 1997).

Chapter 4

1. Thanks to Gail Taylor from The knOwhere Store for the observation about cathedral steps.

2. http://www.steelcase.com/knowledgebase/krci5.htm
3. http://www.steelcase.com/knowledgebase/owens.htm
    These examples from Federal Express and Owens Corning are just two of many you can find on Steelcase's excellent website, *www.steelcase.com*. I highly recommend looking at it if you are planning to redesign your space.
4. Thanks to Carol Gorelick for the introduction to Brad Meyer and help on this case study.
5. http://www.steelcase.com/knowledgebase/clw.htm
6. http://www.steelcase.com
7. Schrage, Michael, *Serious Play: How the World's Best Companies Simulate to Innovate* (Boston: Harvard Business School Press), 2000.

Chapter 5

1. Pine, B. Joseph II and Gilmore, James H., *The Experience Economy: Work Is Theatre and Every Business a Stage* (Boston: Harvard Business School Press, 1999).
2. "BA Puts People at the Heart of Its Brand and Business Plans," Lorrie Hecker, *Agenda 4* (London: The Marketing & Communication Agency Ltd., 1999), 7.
3. Ibid, 8-9.

Chapter 6

1. Harkins, Phil, *Powerful Conversations* (New York: McGraw-Hill, 1999).
2. Trompenaars, Fons and Hampden-Turner, Charles, *Riding the Waves of Culture: Understanding Diversity in Global Business* 2nd Edition (Irwin Professional Publishing, 1998).
3. Knight, Sue, *NLP at Work: The Difference that Makes a Difference in Business* (London: Nicholas Brealey, 1999).
4. Ibid.
5. Senge, Peter M., *The Fifth Discipline: The Art and Practice of Organizational Learning* (New York: Doubleday/Currency, 1990).

Chapter 8

1. "Story Telling: An Old Skill in a New Context," Dave Snowden, personal white paper.

Chapter 9

1. On the topic of reward structures, I highly recommend: Kerr, Steven (ed.), *Ultimate Rewards* (Boston: Harvard Business Review, 1997).

Chapter 10

1. Bunker, Barbara B. and Alban, Billie T., *Large Group Interventions: Engaging the Whole System for Rapid Change* (San Francisco: Jossey-Bass Publishers, 1997).
2. Kao, John, *Jamming: The Art and Discipline of Business Creativity* (New York: Harper Business, 1997).
3. Harkins, Phil, *Powerful Conversations* (New York: McGraw-Hill, 1999), 5.
4. Senge, Peter M., *The Fifth Discipline: The Art and Practice of Organizational Learning* (New York: Doubleday/Currency, 1990), 243.
5. Thanks to Rick Cherwitz of the University of Texas for this reference to "self-risk."

Chapter 11

1. *Inside E-business Communities: Lighthouse '99* (Toronto: Alliance for Converging Technologies, 1999), 1.7. (Private document for alliance members.)
2. "How to Drive an Express Train," Scott Thurm, *The Wall Street Journal*, June 1, 2000, B1.
3. "Special Report: Partners," *Business Week*, October 25, 1999, 106.
4. Tapscott, Don; Ticoll, David; and Lowy, Alex, *Digital Capital: Harnessing the Power of Business Webs* (Boston: Harvard Business School Press, 2000).
5. "Special Report: Partners," *Business Week*, October 25, 1999, 112.
6. Thanks to Jeff Weiss for his contribution to this list of skills for the relationship manager.
7. "Making the Deal Real: How GE Capital Integrates Acquisitions," Ronald N. Ashkenas, Lawrence J. DeMonaco, and Suzanne C. Francis, *Harvard Business Review*, January-February 1998, 10.
8. Ibid.
9. Boone, Mary E. *Leadership and the Computer: Top Executives Reveal How They Personally Use Computers to Communicate, Coach, Convince and Compete* (Rocklin, California: Prima Publishing, 1991), 200.

Appendix 1

1. The Scan, Focus, Act model was originally developed by Frank Burns and Linda Nelson, © 1983 Metasystems Design Group, Arlington, Virginia.
2. For a brief introduction to the concept of Appreciative Inquiry, see Hammond, Sue, *The Thin Book of Appreciative Inquiry* (Plano, Texas: Thin Book Publishing Company, 2nd edition, 1996).

Appendix 2

1. "Unit of One," Jill Rosenfeld, *Fast Company*, June 2000, 128.
2. Meyer, N. Dean, and Boone, Mary E., *The Information Edge* (Ridgefield, Connecticut: NDMA Publishing, 1995) and Boone, Mary E., *Leadership and the Computer*, op. cit.

Acknowledgments

When I started writing this book, I told myself I was going to make a list of the people I needed to thank as I went along in the process. Well, I wasn't as self-disciplined as I planned to be. So, chances are that among the literally hundreds of people I need to thank, I'm going to leave out quite a few. Please forgive me if you're one of them.

Original research is a very expensive proposition in terms of time and money. This project would not have been possible without the independent research sponsorships I received from Teligent and IBM. In particular, I want to thank Robert Stewart at Teligent, who was willing to take the leap of faith first. Mike Zisman and Tony DiMarco of IBM were the next two brave souls. All three of them knew the concept of interactive communication was important, and they made it possible for me to explore it. They were model sponsors—they never interfered with the research process in any way, totally supporting my need for objectivity.

To the entire list of interviewees that is included with these acknowledgments, I thank you for your time, patience, and ideas. Really, you are the creators of this book as much as I am.

Lisa Swayne, my agent, has the two most favored attributes of an agent: patience and responsiveness. Many thanks go to Ruth Mills for her initial editing job, and to Richard Narramore, my editor at McGraw-Hill, whose astute comments and belief in this book kept me energized and encouraged.

Appendix 2 was a collaborative effort. Martin Elton and Richard Dalton made very significant contributions from the initial outline to the final product. Morit Shavelsky and Ron Rice of Rutgers University provided significant research support.

Some people went above and beyond the call of duty. Don Tapscott was extraordinarily generous with both his time and advice. Don Parker listened to ideas in very formative stages and helped me nurse them along until they made sense. Bill Machrone, Phil Harkins, and Larry Walsh did the same. Jim Taylor helped me at a very crucial time in my thinking process and asked some critical questions. Sandy Kyrish and Mitch Dickey provided extremely valuable feedback on the manuscript.

Other people I need to single out for thanks in terms of direct help with the book include Richard Laermer, Billie Alban, Richard Farson, Anthony Goodman, Dave Snowden, Dan Fitz, Ellen Baron, Carol Gorelick, Larry Browning, Barbara McNelis, Rick Cherwitz, Pat Shafer, Cathy Fazey, Elliot Gold, Pat Iglehart, Sheila Blackwell, Sharon Machrone, Enid Mumford, Lisa Kimball, Steve Kerr, Hervey Parke, Lorrie Hecker, Kevin Thomson, Johnny Harben, Mike LeBlond, Jennifer Holzman, and Astrid Perris.

I have an amazing family who has supported every single project I've undertaken for the past 41 years. Thanks to Mom, Dad, Wende, and Rachel.

And to all my friends who understood when I didn't answer the phone and disappeared for months: Thank you *very* much. To Jane Calverley, thank you for helping me build a business in addition to being an amazing friend. Rhona Ceppos, this book would have been impossible without your monumental transcription effort (4000 pages!) To Ray Terlaga, thanks for the ongoing (and emergency) computer support. To Andy Werner, thanks for the carrot cakes. Linda Napier, thank you for the photographs. And to Deb Johnson (aka Gus), thanks for the amazing job on the graphics.

And special thanks go to Tom Pinkowish, who was behind me all the way.

Interviewees

Billie Alban, coauthor, *Large Group Interventions,* Simsbury, CT
Dana Atchley, Founder & Creative Director, Digital Storytelling Conference & Festival, San Francisco
Julie Beedon, Vista, Litchfield, United Kingdom
Anne Bonaparte, cofounder, Buzzsaw.com, San Francisco

Lisa Brooks, Director of Performance Management, Verizon Wireless, Orangeburg, NY

Bob Buckman, Chairman of the Executive Committee of the Board of Directors, Bulab Holdings, Inc., Memphis, TN

Mike Burtha, Executive Director, Knowledge Networking, Johnson & Johnson, New Brunswick, NJ

John Caroselli, EVP Corporate Development, AXA Client Solutions, New York, NY

Larry Cerri, Founder, LCI Communications, New York, NY

Denise Curran, Sr. Manager, Organizational Change Communication, Royal Bank of Canada, Toronto

Richard Dalton, an industry analyst and columnist for Byte.Com, Falmouth, MA

John Easden, Group Marketing Director, First National Bank, Harrow, United Kingdom

Martin Elton, Professor, Interactive Telecommunications Program, New York University, New York, NY

Bill Esrey, Chairman and CEO, Sprint, Westwood, CA

Lindsay Eynon, Director, Change & Internal Communications, Hill & Knowlton Ltd., London

Sarah Fasey, Internal Communications Manager, Microsoft, Reading, United Kingdom

Gloria Feldt, President, Planned Parenthood Federation of America, New York, NY

Sheri Feinzig, Senior Consultant, Internal Transformation Consulting and Services, IBM, White Plains, NY

Rick Fetherston, VP Public Relations, American Family Insurance, Madison, WI

Dan Fitz, General Counsel, Cable & Wireless, London

Scott Gassman, Director, Organizational Development, Empire Health Care, New York, NY

David Gilmour, CEO, Tacit Knowledge Systems, Inc., Palo Alto, CA

Michael Goldhaber, independent thinker and writer on social change, Berkeley, CA

Anthony Goodman, CEO, Smythe Dorward Lambert Inc., Boston, MA

Glenn Gow, CEO, Crimson Consulting Group, Inc., Los Altos, CA

Sandra Gregg, Director, Communications, The Enterprise Foundation, Columbia, MD

Johnny Harben, Senior Consultant, Smythe Dorward Lambert Ltd., London

Phil Harkins, CEO, Linkage Inc., Lexington, MA

Jim Haudan, President, Root *Learning® Inc.*, Perrysburg, OH

Mike Hegarty, Sr. Vice Chairman and Chief Operating Officer, AXA Financial, Inc., New York, NY

Steve Innanen, former Chief Knowledge Officer, AMEDD (Army Medical Command), Converse, TX

Jon Iwata, VP, Corporate Communications, IBM, Armonk, NY

Bill Jensen, President & CEO, The Jensen Group, Morristown, NJ

Kamran Khan, Vice President, Information Technology, Marist College, Poughkeepsie, NY

John Kao, CEO, The Idea Factory, San Francisco

Steve Kerr, Chief Learning Officer, General Electric, Ossining, NY

Lisa Kimball, Founder, Caucus Systems, Arlington, VA

Joe Konecny, Manager, Marketing Public Relations, Royal Bank of Canada, Toronto

Gerry Laybourne, CEO, Oxygen Media, New York, NY

Greg Lee, VP Marketing, ConsumerREVIEW.com, Sunnyvale, CA

Doug Loewe, VP Global Sales, EMEA, UUNet, Reading, United Kingdom

Guy Lometti, Dean, School of Communication and the Arts, Marist College, Poughkeepsie, NY

Alex Lowy, Managing Director, Digital 4Sight, Toronto

Bill Machrone, VP, Ziff Davis Media, New York, NY

Rick and Sue Melvill, cofounders, The Blue Moon Company, Sandton, South Africa (Blue Moon is part of Johannesburg Stock Exchange listed media group Salami)

Brad Meyer, Founder, Collaboration Ltd., Hillingdon, United Kingdom

Ed Miller, President and CEO, AXA Financial, Inc., New York, NY

David Moorcraft, Senior VP, Corporate Communications, Royal Bank of Canada, Toronto

John Moro, Division Manager, Integrated Customer View, AT&T, Piscataway, NJ

Rick Muller, Coordinator, Marketing & Interactive Media, Poudre Valley Hospital System, Fort Collins, CO

Peg Neuhauser, Author, *Corporate Legends and Lore,* Austin, TX

John Old, Director, Information Management, Texaco, Bellaire, TX

Hervey Parke, Director, Investor Relations, IBM, Armonk, NY

Don Parker, President, Parker Consultants Inc., Greenwich, CT

Betsy Pasley, Communications Planner, USAA, San Antonio, TX

Lynn Patterson, Sr. Advisor, Community Initiatives, Royal Bank of Canada, Toronto

Joe Pine, coauthor, *The Experience Economy*, author, *Mass Customization*, and cofounder, Strategic Horizons LLP, Aurora, OH

Bob Pinto, Practice Leader, Knowledge Management, Government Sector, IBM, San Antonio, TX

George Polzer, CEO, Reveal.Net, Inc., San Francisco

Jason Pratt, Director of Product Marketing, Buzzsaw.com, San Francisco

David Reyes-Guerra, Associate Director, Brand Management, Ernst & Young, New York, NY

Liz Richards, Partner, Smythe Dorward Lambert Ltd., London, United Kingdom

Mike Rosen, CEO & President, Philadelphia Virtual Reality Center; Chairman of the Board of Directors, Mike Rosen & Associates Architects; CEO & President, 2Ce. Inc., Philadelphia, PA

Laura Rothman, Technical Controller, DRAM Development Alliance, Southbury, CT

Michael Rudnick, Sr. Vice President, Global B2E & B2B Solutions, XCEED Inc., New York, NY

Anna Russell, Marketing Director, NMTV, London, United Kingdom

Paul Sanchez, formerly Associate Practice Director, the Human Capital Group, and Communications Consulting Practice Director, Watson Wyatt Worldwide; now Executive Vice President, Stoorza Communications, Inc., San Diego, CA

Fred Schoeps, Program Director, Knowledge Management, IBM, Armonk, NY

Scott Schultz, EVP & CFO, United Check Control, Houston, TX

Pat Shafer, Managing Consultant, Xpedior, New York, NY

Bill Sheehan, V.P., Business Development, Suppliermarket.com, Burlington, MA

David Sibbet, President, The Grove Consultants International, San Francisco

Christine Smith, Sr. Director Sales Support & Operations, RIA Group, Catonsville, MD

Dave Snowden, European Director, Institute for Knowledge Management, IBM, Lockeridge, United Kingdom

David Specht, CEO, Seeing Things Whole, Shelburne Falls, MA

Tom Sudman, President, Digital AV, Knoxville, TN

Don Tapscott, Chairman, Digital 4Sight, Toronto

Gail Taylor, cofounder, The knOwhere Store, Palo Alto, CA

Rebecca Thomas, Assistant Professor, Computer Science & Information Systems, Marist College, Poughkeepsie, NY

Kevin Thomson, Chairman, The Marketing & Communication Agency Ltd., London

Betty Turner, former Chief Knowledge Officer, AMEDD, San Antonio, TX

Larry Walsh, Communications Consultant, Osgood O'Donnell & Walsh, New York, NY

Jeff Weiss, Founding Partner, Vantage Partners, LLC, Cambridge, MA

Charlene Wheeless, Vice President, Corporate Communications, DynCorp, Reston, VA

Anne Wylie, President, Wylie Communications, Kansas City, MO

Mary Vertacic, Corporate Communications Manager, American Family Insurance, Madison, WI

David Zelig, Principal, Mike Rosen and Associates Architects, Philadelphia, PA

Mike Zisman, EVP, Strategy, Lotus Development Corporation, Cambridge, MA

Index

About the Author

Mary E. Boone is a leading authority on organizational communication and collaborative technologies. She is also the author of the bestselling *Leadership and the Computer.* Boone is a frequent speaker, executive coach, and consultant on how organizations can improve their performance and strategy execution through better communication. She is president of Boone Associates, a consulting firm based in Norwalk, Connecticut.
Mary Boone can be contacted at:

Boone Associates
50 Washington Street
7th Floor
Norwalk, CT 06854

203-855-0895 (phone)
info@maryboone.com
www.maryboone.com